Memories of Torreón, New Mexico

Memorias de Torreón, Nuevo México

Collected and Edited by Judy Alderete Garcia

Copyright © 2016 by Judy A Garcia All rights reserved.

This book or any portion thereof may not be reproduced or used in any manner whatsoever without the express written permission of the publisher except for the use of brief quotations in a book review.
Printed in the United States of America

First Printing, November 2016

"La Matanza" by Eric J. Garcia

LA MATANZA

*To Marina, Nathan and Sofia
and to all my younger cousins
who didn't get to spend time
in Torreón with our grandparents as I did.*

Judy, Jeanette, Eloy Garcia and Sunshine

I like going to the ranch in Torreón to feed the cows with my grandpa. As soon as my grandpa drives into the ranch the cows follow him. They know it's time to eat. My grandpa fills up the water tank and gives them hay. One cow always comes to visit my grandpa. My grandpa raised the cow at his house and fed him with a bottle. The cow now lives in the ranch, but he hasn't forgotten who raised him. My family enjoys going to the ranch in the summer.

Marina Olivia Garcia Crampton
10 years old

Contents

Preface

Alderete-Garcia, Christella 3
Matanzas, Picking Piñon and Prendorios

Alderete-Garcia, Gloria 11
Comadres and Snowy Winters

Alderete Garcia, Judy 13
My Grandmother Antonia Chavez-Garcia

Alderete, Peté 20
Boyhood Adventures in Torreón, New Mexico

Benavidez, Magdalene 46
My Home in Torreón, New Mexico

Benavidez-Alderete, Florelia 48
Pilgrimage de Nuestra Señora de los Dolores

Benavidez- Lepori, Barbara 52
Natural Healing in Rural New Mexico

Benavidez-Lesperance, Viola 54
Traditional Foods

Benavidez-Zamora, Irene 56
My Love for the Spanish Alabados

Chavez, Feliciano and Regenita Garcia-Chavez 58
Serving in WWII and Herding Sheep

Chavez, Gene 67
Los Garrapatas AKA The Torreón Ticks

Chavez, Gilbert 71
The Torreón Acequia

Chavez, Frank Ruben 72
Mis Recuerdos de Torreón

Chavez-Perea, Susie   76
Wildfires and Working for the United States Government

Chavez-Vigil, Lupe   79
Well-Wishing, Making Butter and Aguinaldos

Garcia, Eloy   84
Fidel's Bar and Playing Sports

Garcia, Fidel Jr. (Sonny)   94
Ross Garcia and Fidel Garcia Sr.

Milton Garcia   101
Growing up in New Mexico in the 1950s and 1960s

Garcia, Raymundo   108
Baseball and Serving our Country

Garcia-Anaya, Carmela   110
Beans! Beans! Beans!

Garcia-Anaya, Carmela   113
Growing up a Cowgirl

Garcia- Lesperance Virginia (Joanie)   115
Spending Time with Grandparents and my Dad Abie Garcia

Garcia-Martinez Rachel   119
My Fondest Memories Growing Up in Torreón, New Mexico

Herrera-Sanchez, Cecelia   133
Capolin Jam

Lujan, Andrea   137
The Joy of my Youth

Lujan, Maggie   138
Riding Goats, Matanzas and Drinking Wine

Olona, Father Richard 152
Parish Priest of the Mission Churches of Mountainair

Perea-Chavez, Imelda 157
Fond Memories of Jose Maria Perea and Carlota Alderete-Perea

Sanchez, Eloy 176
Serving as an Altar Boy

Sanchez, Stella 181
Changes from 1942-2016

Sanchez-Lujan, Ramona 187
First Communions, Funerals and Feast Days

Trujillo, Jesus 194
Running Against Horses and Threshing Beans

Trujillo-Luna, Carmen 196
Trujillo Family Velorio at El Cuervo

Vigil-Lujan, Selina 198
Vigil, Garcia and Lujan Family

Ranch in Torreón by Eric J. Garcia

Preface

Both my parents were born and raised in the small town of Torreón, New Mexico in the Manzano Mountains. As a child, I spent almost every weekend in Torreón. I have fond memories of my time spent there visiting both sets of grandparents, my grandpa Pete (Pedro) and my grandma Candelaria (Candy) Alderete and my grandpa Fidel and my grandma Antonia (Tonie) Garcia. Times have changed since I have spent time there and things continue to change.

I have always wanted to write a book about Torreón and its people. I finally decided, who better to tell the story of this place than the people who lived there, grew up there and spent time there. I wanted this book to be a book about Torreón by the people of Torreón. I love stories, history, writing and I love my culture. I believe the stories of our past and present give us and others a better understanding of who we are.

This is a book of memories and events, and it is a way to preserve the culture, history and traditions of Torreón. The people of Torreón have a long history here in New Mexico and have contributed to the unique culture of New Mexico. In the past, there has been plenty written about the more popular touristic places in New Mexico like Santa Fe, Taos and Abiquiu. Some of the smaller, less known towns have very little written about them. I believe if these stories and memories are not documented a great part of New Mexico history and culture will disappear forever.

Most stories and memories are set in the 1940s and 1950s but some later and earlier. This book does not need to be read in order. However, as you read each story, you may learn more details about certain events or people. Throughout this book, you will see names that show up in other stories, and it may seem that everyone is related in one way or another, and that may perhaps be true. Torreón was a close-knit community, and it still is. Many stories have common themes like *matanzas* and *fiestas,* but this just goes to show you how important these events were in the past or how important some of these events still are today.

A note about some of the Spanish words the people of Torreón used and that you will come across in this book. Some of these words you will find in a standard Spanish Dictionary. Some of these words I could only find in the text A *Dictionary of New Mexico & Southern Colorado Spanish* by Ruben Cobos. Some words I couldn't find in any Spanish dictionary, but just like the culture and traditions that I hoped to preserve, I also wanted to preserve the language of the area, so these are the words that I used. As many will know every Spanish-speaking community here in New Mexico and throughout the Spanish-speaking world have their own unique list of vocabulary words unique to the region.

I have many people to thank for making this book possible. First, my parents for contacting people and helping me pass out letters to family and friends about this project. Of course, I have to say a big THANK YOU to all of the people that contributed stories because without these stories there would be no book. I had wonderful conversations with relatives and friends, and I learned a lot about the culture, history and traditions of my ancestors. I was open to what people wanted to write about and how they went about it. Some stories were recorded, and I wrote them. Some stories, I wrote from notes people gave me. Some stories were a combination of back and forth correspondences. Some people sent me stories that needed little or no editing. However it was done, everyone who contributed a story helped to make this book possible. I found great joy in working on this book, and I hope that everyone who contributed a story found great satisfaction in doing so.

My feeling is that everyone has a story and has something to say. As David Chavez, the son of Ruben Chavez, who contributed a story for this book said, "The people of Torreón have much to be proud of." It's true. The people from this town have not only had an interesting past but have produced some very successful, creative offspring. I know just in my own family of siblings and cousins and second cousins there are professors, teachers, musicians, santeros, artists, school principals, lawyers, engineers, yoga instructors, massage therapists, spiritual healers, many who have completed master's degrees and Ph.D.'s, several police officers and others with great achievements. I am truly proud of my parents Eloy and Christella, my brothers Eloy Jr. and Eric J., my sister Jeanette and of all my aunts, uncles and cousins too numerous to name. They have achieved much, and I know this is also true for the other families of Torreón. I agree, we indeed have much to be proud of.

I also wish to thank everyone who read stories for me after I edited each story. They gave me great advice and suggestions. I tried my best to put commas in the appropriate places and to have stories that flowed well and were easy to follow. Any grammatical errors are truly my errors. Most important, I tried to keep the voice of the storyteller. The purpose of this book was to preserve and tell the stories of the people of Torreón, New Mexico, and in this, I believe my goal was fulfilled. I found out that editing is extremely difficult work, especially when working with so many different voices and at times in two different languages, but I learned a great deal, and I hope this has made me a better writer. A few words about the cover(s) of the book. Yes, I have two covers. My original idea was to use black and white photos for the cover but because there were so many stories about *matanzas* in this book, I decided to use the artwork *La Matanza* by Eric. J. Garcia that I had hanging in my home. I think both book covers are equally important and tell much about the people of Torreón. Lastly, I hope that those who are not familiar with this little village in the Manzano Mountains or for those who do not know much about the culture of New Mexicans will learn something about our past, present and our future.

Matanzas, Picking Piñón and Prendorios

Christella Alderete-Garcia

My name is Christella Alderete-Garcia, and I was born in Torreón, New Mexico in the 1940s. My mother was Candelaria Montoya-Alderete. She was born in Torreón on June 7, 1918. Her dad was Vicente Montoya, who was born in Torreón, and her mother was Pablita Chavez. My father was Pedro Alderete, who was born in Valencia, New Mexico in 1914. His parents were Francisco Alderete and Reyna Marquez. My father passed away in 1984, and my mother passed away November 10, 2010.

My parents had four sons and three daughters. The boys are Vicente, Pedro Jr. (Peté), Dennis and Arturo (Leroy). The girls are Gloria Alderete-Garcia-Serrano, me and then my sister Hilda Alderete-Herrera.

My grandparents Vicente and Pablita Montoya had three kids: Santos, Maximiliano and my mom Candelaria. My mom was only four years old when her mother died. She then went to live with her grandparents Jose and Felicita Montoya in Torreón. When her dad, Vicente, married Adelina Archuleta, my mom went to live with them in Torreón. Vicente and Adelina had five children. They had Catalina, Oralia, Benny, Rudy and Frank. My grandpa provided for his family by farming, and later on when I was in grade school, he was the school bus driver in Torreón. At that time the school in Torreón only went up to the eighth grade, and from there the kids went to high school in Estancia. My grandpa drove the kids from Torreón and the other nearby towns to school in Estancia.

As a kid, I spent a lot of time with my grandpa and my grandma in their home near the *arroyo*. They had a big rocking chair in their house that I liked to sit in. My grandpa would come and sit next to me with an apple in his hand, and he would ask me, "¿*Cómo estás mi hijita?*" He would pull his pocket knife out of his pocket, and he would cut a slice of apple for me and a slice for him. We would sit together eating the apple until it was gone. My grandparents also had a big grandfather clock in their home. I remember the constant sound of the *tick-tock, tick-tock,* and every half hour it was *ding-dong, ding-dong*! I did not like the sound of the clock. It always made me sad.

On Saturdays I went with my grandpa and grandma to Mountainair to buy groceries. This was always fun because we went on the school bus. One time before Easter Sunday, we went to Mountainair, and we went into one of the stores. My grandpa said, "You can pick out a dress for Easter." I looked, and I found a pretty pink, silk dress with black velvet bows. I told my grandpa, "This is the one I like." However, my grandma didn't think buying this dress was such a good idea. She said, "No, that dress costs too much money. You'll have to choose another one." Luckily, my grandpa said, "No, she likes this one, and this one we'll take." My grandpa paid for the dress, and we went on our way. It was not often that I got a new dress, so I was very excited about getting a new one.

Sometimes I helped my grandpa clean the school bus. This I liked to do because I got to keep what I found. I would find money, pencils, pens and other things. When I was done visiting my grandparents, my grandpa brought me back to my house on the school bus, or he would walk with me across the *arroyo*. Sometimes we stopped at Fidel's bar, and he would buy a bottle of wine for himself and bubble gum and penny candy for me.

I loved my grandpa Vicente very much. He was a very kind-hearted man. He was very patient, and everything was always fine with him. He passed away in 1970. He was in his 70s when he died.

All my mom's brothers and sisters moved to Albuquerque and made their home there except for my aunt Catalina (katie). She moved to Albuquerque and lived there for several years. She then came back to Torreón and lived in my grandpa Vicente's house that she inherited. My auntie Katie passed away in June of 2015. She was 90 years old.

My dad was a cowboy. He always wore a cowboy hat, cowboy boots, a western shirt and he loved to read western novels. He enjoyed working with animals, and in the back of our house, we had a big corral where we kept pigs, a horse and chickens. My dad also liked to farm, and he loved riding horses. When I was growing up, my dad worked for the Santa Fe Railroad, and he spent a lot of his time working in Oklahoma and Kansas. We would only see him a few days out of the month when he came home to visit.

In the fall when there was piñón to pick, my dad would take my brothers and sisters and me to pick piñón with him here in the Manzano Mountains. Sometimes my auntie Leonela or my auntie Carlota would come with us. We would get up at about 5 o'clock in the morning and pack a lunch because we would be gone all day. I remember there were times it was so cold our fingers would freeze, and the piñón would stick to the frost on our gloves. My dad was able to pick piñón really fast. Sometimes he would spend a whole week picking piñón. He would pick about 100 pounds, and then he would sell it.

Every year for Christmas or Thanksgiving, my family had a big *matanza*. We would start grinding blue corn to make *tortillas* two days before the event. Because it was such a big event, my uncle Jose Maria Perea and my auntie Carlota always came to help. Many other relatives, friends and neighbors also came to help. The day of the *matanza*, the men got up early in the morning to get everything ready. They would build a big fire outside and boil a huge pot of water. The water was used for cleaning and shaving the hair off the pig. After the pig was killed, one of the first things we did was cut the tail and ears off the pig, and they were then thrown into the hot burning ashes to cook. After they were cooked, they were pulled out of the fire and cut into small pieces. A little bit of salt was added to them, and they were eaten.

Memories of Torreón, New Mexico

After the tail and ears were cooked, it was time to make the pork skins. The skin of the pig was cut into long strips, and then the strips were cut into small cubes. The cubes of fat were thrown into a huge black cast iron pot that sat outside over the fire. Somebody always stood there stirring the pork skins with a long wooden stick so that they wouldn't stick together. The pork skins were ready when they were cooked all the way through but still soft. We then took them out of the pot, added some salt and ate them. They were yummy and tasty! The *chicharrones* were made next. This time, long strips of meat were cut into small cubes and then thrown into the black cast iron pot to cook. Once they were golden brown and crispy, they were ready.

Meanwhile, the women would be in the kitchen making blue corn *tortillas*. The warm *chicharrones* were wrapped into the homemade blue corn *tortillas* and formed into a ball. These were the best *burritos* ever! The women would also be busy in the kitchen making blood pudding, red chile and slicing meat for the chile. The meat would be marinated in the chile and then hung outside to dry a bit, before being baked in the oven. Red chile from a *matanza* was always tastier than the chile we ate every day. By the way, every part of the pig was used. There was no waste. The meat from the head was used to make *tamales*, and the pig's feet were added to *posole*, both traditional foods we ate during the Christmas holidays. The oil that came from the *chicharrones* would harden into lard and was saved and used for cooking and baking throughout the year. Everybody who came to help with the matanza would leave with a coffee can full of lard, *chicharrones*, meat and other feasts of the *matanza*.

A *mantanza* was an all day event, and some people stayed until the final *chicharrones* were cooked and all the oil from the *chicharrones* was canned. The men began the *matanza* early in the morning when it was still dark, and they finished in the dark. By this time, my dad had passed around a bottle of wine or whiskey, and the men were now joking, laughing and sometimes drunk! My dad played the accordion, and they all sang and had a good time. My dad made the best *chicharrones*! He could have won first prize. Once a month my dad also butchered *una borrega*. The ribs he baked would come out brown and crispy. They were so delicious!

My mom was a homemaker, and she kept the family together. She was a good cook, and she never used a recipe. She would add a pinch of this and a pinch of that. She made the best rice pudding and *sopa*. I still make *sopa* the way I learned to make it from my mom, and I take it to potlucks. Everybody always loves it! Before going to bed, my mom always prayed with us, and this prayer stayed with me.

Con Dios me acuesto con Dios me levanto
con la gracia de Dios Espíritu Santo
Dios conmigo y yo con él
Dios por delante yo tras él
Angel de la Guardia dulce compañía

Matanzas, Picking Piñón and Prendorios

velame en la noche
guárdame en el día.

    We lived right across the street from the church when I was growng up, and we attended church often. At that time some of the priests in Torreón were very strict. Women could not enter the church without covering the top of their heads with a veil or with whatever they had at the moment. Women could not wear pants to church or sleeveless shirts. If we were not dressed accordingly, some of the priests would not *ask* us to leave the church but *tell* us to leave the church. One priest didn't even want the girls wearing pants around town, and I remember going to the state fair one year in a skirt.

    My mom's favorite time of the year was summer because she enjoyed getting ready for Corpus Christi. She would often say, "The Blessed Sacrament is coming to bless our home," and she looked forward to setting up her altar outside of her house. The altar was a table covered with a lace tablecloth, and the table was then decorated with fresh flowers and candles. My mom set up her altar for many years until she could no longer because of her age. Several other people in Torreón would also put up an altar. The day of Corpus Christi, we would have a mass in the church, and then we walked in procession from the church to each of the altars. The priest would stop and bless each altar and the people in the procession. In the back of the procession, there were four girls dressed as angels. They wore long white gowns with wings on their backs and tinsel on their heads. Behind these girls were some younger girls. They were about six to eight years old. They wore white or light colored dresses, tinsel on their heads, and they carried baskets full of confetti that they tossed along the way. The confetti was made from pretty colored candy and gum wrapper paper that we saved throughout the year. Our neighbor Doña Josefita Lujan would save lots of decorated paper for us just for this occasion. We would cut the paper into very small pieces and fill up a big box full of the confetti. We would then share it with the little girls in the procession. Sometimes instead of paper for confetti, we used rose petals from the pink or yellow *rosas de castillas* that our neighbor shared with us.

    I went to elementary school in Torreón. When I started school, I had a very hard time because I could only speak Spanish. I didn't know a word of English, and I had a hard time learning the language. At home and in town, everyone spoke Spanish. I also had a hard time spelling my name. Christella Alderete was not a common name. It was two long names, and some people could not pronounce either of them. They would call me "Priscilla" or "Cinderella" or "Cricelda." I was also the shortest one in my class, and the kids would tease me about that. The boys started calling me "Shorty," and I didn't like that name either. After a while, I got used to my nickname. I thought it sounded better than "Cinderella." Today my good friends and cousins still call me "Shorty," and now, I'm just fine with it.

    Each year at the end of the school year, we were happy to see the year end, and we looked forward to summer. This is the song we sang at the end of the year.

Qué Bueno, Qué Bueno, que se acabó *la escuela. Que nunca, que nunca, que nunca más volviera.*

When I was growing up, my best friend was Susie Chavez from Torreón. I also spent a lot of time with my cousins Corrine and Maggie. They were the daughters of my auntie Leonela and my uncle Melcor, who lived right by our house. Imelda was another cousin who I spent a lot of time with. She was the daughter of my auntie Carlota and my uncle Jose Maria, and they were also my neighbors. At that time there was always water in the *arroyo* in Torreón, and we spent a lot of time playing in it. One time I fell into a deep hole in the *arroyo,* and I thought I was going to drown. Luckily, Imelda pulled me out. After that incident, I was scared of the water, and I never learned to swim. Another time while playing at the *arroyo,* Imelda stepped on an old board with a rusty nail. We had to bring her home because she was crying and in a lot of pain. She later got an infection in her foot and couldn't play for a while.

My family got our first TV set in the early 1960s, and I enjoyed watching American Bandstand with Dick Clark. I watched it every Saturday afternoon. I loved this show, and I memorized all the character's names who danced on the show. Dancing was one of my favorite things to do. Corrine had a little record player that played 45 records, and in the evenings, Maggie, my sister Hilda and I loved to listen to music and dance at Corrine's house. We would practice the Twist, the Jitterbug and the Line dance. We got to be really good dancers, and we loved going to the dances at Fidel's Dance Hall. One time when we were about 13 years old, my friend Virginia Sanchez wanted to throw a going away party for a friend who was moving to California. Virginia had a 50 cent piece, and she went and asked Fidel if he would rent the hall to her for 50 cents. He agreed, and we had a party. We took a record player and some food, and we danced. It was a lot of fun. Years later, Fidel became my father-in-law and also Virginias, and to this day, we still love to dance.

I married Eloy Garcia, the son of Fidel and Antonia Garcia. Before we got married, we had a *prendorio*. My parents invited Eloy's family to our house for coffee and probably *biscochitos* and *pastalitos*. Each of Eloy's brothers and sisters came to the house along with their spouse if they were married. Each one of them came to the house to introduce themselves to my family and to me, and they each brought me a gift of money. Of course, we all knew each other because we had all grown up in the same town, and my sister Gloria was married to Abie, Eloy's brother, but that was the custom.

Eloy and I still have a ranch in Torreón and visit often. We are still very close to our family and friends who live there. My brothers Vicente and Leroy and Dennis all live in Torreón, and Vicente and Leroy have very nice ranches there. Leroy is my youngest brother, so he was the spoiled one. I remember he had a brand new bike as a child, and my dad even bought him a nice car in high school. Leroy and his wife, Lorella, have been *mayordomos* of the church several times. They along with my brother Vicente and his wife, Flora, have all been very active in serving the church and the community.

Christella Alderete-Garcia

Pedro Alderete

Auntie Catalina (Katie) Montoya

Vicente Montoya and Pablita Chavez

Christella Garcia and Susie Chavez

Vicente Montoya and Adelina Archuleta-Montoya

Pedro and Candelaria Montoya-Alderete

Leroy Alderete and Jeanette Garcia

Comadres and Snowy Winters

Gloria Alderete-Garcia-Serrano

My name is Gloria Alderete-Garcia-Serrano. I was born in the 1940s in Torreón, New Mexico. I am the daughter of Pedro Alderete and Candelaria Montoya-Alderete. My mom was born in Torreón in 1918, and my dad was born in Valencia, New Mexico in 1914.

Growing up in Torreón in the 1940s and 1950s was not like it is today. We didn't have all the stuff children have today, but we always had food and the important things in life. We had family, friends and faith. As a kid, I always had lots of cousins and friends to play with. I would often visit my friend Juanita at her house, or she would come and play with me at my house. We used to pretend we were baptizing each other's dolls, so we became *comadres*.

When I started school in Torreón, I didn't speak English. My family always spoke Spanish at home, but eventually, I learned English. When I went to school in Estancia, things were very different. We weren't allowed to speak Spanish in school, but things changed for the best. We were able to get involved in school activities and had more opportunities to do things.

The weather was different from what it is today. It snowed all winter long, and sometimes we would get several feet of snow all at once. We all had our rubber boots, scarves and mittens that we wore all winter, and we walked in the snow everywhere. When we got a couple of feet of snow, we still had to attend school in Torreón, and we walked to and from school in the snow. We would make paths to the church, to the outhouse and to the pile of wood in the back of our house. I enjoyed making snow angels in the snow. We would lie down in the snow and spread out our arms and legs and then move them up and down. When we stood up, we could see the angel we made in the snow.

Fiestas in Torreón were the big event of the year. People from the nearby towns like Manzano, Estancia and Tajique would come, and people from Albuquerque would come. One nice thing about *fiestas* is that my brothers and sisters and I got new clothes and shoes. *Fiestas* began Friday night with a Mass, and then it was followed by a procession around the neighborhood. A band led the procession, followed by a few people carrying the Statue of San Antonio. Bonfires lit the way as others followed in procession, and everyone would dance, sing and pray. This procession was followed by a dance in one of the dance halls. *Fiestas* were an event that we always looked forward to.

Comadres and Snowy Winters

back left to right, Abie Garcia, Gloria Garcia, Vicente Alderete, Flora Alderete, Christella Garcia. Middle, Candelaria Alderete, Pedro Alderete, front Melvin and Leroy Alderete

My Grandmother Antonia Chavez-Garcia

Judy Alderete Garcia

Antonia Maria Chavez was born August 20, 1915, in Willard, New Mexico. Her parents were Juan Chavez and Barbarita Campos-Chavez. Juan and Barbarita also had two sons who were Phil and Santiago.

Juan's parents were Feliciano Chavez y Salas, who was born in 1861 and Telesflora Romero, who was born in 1866. They lived on a ranch near Willard, New Mexico, and they had nine children. Juan and Barbarita and their children lived on the ranch with them.

When Antonia was four years old, her father died, probably from the influenza outbreak. A few years later, her mom remarried and had two more sons: Diego and Milton Baca. Throughout this time Antonia continued to live with her grandparents.

Feliciano and Telesflora were very kind, loving people. Feliciano was a wise businessman who owned a large sheep ranch. At one time, he was the treasurer of Estancia and also a school teacher. When he wasn't managing his ranch, he spent his time reading the many books that filled his bookshelves.

Antonia's grandma Telesflora, whom she called Grandma Lola, was a hard-working woman. She spent a lot of time in the kitchen cooking for the hired help that worked on the ranch. She also liked to crochet, and she made many blankets and things for the house.

Antonia's aunt Desideria (Desi) also lived on the ranch with them. Desi never got married and perhaps never worked outside the home. She helped her mom cook and do the chores around the house and helped care for Antonia. Antonia was always well-dressed due to the beautiful dresses her aunt Desi made for her, and she always had matching shoes, hats and gloves to go with her dresses.

Antonia loved living with her grandparents. They lived in a big house, and Antonia had plenty of room to play. Antonia liked to listen to the old Victrola record player, and her grandma had a beautiful brown upright piano that Antonia later inherited. Antonia had her Aunt Ofelia's kids nearby to play with. Ofelia was Feliciano and Telesflora's daughter, and her children were Romelia, Francis, Nicolaus, Rachel, Tellis and Arturo Maez. Antonia and her cousins enjoyed teasing each other and playing pranks on each other. Antonia used to tell them that the cereal they were eating was really dried worms, and she dared them to eat it. Antonia liked to climb up the roof of the barn, and she would jump off into a pile of hay. She would hide there until her cousins came to find her. One day while jumping from the roof, she landed on her back and had to stay in bed for a long period of time. Her

My Grandmother Antonia Chavez-Garcia

cousins would come and visit her and make fun of her. They would say, "*Se quebro la cola.*"

Antonia had chores to do when she was young. She had to feed the chickens, milk the cows and make *tortillas*. When it came time to shear the sheep, the wool was put into big sacks. It was Antonia's job to get inside the sacks and jump up and down on the wool to make room for more. This chore she actually liked. She also enjoyed riding the sheep just for fun.

Spanish was spoken in the home, and Antonia learned English at school in a small schoolhouse in Willard. She liked school, and was good at math and played on the basketball team as a guard. The teachers liked Antonia, and she had many friends. Next door to the school was the general store. At lunch time, Antonio would take her pennies that her grandpa gave her, and she would by crackers and a can of potted meat to share with her friends.

On the day before her First Holy Communion, Antonia's grandma gave her some money to go to the general store to buy herself some shoes to match her First Holy Communion dress. When she got to the store, she found a beautiful pair of white patent leather shoes. The shoes were a size too small, but they were so pretty, she bought them anyway. On the day of her First Holy Communion, she looked so pretty in her white dress and veil, but she couldn't wait to get home because her feet were in such pain.

In 1924 when Antonia was about 10 years old, her grandpa Feliciano died. After her grandpa died, Antonia's uncles managed the ranch. Years later the ranch began to get smaller and smaller, and Antonia moved with her grandma and aunt Desi to a house in the town of Willard. When Antonia was about 14 years old, her grandma died, and she stayed and lived with her aunt Desi.

Antonia has said that she knew that her aunt Desi loved her, but her aunt wasn't always very kind to her. When Desi was a young girl, she wanted desperately to attend high school in Santa Fe with her brothers, but her father wouldn't allow it. Desi always felt that she wasn't smart enough, and she also felt that she didn't speak English well enough. She was a pretty woman and had some very nice boyfriends that wanted to marry her, but she never married. Aunt Desi was unhappy and bossy. Antonia said, "She didn't let me attend school plays or dances, and she didn't let my friends come over to visit." When Antonia was about 17 years old, her aunt Desi died. Antonia believes she may have died of depression.

Antonia soon graduated from high school and was left all alone in the big house in Willard. She was left with some money, and she wasn't sure what she wanted to do next. Some of her friends were finding jobs, and some were getting married. The only thing she knew for sure is that she wanted to be a good girl, and she wanted to do what was right. She got a job in town working for a couple who owned a small store. It was honest work, and she enjoyed it.

One thing Antonia enjoyed was going to the many dances in town, and she always looked forward to the church *fiestas* in the nearby towns. She would buy a new dress and shoes, fix her hair and go to the dances with her girlfriends. She was one of the best dancers around, and sometimes people would make a circle around her and her dance partner and watch them dance.

It is at one of the *fiesta* dances that she met Fidel Garcia, her future husband. Fidel was born in 1900 and grew up in Torreón, New Mexico, one of the nearby towns. He had left Torreón many years earlier to find work in California. He spent 15 years in Los Angeles, California working in a drugstore. He later returned to Torreón and opened up the Golden View Bar with his brother Antonio.

Antonia and Fidel had seen each other a few times at some of the dances in the nearby towns and had spoken briefly, but the next time Fidel saw Antonia, he was ready to propose marriage. Antonia says, "I saw him at the dance, and when he saw me, he came up to me, took the ring out of his pocket, slipped it on my finger and asked me to marry him." They were married in 1936. After the church ceremony, they had a meal of enchiladas, beans and rice, and then they drove to Las Cruces, New Mexico and Juarez, Mexico where they spent their honeymoon. Maybe this began my grandma's love for travel.

After their honeymoon, they returned to settle in the town of Torreón. Fidel had a beautiful pink house built for them right next to his bar, and this is where they raised their eight children: Fidel Jr. (Sonny), Abie, Eloy, Nancy, Carmela, Milton, Jimmy and Cathy. With the savings that Antonia still had, they put a windmill in the ranch.

Antonia kept house, cared for the children and was always busy in the kitchen cooking for the family. She had a busy life but also found time to do other things. In the summer, she picked chokecherries and made *capolin* jam. She also made fresh yogurt. For the Torreón *fiestas*, she would set up a stand and sell hotdogs or hamburgers in Fidel's Dance Hall. During the summer months, she opened up a small ice cream parlor in the little house just north of her home, and she sold homemade ice cream and sodas. At one time, she even worked as a substitute teacher at the school in Torreón. Because Fidel had spent so many years living in California and because Antonia had learned English, they were both able to teach their children Spanish and English. This was not at all common in Torreón at the time.

When Antonia was still raising her kids, her mother, Barbarita, who was getting up in age, came to live with the family. She lived there for many, many years. She was a big lady, and everyone called her "Big Grandma." She was not well and spent most of her time sitting quietly in her chair in the dining room, but when the days were warm, she enjoyed sitting in the front porch watching people as they passed by.

My family and I spent many weekends and holidays at my grandma and grandpa's house when I was growing up. There were always plenty of cousins to play with, and it was always like a big party. During the summer months, we spent time riding horses at the ranch, and every winter we had a *matanza* in the backyard of my grandparent's house. On Sundays my

My Grandmother Antonia Chavez-Garcia

grandma would open the French doors to her fancy parlor room, and us kids got to sit in the room with our parents. The adults drank coffee from dainty coffee cups or drank wine or other alcoholic beverages from elegant glasses from the bar. My brother and sister and I always looked forward to going to grandpa's bar before we headed home because my grandpa would give us bags of candy, gum and chile chips to take home with us.

In the 1970s, my grandpa had a stroke. My dad and my uncles took turns going to Torreón to help run the bar and manage the ranch. Unfortunately, my grandpa did not recover, so my grandma closed up the pink house, the bar and dance hall and moved to Albuquerque. They moved into the northeast heights part of Albuquerque, where they had bought a house years earlier so their children could attend school and work in Albuquerque.

My grandpa died in the late 1970s. My grandma must have been in her 60s at the time. Her mother had died a few years earlier, and her children were grown and married with children of their own. She stayed living in Albuquerque and never returned to live in the Manzano Mountains.

My grandma was very close to her brothers Jimmy, Diego, Phil and Milton, who are now all gone. Milton fought in WWII and died shortly after returning from the war. I believe he died from pneumonia. Diego has been gone for quite some time now. Diego was a great dad to his son Leonard, who was born mentally and physically disabled. Diego loved Leonard very much and took very good care of him. Unfortunately, Leonard died at a young age. Phil has been gone for many years now. My Grandmother was very close to Phil and his wife, Mary Tabet, who was from Manzano, New Mexico. Mary and Phil moved to California many years ago, and my grandma frequently went to visit them. When I was about 13 years old, my grandma took me with her to San Francisco for a visit. That was my first airplane ride, and perhaps that began my love for travel. Phil and Mary's children are Donna, Barbara, Bernadette and Johnny. My grandma's brother Jimmy has been gone now for a few years. His children are Louie, Leroy, Bobby, Sara, George, Karla and Gilbert. My grandma was also very close to Gricelda Garcia-Zamora, my grandpa's sister. Rose, Gricelda's granddaughter, told me that my grandma and Gricelda liked to roll up a cigarette, pour a drink for themselves and listen to Spanish music on the old Victrola record player. I can just picture them sitting in my grandma's fancy parlor room enjoying their time together.

August of 2015, my grandma turned 100, and the family gave her a big surprise party. Many of her nieces and nephews were able to attend. Bobby and Gilbert, Jimmy's sons, attended, and her brother Phil's daughters Donna and Barbara came from California. My auntie Gricelda's family also attended. I'm sure my grandma appreciated so many of her family coming to celebrate her birthday. I know her sons and daughters and I appreciated it. Many of her cousins and friends and family she grew up with have passed by now. Her cousin Arturo who she played with as a child, died while serving in WWII.

My grandma had many interests and hobbies, and she enjoyed

Memories of Torreón, New Mexico

traveling. She traveled to Israel, Europe, Hawaii, Alaska, Mexico City and many other places. When she was about 80 years old, I took her to Washington D.C. to see the Basilica of the National Shrine of the Immaculate Conception, the White House and to many other sights in Washington D.C.

My grandma liked to save things. She saved things that were sentimental to her like souvenirs from her travels or gifts people brought her from their travels. She saved old pictures, letters and cards. She put dates and names on everything, so she could remember when and who gave her these items. She loved to write letters, and she kept in touch with many people that way. She was also fond of plants, rocks and petrified wood. She drove up until her late 80s, and one thing she enjoyed doing was going to the state fair with her friend Placida, who lived down the street from her. My grandma worked up into her 90s for Albuquerque Public Schools. Her title was " grandma," and she enjoyed helping kids read.

Recently in her 90s, my grandma took up smoking again, but as others in the family have said, "She has earned the right to smoke." So every once in a while she gets to have a cigarette. My grandma enjoyed crocheting, cooking, entertaining, going to parties, dancing, and she always enjoyed her glass of wine or shot of whiskey. She loved to read and was curious about the world and others. She was an elegant lady, and she enjoyed dressing up. She always wore her sunglasses, scarves, jewelry, lipstick, stylish clothes and shoes. At 100 years old, she still loved putting on her makeup, having her nails done and wearing her fancy sunglasses.

My grandma baptized me and confirmed me, so I guess I always thought I was special to her. I still have a blouse she brought me from Mexico when I was about eight years old, the rings she brought me from the Vatican, a doll she gave me for one of my birthdays and plenty of other gifts. My grandma Tonie, as everyone calls her, was an elegant, smart, adventurous woman for her time. She turned 101 years old August 20, 2016, and at this age, she is not that active anymore. My grandma was born in a time when women didn't have many choices, but she read, she traveled, she educated herself and was able to do many things.

Telesflora Romero-Chavez  *Antonia Chavez-Garcia*

MRS. FIDEL GARCIA, from the Golden View Bar in Torreon, smiles because she is displaying the best — Coors.

Antonia Chavez-Garcia  *Fidel Garcia*

Desideria Chavez and Antonia Chavez-Garcia

Antonia Chavez-Garcia

Milton Baca

Juan Chavez, Barbarita Campos-Chavez and baby Antonia Chavez

Boyhood Adventures in Torreón, New Mexico

Peté E. Alderete

My name is Peté E. Alderete, and I live in Albuquerque, New Mexico. I was born November 7, 1949, in the town of Torreón, New Mexico in Torrance County, east of the Manzano Mountains and 55 miles from the city of Albuquerque. I am the son of wonderful, hardworking, loving parents, who had a strong Catholic faith they passed on to their children. My dad, Pedro Alderete, was born in Valencia, New Mexico in 1914. My mom, Rosella Candelaria Montoya-Alderete, affectionately called Grandma Candy, was born in Torreón in 1918. I am the fifth child of seven children. My brothers and sisters are Vicente, Gloria, Christella Hilda, Dennis (Dinas) and Leroy.

My dad grew up in Valencia, and my mom grew up in Torreón. My dad would sometimes travel with his sister Carlota and her husband, Jose Maria, in their horse and wagon to Torreón, and this is how he met my mother. My dad must have fallen in love with my mom because getting to Torreón was no easy task in those days. My dad would visit my mom twice a month, and sometimes he would take one of his brothers Lorenzo, Nick or Ernesto with him. My dad would travel on horseback from Valencia to Torreón taking a shortcut through the Manzano Mountains. He would spend the night in the mountains and then go down through the *arroyo*. My dad told me how he would cross through the *piedra lisa* and how his horse would fly off the rock as he passed on top of it. My mom said, she was always staring out the window or waiting outside to see when my dad was coming down the *arroyo* to visit her. Imagine, there were no cell phones at this time or landline telephones. Eventually, my parents did get married and settled down to raise their family in Torreón.

My dad had many jobs in his lifetime. One of those jobs was working for the Santa Fe Railroad. I remember when I was about 10 to 12 years old, and when it was time for my dad to leave for work, my sisters Hilda, Christella and my brothers Vicente, Dinas and I would all cram into our green International truck to take my dad to the train depot in Mountainair. I remember Vicente would have to hand crank the truck to get it started. My dad would catch the train to go work in Kansas City, and he would be away for about a month at a time. He would travel with his friend Fidel Sedillo, also known as *Pájaro*. My dad leaving was always hard on us. We would watch him board the train with his *mochila*, which was a rolled up mattress with his belongings inside. We were all so sad to see my dad go, and we would wave goodbye to my dad as he waved through the window.

We were always anxiously awaiting the return of my dad. He could come day or night. When he came back into town, he would arrive at the Willard train station, and from there he would get a ride from a friend to our house in Torreón. As soon as we saw a truck pull up to the house, we got all excited, but we were never sure if it was my dad until we saw his *mochila* in the back of the truck. This was the signal that dad was home. As soon as we saw the backpack, we would all run outside to greet him. My dad would get out of the truck, walk around to the bed and pick up his things. We would grab his *mochila* and open it because we knew there were lots of goodies inside. He would bring us big boxes full of candy bars. One time when Dennis and I were young boys, he brought us two little railroad suits. It was the *pachetas* and the hats to match. We were all happy wearing our suits.

When my dad was gone, my mom was left with a bunch of children and was always busy. It wasn't easy raising the more than half a dozen kids. Vicente, the oldest, was away a lot of the time working with Manuel Brown on a windmill, sometimes staying overnight. My mom didn't like staying alone at night even though she had a house full of children. I guess we weren't old enough for her. Sometimes she would let us invite someone to sleep over. I always invited my cousin Pablo Perea, the son of my *tía* Carlota and my *tío* Jose Maria, who lived next door to us. Other times my sister Christella would invite our cousin Corrine, the daughter of my auntie Leonela and uncle Melcor, who lived within walking distance to the south of us. We always had a full house of kids, and every day was an adventure.

One time when my dad was working out of town, Christella invited Corrine to spend the night. Christella, Corrine and Hilda loved to make fudge, and Dinas and Leroy and I loved the fudge they made. Sometimes the fudge would come out really sloppy or hard or all *caramelo* because they heated it too long on the woodstove. One night, we were all enjoying our fudge when Corrine started yelling, "Look! Look! There's a man outside the house." The curtains in the kitchen didn't close all the way, and she said she could see a man standing outside, pointing towards us. Chris and Hilda came running to look out the window, and they said, "Where?" Corrine said, "Over there! Over there!" She pointed towards the man. Christella and Hilda said they could see him too. Dinas and I came running to look out the window, and we saw him too. I remember there was a full moon out that night, and we all started to panic. Corrine ran to tell my mom, "¡Tía! ¡Tía! There's a tall man standing outside over there by the corral, looking through the window." My mom became worried and said, "*Treame la farrola o una vela y enciende lo,*" and she got her broom. She said, "Vamos *afuera para ver quien es.*" By now, Corrine was really scared, and she said, "No way, I'm not going out there," but we all got our hands together and walked outside in a line. First, it was my mom, then Christella, Corrine, Hilda, me and then Dinas and Leroy. All of us walked real slow and quietly out the door towards the corral. When we finally got closer and closer to the corral, my mom said, "Oh, my goodness look what it is?" It was a pair of coveralls that my mom had washed and were hanging on the clothesline. The coveralls were blowing in the wind, and the hands were blowing back and forth, so we thought the man's hands were pointing at us through the window. We were really relieved when we found out what it was because Corrine had us really scared, but Corrine was that way. She was always yelling and panicking. We really miss Corrine. She was a good cousin who's gone now.

My parents had seven children, and the house we lived in wasn't very big. We didn't have a lot, so we often had to share what we did have, and sometimes this led to arguments. Dennis, Leroy and I had to share the same drawer for our clothes, and we could never remember what socks belonged to who. Hilda and Christella also had to share the same drawer, and they also had arguments.

Our house had two bedrooms. One room was where all the kids slept. When Pablo and Corrine came to sleep over it would be Vicente, Gloria, Christella, Corrine, Hilda, Dinas, Pablo, Leroy and me, all sleeping in one crowded room. My mom had the other room to herself. Every night my mom was ready to go to sleep by eight-thirty. By five-thirty or six o'clock in the morning, we could hear her in the kitchen making coffee. She would say to us, "Get up now that the sun is up," and she would make us get up early.

Sometimes Dinas and I would wake up in the middle of the night because we could hear the sounds of crumpled candy wrappers. Vicente, Gloria or Christella would steal the candies that my dad brought from Kansas City, and they would eat them under the covers. We would wake up and say, "Hey, I hear some noise, somebody is eating candy that's not fair," and we would get into arguments over the candy. My mom would hear us fighting in the middle of the night and get mad at us. She would yell from the other room, "Shut up! Be quiet! I'm trying to sleep!" Sometimes in the middle of the night, someone would need to go to the bathroom. We didn't have an indoor bathroom, so whenever someone had to use the bathroom someone had to walk outside to the outhouse with them. The outhouse was away from the house, and we were afraid to go alone. We had to light a candle, walk outside and wait for each other to use the bathroom. Sometimes we didn't have toilet paper to use in the outhouse, so we had to use old magazines and catalogs.

As a boy, I went to school in a four-room schoolhouse, which is now the community center. Because the winters in Torreón were very cold and snowy, someone would have to go and build a fire in the school every morning before school started. I think it was the county who would hire one of the families to do this, and one year it was my dad's turn. Christella and Pablo and I would wake up early in the morning, and by six o'clock we were walking through the *arroyo* to go help my dad. We would help bring in wood from the shed that was located next to the school, and we would make a fire in Mrs. Herrera's room, Mrs. Aragon's room, Mr. Perea's room and in Ms. Otero's room. These are the four teachers that I remember when I was in school.

We didn't like winter afternoons because there was always a lot of work to do. Every afternoon we had to pile up wood inside the house to make sure we had enough wood to make it through the night. We had the kitchen stove plus two other stoves in the house that we kept lit all night.

It seemed that every year the water pipes in Pablo's house and my parent's house would freeze. By the time Halloween came around in October and in November and December, we didn't have running water in the kitchen. We had to get water from Roberto Lujan's well that was between my house and my *tío* Melcor's house. Almost everyone in my family and Pablo's family would have to walk with big buckets full of water from the well and back home, back and forth, back and forth. It wasn't too far, but with buckets full of water and in the cold, we got tired. The well had a big lever, and we would pop it. We all took turns popping water *POP, POP, POP, POP!* This well was so rich it gave water to everyone in Torreón, but it was a lot of work. To take a bath we had to warm up buckets and buckets of water on the woodstove and then toss it into the *cajete*. We would take our bath in the kitchen near the stove where it was warm. However, the *cajete* was so small and round, we didn't have much room to sit. Later on my dad bought us a better *cajete*. It was a longer one where we had room to sit.

I spent a lot of time with my cousin Pablo when I was a kid. I also spent a lot of time with my friends Frank and Eloy, who lived near the *arroyo*. They were the sons of Mrs. Sanchez, who ran the post office out of her house in Torreón. The Sanchez family had a separate large room right next to their main home that everyone called *la galera*. We spent a lot of time in *la galera*. We also spent a lot of time playing outside.

One summer Pablo and I decided we wanted to build a little shack where we could hang out. Pablo and I went to find boards in an old abandoned house. When we found a board we liked, we would throw it outside through the broken windows of the abandoned house. We brought the boards back to my parent's house and built a shack in the backyard near the big corral and the stable. Dinas, who was three years younger than me, helped us build the shack. We even put a woodstove in the shack that we found in my backyard. My dad had left the stove there because it had a crack in it. He was going to weld it and fix it one day, but we decided to put it in the shack. In the winter we made a fire in the stove and slept in the house we built. Sometimes the rain would come, and we could feel the water dripping through the roof on our heads. Pablo and I decided to call the shack "The Sugar Shack." There was a Sugar Shack restaurant in Mountainair that we thought was so cool. Teenagers would come and hang out there in their fancy cars and buy ice cream and hamburgers. So that's what we called our shack "The Sugar Shack."

In those days the houses in Torreón were never fenced, and people would use the land in the back of our house as a shortcut to get to their homes. They would walk or ride through on their horse or on their horse and wagon. The Pereas, the Sedillos and the Sanchezes would all come through to get to church. One day a neighbor was passing by, and he stopped to look in the Sugar Shack. He said, "Hey, I like that burrito stove you got in there," and he asked me how much I wanted for the stove. He said he would trade me a *maranito* for the stove. I was a young boy, so I thought it was a good deal. I thought, I'm swapping the stove for the pig. Anyway, during the winter we weren't spending much time in the shack because we were spending more time with Frank and Eloy in the *galera*. Right away, my neighbor came with his sons to pick up the stove, and he said, "I'll bring you the pig later." A few days later he showed up with a tiny baby pig. He was so tiny, I had to build him a small pigpen. When my dad saw the pig and noticed that the stove was gone, he asked, "What happened to the stove?" I told him, "I traded it for the little pig." He was very upset. The first thing he said was, "Oh, shit." Then he said, "That piece of shit is too small. That burrito stove was worth way more than that *maranito* you got there." Anyway, I took care of the pig until he grew up, and then we butchered him. In the end, he turned out to be a really good size pig.

Summers in Torreón were always fun, and we always had plenty to do. Pablo would say, "It's time for the *zancos*." We would make the *zancos* out of two by four pieces of wood. The people of Torreón used to say that there was an old sawmill there at one time. I never saw it, but maybe my older brother Vicente remembers it. Anyway, there was a big pile of *escapotes* thrown near the *mantoncito,* and Pablo, Eloy, Dennis, Liberty (Frank and Eloy's younger brother) and I would get the *escapotes* and bring them home. Pablo would cut the wood with a *serruche* that he borrowed from his dad. Then he would nail the wood for us, and we would go find something to use as the straps. At that time, my dad had stopped using his wagon, so he had the *gauriniciones* hanging in the big stable. We would get a knife and cut pieces of the leather and use them as straps for the *zancos*. We would hear my dad say, "What's happening to the *gauriniciones*? The leather is all gone. There is nothing but chains left." We would laugh because we were stealing it. When there was nothing left of the *gauriniciones*, we got some knives and cut some old used tires, and that's what we used for the straps. When these *zancos* wore out, Pablo would help us make the stilts out of old cans and wire. We would go to *el basudero* out there by the *mantoncito,* and we would find old cans of orange juice or Pet milk. Pablo would poke a little hole in the can and pull some bedding wire through the can. We would hold the wire up to our knees, and we would walk with the cans on our feet. We could hear the *zancos* go *plunk, plunk, plunk, plunk!* We thought it was so cool to see everybody with their *zancos* running around town. It was a tradition.

Pablo was one of the oldest kids, and he taught us all how to walk on the *zancos*. We would walk on the road to the *mantoncito*. We all walked in a row, following the leader, one after another. Pablo was also one of the best ones on the *zancos*. My *padrino* Nicanor, my *tío* Lorenzo and my cousin Junior would come and drink a beer with my dad, and they would say, "Son of a gun, look how good Pablo is." Pablo would jump on one leg, and he would jump from the porch down to the floor and do all sorts of tricks on the *zancos*.

Sometimes in the summer, our toys would be old tires. We would roll tires all over the little roads. There were little trails all over the back of our house to Pablo's house and to the *mantoncito*. My dad had one of the biggest stables in Torreón, and the kids liked to play in the stable because it was tall, and it had *vigas* that enclosed the corral on all four sides. The kids would jump from one *viga* to another. Outside near the stable, we also had a tire swing. We liked to sit on the tire and spin and spin until we were so dizzy we could barely stay on the tire. We would laugh and have fun.

We loved to go camping during the summer. Pablo would say, "Let's go camping," and he would get the ax from his dad and we would go. We went deep into the *mantoncito,* and when we found a spot, Pablo would say, "Ok, this is a perfect place to make a little *campito.* We would cut greens and junipers and tie them together and pile them on top of each other and make a little tent. We would bring a candle to build a fire, and we would cook the best food. Before we went camping, Pablo would say to us, "Remember you have to steal whatever potatoes from your house that you can. If you can get two potatoes, get two, or three or four, whatever you can." Frank and Eloy would come with red potatoes. I would come with white potatoes, and Pablo would come with brown potatoes. Pablo would also steal a salt shaker from his mom's house. We would throw the potatoes in the fire until they got dark black. Then we would get the steaming, hot potatoes out of the fire, open them up, put salt on them and eat them. Boy, was it a good supper. We really enjoyed it.

We went camping maybe twice a week during the summer months, and Eloy, Frank, Pablo and I enjoyed playing tricks on Dinas, and Liberty. We would all agree to go camping, but we wouldn't tell Dinas and Liberty. We would send them to go do something, and we would take off on our camping trip without them. When they noticed we weren't around, they would come looking for us in the *mantoncito*. They would come walking together, really slowly and sad, dragging a little blanket behind them. They would yell, "Hey, Peté, Pablo, Eloy where are you guys?" The whole time we would be hiding, laughing and watching them come through the *arroyo* or around another way, and we couldn't stop laughing.

My mom worried about us when we camped outside. Early in the morning, she would stand near the *mantoncito,* "¿*Pablo, Pedro donde están?*" We would yell back, "¡*Hay vamos!* We're ok! We're ok!" She would be worried that we had got caught in the rain or something had happened to us. We would come back all dirty. Our hands and face would be all black from the fire and the dirt. It was so much fun and a beautiful time.

One summer when I was about 12 years old, Frank, Dinas, Pablo, Liberty and I were coming from one of our camping trips, and we stopped to swim in the *jondable,* which was irrigation water that would spill over at the *arroyo,* right next to the store that Mr. Salas owned. The water wasn't really that deep maybe about four feet deep, but to us, it was deep because we were all shorties. We spent the day swimming, and we were hot, tired and hungry. For some reason, Pablo had a little money with him. He had some quarters and some change. When Frank and I saw the money, we said, "Damn!" It was not common for any of us to have money, but since Pablo had money, we decided to go to Mr. Salas's store.

Boyhood Adventures in Torreón, New Mexico

We went inside the store and on top of the counter was a big square chocolate sheet cake. Frank and I saw the cake and said, "Oh, that looks good!" The cake was about a dollar and some change. Pablo saw us looking at the cake, and he said, "I'll buy the cake for you, but you have to cut the cake in half, and you both have to eat it." He said, "You have to eat it without water, nothing." Frank asked, "Not even a coke?" Mr. Salas used to sell those small, short bottles of coke. Pablo said, "No, nothing." Frank said, "*hijole*, it's so hot, and I'm so hungry." Frank and I looked at each other. Then Frank said, "I dare you," and I said, "I will go for it, if you do." Pablo said, "If you guys don't eat all the cake then you guys have to pay me back for the cake. I got my witnesses." It was Liberty and Dinas. So, we said, "Ok." Pablo bought the cake, and we went behind the store to eat it. Pablo got out his knife that he always carried with him, and he cut the cake in half. Liberty and Dinas were there looking at us, hungry and staring at the cake. Frank and I started to eat the cake, slowly. When we were both about three-quarters finished with the cake, I took a deep breath and asked Pablo if I could have some water. Pablo shook his head and said, "Ah, Ah, No, No, No!" Dinas and Liberty kept watching us and would ask us, "Hey, do you want us to help you?" Pablo would say, "No *chica* bites for anybody, no *chica* bites, no nothing. Frank and Pete have to eat it all, or they have to pay for the cake." I remember I would take a deep breath and crumbs would fly out of my mouth into the air. Frank would take a deep breath and say, "I can't breathe! I can't breathe! I think I'm gonna get sick." He was breathing in and out like a horse, and the crumbs would fly out of his mouth to the floor. Every time we tried to breathe, we would spit out crumbs, and Pablo would make Dinas and Liberty catch all the crumbs or pick them up from the floor. Pablo would tell Liberty and Dinas, "Get those crumbs from the floor," and they would pick them up and put them in Pablo's hand.

Finally, we finished the cake and Pablo said, "Wait! Hold on. You're not done. Look at these crumbs in my hand." He said, "Open your mouth," and he took the crumbs and dropped them in our mouths. If we spit them out, he made the boys pick up the crumbs again. Pablo would tell Frank, "Open your mouth *güero*," and he would throw the crumbs back into his mouth. Pablo made us eat all the cake and the crumbs, and when the cake and crumbs were gone, he was still looking around for crumbs. Finally, Pablo said, "Ok, you guys did it. Go ahead and get some water." We ran like crazy into the little irrigation canal, and we dropped ourselves into the water. The water was crystal clear, and we stayed there laying in the water. We drank the water like dogs, holding our stomachs, saying, "Thanks to God. Thanks to God." Eating all that cake on a hot summer day was torture.

If we weren't sleeping in the *mantoncito*, we would sleep with Frank and Eloy in the *galera*. When Pablo and I would come home from a basketball game or from some other place, we would stop at my mom's house and Pablo's house, and we would shout through the windows because the windows were always open. We would yell, "Mom, we're going to sleep in the *galera*," and our moms would say, "Ok, go ahead, *mucho cuidado*," and we walked to the *galera*. We slept three to a bed. Liberty, Dinas and me in one bed and Frank and Pablo and Eloy in the other bed. Sometimes at two o'clock in the morning, Frank or Pablo or I would wake up. There was electricity in the *galera,* so we would pull the light switch and turn on the light. We would pick up Liberty's socks and put them in his mouth, and we would laugh and laugh. We were all just having a good time. We teased and played tricks on each other, but we always knew it was all for fun.

At some point the school was moved from Torreón to Estancia, so the school building was used for other things. A big, tall man named Mr. Benedict would come from Albuquerque to Torreón and give us religious classes in the old school house. He was part of an organization that would come to help the families in the east mountain because most of the families in the area at that time were poor and didn't have much. The organization brought us food and clothes. They brought army clothes and canned foods like pork in beans, tamales in a can, green beans, cereal and other foods that wouldn't spoil. The organization stored the food in the old school house building, and then the food and clothes were passed out to the residents. There was a set amount of food that each home could receive.

One year Eloy and I decided to plan for the winter. I don't know how or why we got this idea into our heads, but we thought before the food was passed out, we should stash some food for ourselves. We thought we would get our own can opener, and in the winter when we woke up in the morning, we could open up a can and have a little bit of food for ourselves in bed. I remember Eloy said, "This food will never go bad." So I said, "Ok, this is a great idea let's do it." There was a partition in the building made out of plywood, and so we decided to store the food behind the plywood wall. We stacked a little bit of food behind the partition, and then we started to get greedy. We looked at the stash and said "We need more. The winters here are very heavy," so we hid more food. We kept coming back and hiding more and more food until the pile was about four feet high and four feet wide. When we were done stacking up our food there was a bed in the school house that we would move in front of the partition. We thought this was a good hiding place for our food and nobody would find it.

Eloy's mom, Mrs. Sanchez and his sister Ramona were the ones in charge of separating the clothes and the food at the old school house, and they helped distribute the food. Sometime after we had stashed away the food, we heard Mrs. Sanchez ask Ramona, "*Oye,* for some reason, it seems like the food is disappearing. How many cans have you been giving away?" Ramona said, "I don't know what's happening to the food, I'm only giving out what I'm supposed to give." Eloy and I looked at each other and didn't say anything.

One day Mrs. Sanchez and Ramona were moving the furniture and the beds around in the building, and they noticed a bulge coming from behind the plywood. They started to feel around, and they heard something fall from behind the plywood. They started to pull open the wall, and as they were opening it, the cans started to fall from the wall. I don't know who told

Ramona that it was Eloy and me who were stashing food for the winter, but we got in big trouble. Ramona was very mad at us. One day Pablo and I were walking to the post office to pick up the mail. I was happy, whistling but when I got to the post office, Ramona saw me. She said, "Peté come here! I want to talk to you. It's very embarrassing what you and Eloy were doing." At first, I didn't know what she was talking about, so I said, "What?" She said, "You guys were hiding food in the wall that is supposed to go to the people. That was a terrible thing to do, and you guys should be ashamed of yourselves." I said, "Ok, Ok" because she started to tell me off. I told Pablo, "Let's go. Let's go." I was pretty embarrassed.

As I was growing up, the older guys like my cousin Pablo would go work on the ranches in the valley shucking alfalfa and cane. I was still too young to go work with them. Maybe I was about 13 years old, but I wanted to work. Frank and Eloy wanted to work too, so we decided to go look for a job. We went to Manuel Brown's house, who was the blacksmith in Torreón, to see if he had a job for us, but he didn't. While we were at Mr. Brown's house, we ran into his friend el *Coronel*. Everyone called this man el *Coronel* because he was a retired colonel. He always drove a tractor with a wagon attached to it, and he always had about six little white dogs with him. I think they were a dachshund mix. Anyway, Frank, Eloy and I helped el *Coronel* unload some boxes of bolts and other things from his wagon, and we told him we were looking for work. He told us to come up to his ranch tomorrow, and he might have some work for us. He said his name was Paul McVay. We asked him where the ranch was, and he said it was by the Sandia Summer Camp. We asked him, "Is it near the apple orchards?" He said, "Yes." It turned out that the ranch used to be the ranch of Don Francisco, a relative of Frank and Eloy's. So, anyway, we were happy to find a job.

The next day we got up early and walked towards the ranch. We walked and walked until we got to the *questasita de pierda*. Everybody knew that once you were at the *questasita de pierda*, you were halfway to the ranch. We kept walking, and we finally got up to the ranch. Once we were there, Mr. McVay asked us what our names were, and we said, "Peter Alderete, Frank Sanchez and Eloy Sanchez." For some reason, Mr. McVay never remembered our names. He would say, "Ok Frank, you take the boys and do this and that." Maybe he remembered Frank's name because he was the oldest. So that day, he told Frank to take us to the corral and clean up the manure. We did the work that day, and he told us to come back the next day. He never told us how much he was going to pay us, but we knew we had a job, so we were happy. Still, we were wondering how much we were going to get paid.

When we returned to work at the ranch, Mr. McVay had just gotten back from Albuquerque, and he had us unload some things from his truck. He gave Frank some brand new work gloves to give to us. They were really nice gloves that fit our hands perfectly. Mr. McVay then told Frank to take us to the barn and have us clean out the manure from the chicken coop. He wanted us to break up the manure, put it into a wheel barrow and take it and dump it near the *arroyo*. *El Coronel* then jumped on his tractor with his little dogs, and we could see him chewing his tobacco as he took off.

We kept coming back each week. Once we got there, Mr. McVay would tell Frank what we needed to do, and then he would take off on his tractor. We would watch him drive away until he would disappear. He would be gone for a long time, so we worked there by ourselves. We laughed, talked, took our time and worked comfortably. Later in the day, Mr. McVay would come back, and say, "Ok, good job. I will see you guys tomorrow."

Sometimes when we were walking to the ranch, Mr. McVay would pass us on the road, and he would say, "I'll be back later. I'm going to Manuel's house. When you get to the ranch you can start cutting weeds around the barn," or he would have another job for us. He would say, "All the tools are there. You can start working." He still hadn't said anything about how much he was going to pay us or when he was going to pay us. So, we were still wondering about our money, but we kept going back.

Finally, it came time to pay us. Mr. McVay got out his checkbook and said, "Ok, to Frank Sanchez," and he wrote the check out to Frank. Frank went to cash the check, and we were each making about $5.00 a week. We were happy with our $5.00.

One time when we were working at the ranch, Frank said, "Look, Mr. McVay leaves the keys in the tractor, he trusts us." Then he said, "I wonder how hard it is to operate this tractor." Frank and I decided to get on the tractor, and Eloy stood there watching us. Frank started the tractor, and it cranked right up, but the power lift was down, and we didn't know how to raise it up. Frank said, "First gear is here," and he slipped it into gear, but when he let go of the clutch, the tractor started to plow a big hole behind us. I remember Eloy was yelling, "Stop! Stop! Stop! Look what you're doing!" Finally, Frank was able to shut off the tractor, and we got off and looked at the hole. We left about a six or seven-foot long hole in front of the house. For this incident, Mr. McVay cut us some slack. The next day, he came to talk to us and said, "I know you guys were playing on the tractor. You made a giant trench that I had to cover." He said, "I don't want you guys playing on the tractor again." We said, "Ok, we're sorry," and he gave us another chance. That was the last time we played on the tractor. We continued to work on the ranch, and pretty soon each of us had about $20 to $30 saved. We were saving our money for the Torreón *fiestas*. At that time there was really no other way to spend our money.

While we were working at the ranch, Mr. McVay would leave the door of the house unlocked, so we could go in and get some water. One Friday afternoon, we went into the house to get some water, and we noticed a big birthday cake on the kitchen table. We stopped to look at the cake. We looked at the cake, and then we looked at each other. Eloy said, "I'm hungry." Frank said, "So am I," and I said, "Me too," and we couldn't stop looking at the cake.

Finally, Eloy reached out his hand and touched the cake with one finger. He got some frosting on his finger and put it in his mouth and said,

"Boy, this is good." Then Frank said, "Let me see," and he tasted the frosting. I tasted it, and then we all started tasting the frosting from a corner of the cake. It was really good. Frank said, "Mr. McVay is going to notice what we did to the cake." Eloy said, "I don't think he'll mind," and we all grabbed a piece of cake with our hands, and we tore up one side of the cake. While we were eating the cake, we noticed there was a big, tall, brown barrel on a shelf. It was one of those barrels made out of old-fashioned oak with bands around it, and the top was covered with a white dish towel. We climbed on a bench, looked inside the barrel, and it was full of beer. Frank said, "I'm going to taste it," and he grabbed a glass and tasted it. I told Frank, "I'm gonna taste it, too," and I tasted it and so did Eloy. We all had a little mustache of beer around our mouths. One of us said, "Should we get another drink?" We all agreed to have one more little drink. We thought Mr. McVay wouldn't notice. Frank got another drink, and I got another drink, and Eloy got another drink. Then we went and rinsed the glasses and put them upside down on the shelf, closed the door and we walked home.

    Saturday morning we were walking to work, and we ran into Mr. McVay on the *questasita*. He was going towards the ranch, and we thought he was going to stop and give us a ride back to the ranch on his wagon. He stopped when he saw us, and he got out of the truck. He said, "I want to talk to you boys," and he said, "Frank, give me those gloves." He took our gloves away, and he said, "You guys are fired." We said, "Mr. McVay what happened?" He said, "You know what happened. You guys destroyed my birthday cake. I gave you another chance when you guys got on the tractor and made that hole, but what you did to the cake, that was it," and he fired us. So, unfortunately, we lost our jobs that year.

    As we got older, we would see Parras, who was a little bit older than Pablo, playing his guitar around town. When we saw Parras coming, Pablo would say, *"Hay viene Parras con su guitarita."* Pablo, Liberty, Dinas and another friend Clemente (Blues) Perea loved to watch Parras play the guitar. He was learning to play the guitar from a guy in Manzano, one of the Padillas. He would play some songs in Spanish, and I really liked the way the guitar sounded. I had grown up with my dad playing the accordion, and one day I decided I wanted to play the accordion too. I would go into the bedroom, close the door and practice playing the accordion, and I taught myself to play. Now, I wanted to learn how to play the guitar.

    One day Parras said, "If you guys get a guitar, I'll teach you guys to play." I thought it was a good idea. I said to Pablo, "I wonder how we can get a guitar, and how much would one cost?" Pablo said, "Look, it's very easy to get a guitar," and he brought me a Sears Catalog and an Eldens Catalog. These were the magazines we used to get in the mail, and a lot of people had them to order things. They were big and thick, and when they were old, it was these catalogs that we put in the outhouses, and we used them to clean our behinds. These catalog pages helped us make it through the year. Pablo showed me the guitars in the book, and I saw one for $12.00. That would be my first guitar. I don't remember if it was a Stella or a Silvertone. Eloy said he also wouldn't to buy a guitar, so he found one in the catalog he liked, and since he had money, he ordered his guitar first.

We had already been fired from e*l Coronel's* ranch, so I didn't have any money. I told Eloy and Frank I needed to look for a job, and they decided to go with me. We walked to Earl Lundy's ranch. It wasn't too far from Torreón, maybe half a mile. Earl Lundy had acres and acres of pinto beans. Liberty, Eloy, Frank and I all got jobs there. I can't remember if Pablo worked there too. We worked hoeing beans and cutting weeds, and it seemed like it would take forever to get to the end of each row. The rows would last forever. We would go down one row and up another row and then back down again. We would walk to work in the morning past the cemetery and walk back in the afternoon. We did this every day for a few weeks. I can't remember exactly how much we got paid. It wasn't that much, and the job only lasted a couple of weeks, but I saved about $20.00.

Eloy helped me fill out the paperwork for the guitar, and I ordered my first guitar. Every day we would stand and wait for Valeras, the mailman, to bring the mail to the post office. The first guitar he brought was Eloy's because he had ordered his first. One day we saw Valeras drive up to the post office, and we saw a big box in the back of his truck. As soon as he got the box out of the truck, we knew it was the guitar, and we ran over to see it. Eloy got the guitar, and we all ran over to the *galera* to open the box. There were about ten guys around Eloy, all anxious to see the new guitar. We didn't know anything about it. We didn't know how to tune it or anything. Somebody called Parras, and he came and tuned the guitar for us, and we liked the sound of it.

Pablo decided he was going to order a guitar too, a bigger and fancier one because he had a little bit more money. He ordered a Spanish guitar. It was a pretty, gray one. The guitars Eloy and I ordered were brown. Again, everyday, we waited for Valeras. We would wait by the *arroyo* or by our house or at the post office. Each day he would come with a big duffle bag full of letters but no guitar. "Maybe today the guitars are coming," we would say. We couldn't wait to get our guitars. The guitars took about a month to arrive, which seemed like forever. Finally, the guitars arrived, and we all had one. I had a guitar. Pablo had a guitar. Eloy had a guitar, and Blues ordered two guitars. So now we had several guitars to play. Parras was our teacher. He would say, "Ok, line up here," and he would help us tune our guitars. He would teach us something, and we would practice and practice, and we couldn't get the hang of it. *POUND, POUND, POUND, POUND*, back and forth, back and forth, we would play. Parras would say, "Ok, that's enough, I'll see you guys again tomorrow afternoon." We kept coming back and practicing, and little by little, Blues and I started to get the hang of it. I really liked playing the guitar, and I practiced a lot. I wouldn't stop. I would sit by myself in the corral and practice, and Blues would come to my house, and we would practice together. We would go to Parras's house when we needed help, and he would say, "Ok, show me what you guys have learned," and we would show him what we learned. Pablo would practice with us too, but he had other things to do. Pablo always liked school, so he would rather study. I didn't care for school that much, but I was very interested in the guitar. Once I learned the keys on the guitar, I started getting faster and faster. I started following the keys on the Spanish guitar, and Blues and I would compete with one another. Blues and I were getting really good on the guitar, and we started to play rock and roll music and cumbias.

One day Parras said, "We should see if we can get some electric guitars and put a band together." I said, "That's a good idea," and Blues thought it was a good idea too.

Then one day we saw Blues, and he told us, "You won't believe what I got. Let's go to my house, so I can show you what I got." We went to Blue's house, and his dad had bought him an electric guitar and a deluxe amplifier. He plugged in the electric guitar and played it, and it sounded beautiful. We all got a chance to play on it. Blues played the guitar, Parras played it and then I played it. I told Blues, "Watch, I'm going to get me one too." Jose Manuel really liked the guitar too. He was another friend from Torreón, who had ordered a guitar and was also playing the guitar with us.

At this time a bunch of kids my age had dropped out of school, including myself, so I needed to find a job. I was now about 16 years old, and my *tío* Melcor asked me to go work with him at the Crider ranch. It was Barry Crider's dad's ranch. They had a lot of *terrenos* full of corn and other crops, and they had pigs and cows. They had this machine that would dump the corn into a truck, and then my *tío* Melcor and I would shovel the corn into a big quonset tank house. When we weren't shoveling corn, we worked in the field shucking cane. We would gather all the cane into the middle of the field, and we would make some big *montones grandotes*. We also worked cleaning manure because of the *marranos* in the corral. It was hard work, but my *tío* Melcor was strong at the time, and I was getting strong too. We probably made about a dollar an hour, and we worked there for a couple of months.

I was saving my money, and I saved about $60.00. Jose Manuel also had money for an electric guitar, so I told him, "We should go to Albuquerque to see how much the electric guitars cost." We thought about looking at used electric guitars because they didn't have to be new. The only problem was, we didn't have a ride to Albuquerque. Jose Manuel remembered that there was a bus that went from Estancia through Willard to Moriarty and then to Albuquerque, but we would need a ride to Estancia. I thought we could get a ride with the mailman Herbert Moore in his Volkswagen. Herbert Moore would come to Torreón from Estancia to bring the mail. Barreras, the other mailman, would come from Mountainair, and they would both exchange mail here in Torreón. Herbert would take the mail back to Estancia, and Barreras would take the mail back to Mountainair. One day, we waited for Herbert at the post office. We asked him for a ride to Estancia to catch the bus, and he said, "Yes."

When we got to Estancia, we waited for the bus. Finally, it came. The bus drove us to Albuquerque and let us off downtown on Central. We were kind of lost, so we walked around for a while trying to find our way around. We started to walk north a few blocks on Fourth Street, not far from Central when we saw the sign that said "Dock Holidays Hock Shop." We went into the store, and there were all kinds of things in the store like guns, violins, rings and knives. We looked around for a while, and then we saw the guitars on the wall, and we ran over to see them. I found a guitar I really liked. It was a Gibson Melody Maker, a yellow and dark brown one. I asked the clerk how much the guitar cost, and he told me $60.00. I had about $65.00 or $75.00. Without even trying out the guitar, I told him, I would take it. I asked him if he had a case for the guitar. He had one that didn't even match the guitar, but the guitar fit perfectly. I also asked him for the electric wire that goes from the guitar to the amplifier. I think it cost about $1.00 or $2.00, so I bought that too. Jose Manuel bought a red Gibson guitar that cost about $75.00 with a case. I told Jose that I also wanted to buy an amplifier. The man at the store had a yellow old style used one. It was $30.00 or $35.00. I didn't have any money left, so I asked Jose if he had some money he could loan me. He loaned me some money, and we got the amplifier. We walked out of the store that day very happy, carrying our guitars. We took the amplifier back to Torreón, and we shared it for a while. After I had paid Jose Manuel the money that I owed him, the amplifier became mine.

We had a good time playing our electric guitars on our amplifiers. Parras loved my Gibson guitar. He would come around and say, "Hey, let's play the Gibson." We would get together with Blues and Jose Manuel, and we would plug our guitars into Blue's amplifier because we could plug two or three guitars into it at a time. I really liked the amplifier that Blues had. It was a deluxe reverb, and my Gibson sounded beautiful on it. I told Blues, "I'm going to get one like that." I liked the amplifier I had bought, but it just wasn't as nice as the one Blue's had. I had already told my mom I was saving my money to buy a new amplifier.

Good thing I was saving my money for a new amplifier. One day I was playing my guitar with Liberty, Pablo, Dinas, Parras and some other guys when all of a sudden my amplifier just stopped working. It looked like a fuse had burnt out. We didn't have anywhere in Torreón to buy a fuse, so Parras suggested we wrap a piece of foil around the broken fuse to see if that would work. We used the foil from Parras's cigarettes and wrapped it around the fuse and it worked. I was able to continue playing my guitar for a good while. After a while, though, smoke started coming out of the amplifier, and it completely burnt out, so I no longer had an amplifier.

I continued to work with my *tío* Melcor on the ranch, and I had saved about a $100.00. One day my mom was coming to Albuquerque with my sister Christella and Christella's husband, Eloy. I told them I wanted to come with them to buy an amplifier. I can't remember how I got to Don Lesmans Music Store downtown once I got to Albuquerque, but somehow I got there. I went into the store and looked at the amplifiers and the prices. The amplifier I wanted to buy was $250.00. It was the same one that Blue's had. Christella was already living in Albuquerque, so I remember I went and asked her if I could borrow $100.00. The first thing she asked was, "Why?" I

Boyhood Adventures in Torreón, New Mexico

told her I wanted to buy an amplifier that cost $250.00, and I only had a $100.00. I told her I would pay her back, and she agreed to loan me the money. I went back to Don Lesmans, and I bought the amplifier. I remember Eloy took my mom and me and my brand new amplifier back to Torreón. I was so excited with my amplifier. As soon as I got to Torreón, I went to tell my friends what I had bought. Then I went home and plugged in my Gibson guitar to the amplifier, and boy did it sound great. Blues went and got his amplifier and brought it to my house, and we had both amplifiers plugged in at the same time. All of a sudden, all the kids from Torreón were gathered at the front of my house, listening to us play. The amplifiers were blasting the house. It was so loud, and it sounded so nice.

My mom reminded me that I had to pay back Christella the money that I had borrowed from her. It was in the back of my mind too. I got lucky because my uncle Melcor said that there was more work on the ranches in the area. We would ride together in his old, gray Chevy to the valley and work there. I finally got enough money to pay back Christella, and I was happy, and she was happy.

At this time Parras started singing, and he asked Blues and me to try and follow him on the guitars. He would sing James Brown music, which was very popular at the time. Parras became a really good singer, and Blues and I were playing really good music, so we decided we were ready to put a band together. One day we were trying to think of names for the band, and Parras said, "How about Parras and the Soul Parakeets?" So that's what we named our band. We also thought that if we were going to have a band, we would need a drummer. We knew that Bolesslo Perea from Estancia had a son named Boy that played the drums. I don't even remember Boy's real name, everybody just called him "Boy". We took our guitars to Estancia and went to Bolesslo and Boy's house. Bolesslo had a little room on the side of his house where the drums were set up, and Boy would practice the drums there. He was only about 13 years old, but he was learning to play from his dad. Boy joined our band and Parras, Blues and I started to teach him the beats, and he became a hell of a drummer. So now we had a band. The first time we played was for Tony Maldonado and Ida's wedding dance. After that dance, word got around that we had a band and that we played really good. We played at a couple of dances in Torreón, and the kids loved the music.

We heard that the high school in Mountainair needed a band for prom, so we went and asked if we could play, and we got the job. We played at the high school, and the teachers paid us for playing. That night we tore it up. Parras was sliding all around on the stage like James Brown, and everybody loved us. After that dance, we played at other dances, and our band kept getting better and better. With the money we made, we were able to buy some strobe lights and a couple of microphones. One of the microphones, we put in the background, and Parras had his own microphone because he was the singer. He had to be careful with the microphone, though, because one time he hit me in the face with it while dancing around on stage. Our band got more and more popular, and we were getting a lot of requests to play. We played at the wedding of Juan Chavez and Dalia Herrera at Fidel's hall in Torreón. The hall had hardwood floors, and the music sounded beautiful. We also played for the wedding of Orlando Lopez and Dolores Sanchez and several other weddings. One time we played for the Torreón *fiestas*. We were playing our music and making money, so we were happy.

One summer a new priest came to Torreón, and at this time there were a lot of guys in the area without jobs. This new priest said that he knew some people in Yosemite that would hire young kids to work for the summer. He said we were pretty much guaranteed a job once we got there. The Job Corp had also come into town, and they were also hiring young people for jobs. Frank decided to join Job Corp. Henry Sedillo and some other guys from Torreón also joined Job Corp. I decided to go to Yosemite and so did a friend named Bellamah. Pat and Louie, two other guys about my age from Tajique, were also going to Yosemite and said their dad was going to drive them in his Pontiac. I think it was a Pontiac. So Bellamah and I were able to get a ride with Pat and Louie and their dad to Yosemite. The priest had already called his friends in Yosemite, and they were expecting us.

We took off on a Saturday afternoon, and we drove until late into the night. I remember we stopped somewhere and rented a room, and the next day we drove all day. We finally got to Yosemite late that night, and we called our contacts to let them know we were there. I think we called from Fresno or Mercedes, and they said they had dinner ready and they were waiting for us. It was March when we got to Yosemite, and boy did we have a good time there. We lived in dorms. The boys stayed on the first floor of the building, and the girls stayed on the second floor. The dorms were within walking distance from Deckman's restaurant. From the restaurant we could stand there and look up and see Yosemite Falls, we could see it close. We could see people mountain climbing with their ropes on the mountain. I had never seen such huge canyons and such high mountain peaks. Coming from a small town like Torreón, all this was amazing to me.

Some of the guys that had come from back home didn't like the work very much. They only stayed a couple of weeks then returned home. They said they could make more money cutting and selling wood. I started to panic a bit because I wanted to make sure I was going to have a ride back home. Louie and Bellamah said they were staying. We heard that more guys from Mountainair were coming, so we thought if anything, we could get a ride back home with one of them, or we could go back home on the train, so I decided to stay.

I started working as a busboy in the restaurant, and I liked it. Then the manager asked me if I wanted to cook, so I started making hamburgers at night. They had really good food in the restaurant, and they had the best chocolate malts. In the morning for breakfast, I would eat a couple of bear claws. I had never seen so many bear claws before. I started gaining a lot of weight, and I got really big. I still exercised, and I was in good shape, but I still gained weight.

Boyhood Adventures in Torreón, New Mexico

I had already been there about two months when Bellamah got a letter from his sister saying that my family was coming to visit me, and they were on their way. The letter said my mom, dad, Dinas, Leroy, my older brother Vicente and his wife, Flora, and their son Melvin were all coming to visit me. Before I left to California, my dad had just bought a new 1965 Chevy truck. I wondered how they were all going to fit in that truck. Well, somehow they managed.

I had been expecting my family to come, but I wasn't sure what day they would arrive. The day they arrived, I had got word that someone was looking for me. I remember I was in my t-shirt and jeans and Bellamah and I were walking outside, when I heard someone call me, "Peté, Peté." It was Dinas. I remember he didn't have a shirt on, and he looked really dark and skinny. Dinas, Leroy and Melvin were all dark and sunburnt from traveling in the back of the truck. My dad had rigged up some homemade seats in the back of the truck. He put some two by four pieces of wood in each corner of the truck, covered them with a *tapolio* and secured them with some wire. Vicente drove the truck, and Flora and my mom and dad were all cramped together in the front seat.

My dad got out of the truck and put his summer cowboy hat on his head and said, "Oh, shit, you don't look like Peté, what happened to you?" He said, "You gained about 70 pounds." Vicente said, "You look healthy." I had been living high on the hog. I had been drinking all those malts and eating all those sweets. After we talked for a while, we got in our cars, and they followed us to the dorms. Bellamah had saved some money and had bought an old, small 1953 Chevy. The car was so old, it made a lot of noise as we drove to the dorms. Once we got there, I took my family to meet my bosses. They were Dutch men and they spoke with a Dutch accent. They met my family and right away, they gave my family a room for the night. It was a room with some little beds. The next day, Louie and I showed my family around. The animals were tame, and they would walk around all over the place. There were also lots of bears and deer everywhere. We took my family to a place where there was a little beach. The water was about five feet deep, and people would swim there. The next day we took pictures with my family, and then they took off, but it was a nice visit.

A week later some more kids from Mountainair came to work in Yosemite. It was Severo and Edwina and Roshina. The girls got jobs as waitresses. We all liked are jobs, and we were making good money. Severo started to save his money, and he bought a car. It was a really nice 1948 Chrysler. A guy we were working with was selling it, and Severo ended up paying about $400.00 or $500.00 cash for the car, which was a really good deal. One weekend, Severo, Bellamah and I went to Mercedes for the weekend. We went into some stores, and I found a box guitar, so I bought it. It was about $15.00. In the evening, I would play my guitar, and we would sing songs. We spent the whole summer working and having fun at Yosemite. It was now getting close to August or September, and the restaurant was going to be closing soon for the winter. Mr. Deckman said in his Dutch accent, "Peeta if you ever need a job again you come back next summer." He said I was a very good worker, and I could bring some friends with me the following year.

Severo, Bellamah, Roshina, Edwina and I packed up our stuff, loaded it in the cars, and we left. We spent one night at a hotel somewhere along the way and then we spent one night in Albuquerque with Severo's brother. We got back to Torreón in September on a Sunday morning. When we got there, I saw Pablo and Parras riding around in Pablo's car. Before I left, Pablo had bought a new car. They didn't even recognize me when I waved at them. Severo dropped Bellamah and me off in Torreón, and he and the girls took off to Mountainair.

That fall and winter I continued to do odd jobs, here and there. I was about to turn 17 years old. Some of my friends, the ones that didn't drop out of high school were graduating or about to graduate. I had dropped out of school, so I didn't graduate. Jimmy Garcia, my brother-in-law Eloy's brother, had just graduated from high school. One day Jimmy and I went to visit our friend Jose Manuel at his house, and he was gone. His dad said he wasn't there. He had just left. He said he had just taken off to California with some cousins. Jose Manuel's cousins from California had come to visit him, and when they were on their way back home to California, at the last minute, Jose Manuel decided to take off with them. We were surprised because he wasn't planning on leaving, he just got up and left.

Jose Manuel had been gone about a month when Jimmy said, "We should go and look for Jose Manuel and look for jobs in California." He said, "We can go in my car." At the time, there weren't any jobs near Torreón or in Albuquerque, so it sounded like a good idea. Frank had just gotten back from the Job Corp and was unemployed, so he wanted to go too. It was almost spring again, and I said, "I bet if I call Mr. Deckman he'll give us a job." So we all agreed to go. My parents weren't home, so I couldn't tell them I was leaving. They had taken Dinas and Leroy and had gone on a little trip to Colorado. I went and told Vicente that I was leaving the next day to Yosemite and to tell my mom and dad. I told him to tell them, I loved them and that I already had my *valise* packed, and I was ready to go. Vicente and Flora said, "Don't worry," they would tell him, and so we left the next day.

We all had a little money saved, so we spent one night in a hotel in Barstow. The next day, we made our way to San Bernardino, California, and when we got there, we were a little lost. We stopped at a phone booth and made some calls to some relatives. We ended up in Los Angles, and then somehow, we ended up in Compton. We went into Watts, and we got chased out by some big black guys. They didn't want us there. They looked like older guys, maybe about 30 years old. One guy would open up his car window and blow smoke at us. Finally, Jimmy got us out of there.

We stopped and made some more calls, and then we made it to the neighborhood we were looking for. We were driving around real slow in the area looking for Jose Manuel's relatives house when some older guy with gray hair stopped us. He said he had noticed the license plate on the car was from New Mexico, and he said, he was from Torreón, New Mexico. We told him we were from there too. His name was Daniel Otero. He knew my dad and Pablo's dad and a lot of people from Torreón. He asked us who we were looking for, and we told him the names of Jose Manuel's relatives, and he said, "They live right there." They were his neighbors. We were happy to finally find the house. We pulled into the driveway, and we honked and Arturo, Jose Manuel's cousin, came out of the house and walked toward the car. He looked at the car and then stared at me, and then he looked at Frank and then at Jimmy. Frank said, "Hey, Arturo," and then he recognized us. It had been years since we had seen each other. We started talking about my sister Christella and my cousin Corrine because they were closer to his age. Then Jimmy said he was Eloy's brother, and Arturo said, "I remember Lollie," which was Eloy's nickname, and he also remembered Jimmy's other brothers Abie and Fidel. We talked for a while, and then Felix, another *carnal,* came to talk to us. We asked where we could find Jose Manuel, and he said that he had gotten a job at a furniture store, and he had his own little apartment that was not far from here. We also found out that Johnny Perea, Blue's brother, was working nearby as a foreman in a factory. We thought maybe we could get a job in the factory.

First we went to the furniture store that Jose Manuel was working at. When we got there, we saw some guys working outside. We didn't see Jose Manuel, so we walked inside the store. As soon as we walked in the store, we saw him. He was there putting some legs on some furniture. We all yelled, "Jose Manuel!" He turned around, and as soon as he saw us, he jumped up and was happy to see us. He hugged us, and he asked us when we had arrived, and we talked for a while. We told him, we needed to find a place to stay for the night, and he said, "Don't worry. You guys can stay with me. We can go right now." We said, "Well, don't you have to work?" He said, "No, I quit right now. I'm quitting right now." He was happy to quit his job and said, "I'm going with you guys wherever you guys are going, back to Torreón, or wherever, I'm going." He quit his job and took off with us.

We went back to Arturo's house and drank a few beers with him. We asked him where Johnny Perea worked, and he took us and showed us. In the morning, we went to the factory, and we asked for Johnny, and he came outside to meet us. Johnny was a lot older than us and didn't know us, so we told him who we were and who are brothers and sisters were. He remembered Carlos, Frank's brother, and my brother Vicente. He asked us, "Are you guys looking for a job?" We said, "Yes," and he asked, "Are you sure? The work isn't that easy here?" We said, "We don't care. We need a job." He said, "Ok, let me show you around the place." It was a factory with an assembly line that filled bottles of shampoo, lotions, mouthwash and other liquids, and then the bottles would be put into boxes. He had us watch some guys that were working on the assembly line, and it looked pretty easy. He asked us if we wanted to try it, and we said, "Yes."

Our job was to open up the boxes of glass bottles, get them out of the boxes, put them on the assembly line and get them filled. Well, the bottles were in the boxes upside down, so when we got them out, we had to flip them over and get them on the assembly line. We had to move fast because the line was moving fast. The job wasn't easy. Before we knew it, we had broken bottles on the floor and liquid all over the place. We would have to stop and get a broom and sweep up the mess and then mop it up. We just got further and further behind. We tried to work faster, but we just couldn't get the hang of it. So that job didn't work out for us.

    We decided to call Mr. Deckman at Yosemite. I looked up the phone number in a phone book, and I called the restaurant where I had worked. Mr. Deckman got on the phone, and with his Dutch accent he said, "Ya, Peeta, I remember you Peeta. Where are you?" I told him I was in Los Angeles and that I had some friends with me, and he said, "Bring them over Peeta. Bring them over, and I can put everyone to work." I said, "Ok, great! We will be there tomorrow." Jose Manuel wanted to leave right away that way he wouldn't have to pay any more rent on his apartment. Jose Manuel had bought a car in California, but he didn't want to drive it to Yosemite. It was a Chevy, and he was worried about driving the car because he had put some really loud pipes on it that may have been illegal, and he didn't want to get a ticket. I remember Frank saying, "Well, danger is my business, so I will drive the car." Frank and I got in the Chevy, and Jimmy and Jose Manuel got in Jimmy's Impala, and we took off. We got the freeway north towards Fresno, and we traveled all night with Jimmy and Jose Manuel following behind us. All along the way, we could hear the pipes on the Chevy *brrrrr, brrrrr, brrrrr*. We drove through Fresno, through Mercedes and from there, we drove through all of the turns and canyons until we finally made it to Yosemite.

    It was late night when we got there, and we went to the restaurant where I had worked the summer before. I saw the cook, and he recognized me right away. I told him I had brought three other guys with me to work. He asked us if we were hungry, and right away, he invited us to eat. We ate, and then we were given some dorm rooms. Frank and I shared a room, and Jimmy and Jose Manuel shared a room. We took showers and went to bed. We got up early the next morning to have breakfast. We went to eat at the smorgasbord on the second floor, and the guys really liked the food. I talked to Mr. Deckman, and he asked me what we wanted to do, and I said, "Whatever you have. We just need to work." He gave me a job as a busboy, and I think Jimmy was also a busboy. Jose Manuel was a night dishwasher in the bakery, and Frank was also a dishwasher. We started work, and we all liked our jobs. We got paid every two weeks. I don't remember how much we got paid, but it was good money, and we didn't have to pay for food or our dorm rooms.

    Every night Jose Manuel wanted someone to walk with him from the dorms to the restaurant because there were a lot of bears in the area, and we could hear them walking around at night. There was always a huge mother bear with her cubs that would get in the big dumpsters and eat all the food that had been thrown away. One time I remember we saw a little bear out at night, and Jimmy went and got his flashlight and followed him way up into the mountain until he couldn't see it anymore.

When we weren't working, we went riding in Jimmy's Impala. We liked driving the car through the huge tree that had a big tunnel carved out at the bottom of it, and we would stop to take pictures. It was a fun summer, but it was getting close to August or September, and the job was about to end. Jimmy thought that we should go visit his uncle Phil and auntie Mary in San Francisco before going back home. I had never been to San Francisco, neither had Frank or Jose Manuel. We had been saving our money, and we wanted to see the Golden Gate Bridge, so we decided to go. When our job was over, we loaded our things into the cars, put on our shades, and got in our cars and left. At that time, we didn't have to worry about wearing seatbelts.

We got to San Francisco, and we crossed the Golden Gate Bridge. We went down to the water where all the fishermen were, and Jimmy asked, "How would you guys like to take a ride on a boat?" None of us had ever been on a boat before, so we took a ride on a boat to Alcatraz. It was a tour boat that told us all about the history of Alcatraz. We were having a good time on the boat when, all of a sudden, we all started to get sick. I know someone threw up, but I can't remember who it was. That evening we finally got to Jimmy's uncle Phil's house in San Francisco. It was a big, nice house, and we stayed there for the night.

The next day Jimmy said, "Since we're here in California we should also go to Long Beach," and we all agreed. We thought we might not get another chance to come back, so we might as well go now that we're close and have the time and money, so we drove to Long Beach. Long Beach had a big roller coaster. It was one of those big roller coasters that was made of wood. Jimmy and Frank wanted to go on it. I didn't want to because I thought I would get dizzy, and Jose Manuel didn't want to go on it either. So Jimmy and Frank went on the roller coaster, and they came back laughing and talking about how we had missed all the fun. They said, "Come on! Let's all go on it together, it was really fun!" I thought I may never get another chance to come back, so I decided to go on it. Jose Manuel also decided to go on the roller coaster. I said, "*Bueno,* Frank, I'm going to hold on to you," and he said, "Don't worry! Don't worry! It's going to be ok!" Jose Manuel said, "I'm going to hold on to you too, Jimmy," and Jimmy said, "Ok, Ok." We got on the roller coaster, and it started to go up *tr tr, tr, tr, tr, tr* and up, up it went. Frank and Jimmy started laughing, and they said, "Do you see that sign over there? Watch out beyond that point." We kept getting higher and higher, and I could see the ocean on the side of us. Jose Manuel looked down at the ocean, and he said, "No way! We're so high! I don't want to look down!" He looked the other way. Then Jimmy said, "Hey you guys better hold on! Watch out!" I grabbed hold of the bar in front of me, and all of a sudden, we dropped. *Woop!* We went down so fast. It felt like my head was going to stay up there. Jose Manuel was yelling, "Ahhhhh!" And I was yelling, "Ahhhhh!" And Jimmy and Frank were laughing. I had my eyes closed, and I would peak from one eye, and I could see the tracks. We were moving fast. How fast? I don't know, but to me, it seemed really fast. We kept going up and down and around curves, and Jose Manuel was yelling, "That's enough! ¡Para lo! ¡Para lo!" Finally, the roller coaster started to slow down, and I asked, "Are we here? Are we here?" Jimmy said, "We're here. Pick up your head, and open your eyes." The roller coaster was scary but fun, and we were happy we tried it. Before we left Long Beach, we decided to take a picture for memories. There was a fake jail front on the beach, and the four of us took a picture there in the jail. I can't remember how much the picture cost, but we all got a picture.

    Before we headed home, Jimmy had another idea. He said, "You know, we don't have to be in a rush to get home. We worked all summer, we got paid and we saved some money, so let's tour a little bit." He said, "Let's go to Las Vegas and spend the night there." We thought that was a great idea, but before we left Long Beach, we decided to get some beer to celebrate. We made it to Las Vegas and had a fun time there. We walked along the strip and went into some casinos and "what happens in Vegas stays in Vegas." A few days later, we made it back home to Torreón, New Mexico. It was good to be home.

    As time went by, I still worked and played with the band, but after a while, Parras and Blues decided they were going to play with Bolesslo's band, and they didn't need two guitarists. So I went to talk to my cousin Mel Lujan, who played the saxophone and had a band in Albuquerque. I asked him if he needed a guitarist, and he needed one every weekend. I had been saving my money, and I bought a 1956 Chevy, so I was able to drive to Albuquerque on the weekends to play with the band. When I was in Albuquerque, I would stay in the little house that Eloy and Christella had in the back of their house. I would play with Mel at Me Gusto Bar on Saturday nights, and I made about $15.00 for four hours. We also played at La Pompita Lounge, at the Needles Lounge and at Saguaros Lounge, all in Albuquerque. At one time, we were even going to Grants to play. Mel always had a job for me on the weekends, and on Sunday I would drive back to Torreón and stay there for the week.

    I moved to Albuquerque several years ago. I still love playing the guitar and still play for the Torreón *fiestas* or other parties, and now my children play in a band with me. To this day, I enjoy going back to Torreón and spending time on the land I have up there. I enjoy spending the day or weekend up there with my wife, our kids and grandkids. If I could, I would spend every weekend up there.

Boyhood Adventures in Torreón, New Mexico

Peté Alderete

Jimmy Garcia, Peté Alderete, Frank Sanchez and Jose Manuel Zamora

Norbert (Liberty) Sanchez, Pablo Perea and Peté Alderete

Jimmy Garcia, Eloy Sanchez, Nash Salas, Dennis Alderete, Milton Garcia, outside of the galera

Pedro Alderete and Candelaria Montoya-Alderete

Peté Alderete's car 1956 Chevy

left to right, Eloy Garcia, Abie Garcia, Vicente Alderete, Pablo Perea, Dennis Alderete

Pedro and Nicanor Alderete

Vicente Montoya

My Home in Torreón, New Mexico

Magdalen Benavidez

My name is Magdalen Benavidez, and I was born in Torreón, New Mexico in 1953. My father was Estanislado Benavidez, who was born in 1901, and my mother was Nicolasita Chavez-Benavidez, who was born in 1912. I grew up in Torreón, and I inherited the house I grew up in from my parents. This house is at least 150 years old, and it may very well be the oldest standing home in Torreón.

As you drive from Tajique toward Mountainair in the Manzano Mountains, you will come to the small village of Torreón. Once you get there, if you turn right on Rocky Road, the house is about a fourth of a mile down the road.

My grandparents Tircio and Adellada Chavez lived in this home for many years. When my parents married, they lived in the home with them. When my grandparents passed away, my parents inherited the home, and this is where they raised their children. It is a house with thick adobe walls, and the house was originally the shape of an L. The whole house was only three rooms, and as my parents had more and more children, additional rooms were added.

Being the youngest of 17 children, I never knew my grandparents, but the wonderful stories my parents left behind will forever be a part of me. Of the 17 children my parents had, eleven of us survived. My parents raised nine girls and two boys in this small home. There were so many of us that we all slept two or three to a bed.

My father was a farmer, and I remember his hands bleeding from peeling *vigas* to sell so that he could put food on the table. My mother spent a lot of her time cooking. She would make piles of *tortillas*, rice and beans to feed our large family. On Good Friday, it was the custom to make food to share with the neighbors, and they, in turn, shared their food with us even though everyone had the same menu. On Sunday it was not uncommon for the parish priest to come and eat lunch with my family after mass.

The house did not have a cellar, but we did have a *dispensa* that was very cold, and this is where we kept our meat for the winter. After a *matanza*, my parents would hang the fresh meat from strings and then hang the strings of meat to hooks attached to the ceiling. When my mom was cooking, she would ask one of us kids to get a piece of meat from the *dispensa*. We would take a knife and cut the meat off the string. In this room, we also kept our fruits and vegetables. We would pick apples from the nearby trees, and we would wrap each apple in newspaper or pages from a catalog. We would then put the apples in a big basket in this room.

Memories of Torreón, New Mexico

I have both good and sad memories of my home. As years went by and my older siblings left for marriage and the world outside of Torreón, I was the only one left in the home with my parents. I missed my brothers and sisters, who to this day, tell me how spoiled I was as the youngest child. My family was very poor but rich in the things that mattered in this life like love, faith and charity. My home in Torreón is rich in tradition and heritage, and I hope someday my children and grandchildren can appreciate this fourth generation home in the future.

Pilgrimage de Nuestra Señora de los Dolores

Florelia (flora) Benavidez-Alderete

My name is Florelia (flora) Benavidez-Alderete. I was born in the year 1940, and I was born and raised in the small town of Torreón, New Mexico. I am the ninth child of Nicolasita Chavez-Benavidez, who was born December 30, 1912, and Estanislado Benavidez, who was born May 21, 1901. My husband Vicente Alderete was born in Torreón in 1938 and was raised in Torreón. Our son Melvin Alderete was also raised in Torreón.

My story is about a tradition that has been carried on by the people of Torreón for many years. Each year in June, the people of Torreón make a pilgrimage from Manzano, New Mexico to Torreón carrying the Statue of *Nuestra Señora de los Dolores*. She is the Patron Saint of the Catholic Church in Manzano.

As a young child, I remember my mom telling me about this pilgrimage. The parishioners who made the pilgrimage walked with a lot of devotion and faith, and they prayed and sang *alabados* along the way. There were no paved roads at the time, so people walked on the dirt road to Torreón, taking turns carrying the Statue of Our Lady of Sorrows. Some of the participants of the walk took their shoes off and walked barefoot as a sacrifice. People also made promises or asked for special favors of *Nuestra Señora* in times of need. As a result of their dedication and devotion, many miracles and prayers were answered.

The distance from Manzano to Torreón is seven miles. There is a rest stop at Los Pinitos which is about halfway between Manzano and Torreón. Here the pilgrims stopped for food and water. After everyone had rested and eaten, the pilgrimage continued with everyone singing *alabados* and praying the rosary until they arrived at the church in Torreón.

As a child, I made this pilgrimage with my mother and my sisters. I rang a little bell as I walked, and I shared this task with the other children along the way. Ringing the bell was to let the people know of the arrival of *Nuestra Señora de los Dolores* at the San Antonio de Padua Catholic Church in Torreón. Here Our Lady was brought into the church as the people sang and prayed. Our Lady stayed in Torreón for a week, and then she was returned to her home in Manzano.

While the Statue of Our Lady was in Torreón, people came and took her into their homes for a visit. Some took her during the lunch hour, which we called a *cesteo*, and there was praying and singing during this time. Some people took her into their homes for a *velorio,* where she would spend the night, and many people attended this event. *Nuestra Señora* would be placed on a beautiful lace covered altar, and the altar would be decorated with lots of beautiful flowers. The rosary was prayed, and *alabados* were sung. Refreshments were served which included homemade *pastelitos, biscochitos, mollotes* and other goodies. The visit of *Nuestra Señora de los Dolores* was and still is very special for the people of Torreón. There is a lot of faith and love for Our Lady here.

One *velorio* that I will always remember was in the month of May 1972 when my family had an all-night *velorio* (as a *promesa*) in honor of Our Blessed Mother for my father's health. At that time my dad had been diagnosed with cancer. Sadly, he passed away that year.

This Statue of *Neustra Señora de los Dolores* is very old and has been kept at Manzano for many years. She was once stolen from the church in Manzano and later found and returned, thanks to so many prayers from the people. While she was missing, her delicate hands were broken off and had to be restored.

This tradition in honor of Our Lady is still taking place to this day. My cousin Lourdes Chavez was devoted to the pilgrimage and kept the pilgrimage going. On June 3, 2006, Lourdes went home with our Lord where she will be with Our Lady in Heaven. After her passing, Imelda Chavez, who was the daughter-in-law of Lourdes, and I have continued this beautiful tradition. I hope further generations will carry it on as we have.

Pilgrimage de Nuestra Señora de los Dolores

Flora Benavidez and Imelda Chavez with Nuestra Señora de Los Dolores

Nicolasita Benavidez, Lourdes Chavez and Carlota Perea with the Blessed Mother

Back L-R Candelaria Alderete, Lourdes Chavez, Maria Chavez, Tomasita Chavez, Front L-R Fedalina, Irene Benavidez, Magdalena Benavidez, Nicolacita Benavidez

Natural Healing in Rural New Mexico

Barbara Benavidez-Campos-Lepori

My name is Barbara Benavidez-Campos-Lepori. I am 67 years old, and I was born and raised in Torreón, New Mexico. Many of us have heard of *Curanderismo*, a natural way of healing. *Curanderismo* is a form of folk healing that includes the practice of ritual spiritual contact, energy work, prayers, healing herbs, plants and other natural substances. When healing the body, one must also heal the mind and spirit because they work together. Some may be skeptical of *curanderismo*, but others like myself have a strong belief in natural healing. In the past, most families in rural areas of New Mexico relied on a *curandera* or *curandero* for medical assistance because there were not many doctors available.

As a young child living in the small community of Torreón below the magnificent Manzano Mountains, I was curious about a woman who lived next door to our family. She would come to our home every morning to drink coffee with my mom, Nicolasita. My curiosity would peak when my mom would call the *curandera* when one of her children were sick. The *curandera* would come with a small black bag much like a medical doctor. She would pull out small vials and pouches of dried leaves and boil the contents in water. We would either have to drink the mixture, or she would apply it on us. When we had to drink it, it usually tasted awful.

The *curandera's* name was Angelita. My mom taught us to call her "Aunt Angelita." Angelita was a small, stout woman in stature with dark skin and big piercing eyes. She always wore a dress with an apron tied around her waist and a bandana around her head. She spoke in soft tones in Spanish, of course. My mother relied on Angelita for the care of her 17 children. I recall a time when I was sick with a rash all over my body. I had a high fever, and I was kept in a dark room for three days. Angelita would come to our house maybe twice a day and give me something to drink, and I remember I slept a lot. I also remember hearing my family say that I was very sick and might have scarlet fever. Wow! And of course, I prayed a lot as my family also did for my recovery. To this day, I truly believe that this gentle woman healed me through the power of natural herbs, prayer and faith.

Angelita believed in her God given gifts. She trusted in her intuitive nature, her knowledge of herbs and her ability to channel her resources to aid a person back to health. Angelita was not an educated woman. She merely accepted her gifts from the Great Creator. Where she came from or where she learned to heal, I don't remember. I do remember, she would go up into the mountains and collect her herbs and dry them. She had natural remedies for everything. Some people were a little suspicious of Angelita, but because

Memories of Torreón, New Mexico

there were no doctors in the area, everyone used her services. Not only did the people from Torreón come to her to heal their ailments, but people from the nearby towns came as well. It was also Angelita who helped to deliver the babies in town.

One of the common ailments that Angelita cured was *susto*, which was known as becoming ill from a terrible freight. Some of the symptoms could be anxiety, insomnia, irritability and depression. Another common ailment was *mal de ojo*, which usually affected an infant or young child. If someone stared admiringly at a child for too long, the child could become sick with *mal de ojo*. This would cause the child to cry, become fussy, have a fever, vomit and have aches and pains. *Empacho* was another ailment that had to do with the blockage of undigested food in the stomach. Sometimes a raw egg rubbed over the stomach was used to relieve *empacho*.

Curanderismo is a very spiritual practice with a strong religious faith. *Curanderas* use a variety of objects for healing that includes spices, eggs, lemons, limes, potatoes, holy water, saints, crucifixes, prayer, candles, incense, oils, herbs such as *manzanilla and yerba buena*, divination tools and spiritual assistance. On a healing level, the *curandera* views life as a whole, mind-body-spirit. The three connected is what creates life.

I know for our family 10 of the 17 children are still alive, and we still remember Angelita coming to our home to help our mother with her sick children. Having faith in what works to heal our body, our mind and our spirit was a very important part of the healing process. To this day I still use some of the remedies on my children, grandchildren and myself that I learned from my mom and Angelita. I rub eggs on my grandchildren's stomachs when they have a stomach ache. I use potatoes with vinegar for migraine headaches, *manzanilla* for relaxation and *yerba buena* for aches and pains. I am very thankful for being exposed to Angelita in our village of Torreón. It has made me a strong believer of *curanderismo*/natural healing. I am convinced that given the opportunity and experience of being treated by a *curandera* more people would have faith in the natural healing process.

Barbara Benavidez

Traditional Foods

Viola Benavidez-Lesperance

My name is Viola Benavidez-Lesperance. I was born and raised in the small town of Torreón, New Mexico, and I am the daughter of Estanislado and Nicolasita Benavidez. I came from a family of 17 kids, and I am the third to the youngest. Growing up in Torreón was amazing! Everyone I grew up with came from big families. We always had something to do, and there was never a dull moment!

Our home was filled with lots of love. My parents were strict, and our values and morals were something we learned growing up. Having so many sisters, I was always learning something new. My sisters and I always took turns cooking, rolling *tortillas,* washing and ironing clothes early morning before school. These were just some of our many chores we had to do, and this is how I learned everything I know today. Sometimes we complained, and thinking back now I have to laugh. If we said it wasn't our turn, my mom would say, "¡Qué turn, ni qué turn! Do your work and don't complain!"

My mom taught me how to cook at a young age and baking was my thing. I had to bake a cake from scratch every Saturday for our Sunday meal. On Sunday we usually had a special meal of chicken, mashed potatoes and corn and we had our cake for dessert. Our daily dinner usually consisted of beans, *papas con caldo* or macaroni and *tortillas* and chile. In the summer my dad always had a garden, so my mom made *calabacitas* to eat in the summer.

For breakfast we usually had hot chocolate and oatmeal or *atole* or maybe a *tortilla* with butter. In high school, we had to be at the bus stop early, at about 7:00 in the morning, so we didn't have much time for breakfast.

I often took lunch to school in Estancia. My lunch usually consisted of a fried egg in a *tortilla* or a potted meat sandwich. Often my friends from Torreón and I would eat in a place where there weren't too many kids around so that they wouldn't see our lunch. If there were other kids around, I would take a bite of my sandwich and then quickly put it back in the brown paper bag between bites.

Christmas was a favorite holiday. Our traditional foods were *tamales, posole, biscochitos, pastalitos* and *molletes.* My mother also made *empanadas.* These were made from the boiled tongue of the pig which we saved after we had a *matanza.* My mother would grind up the tongue in a little grinder that she attached to the side of the table. Then she would take the meat and mix it with cinnamon, sugar and raisins. We then rolled out small round pieces of pastry dough and filled the dough with the meat. We folded the pastry dough into a half moon shape, sealed the edges and then deep fried the pastry. They were delicious!

Another tradition I have carried with me are the different foods that we prepared for Lent. We prepared *chile con torta*, pinto beans, *quelites*, tuna patties and of course, we had homemade *tortillas*. Our dessert was *sopa, natillas* and sweet rice. We ate these foods for Ash Wednesday and Good Friday. On Good Friday these foods were prepared and ready by early noon. Then my mom would have us fill small bowls of each food, and we would take them to our neighbors. They, in turn, would send us food that they had prepared. It was a big feast for all of us, and it was fun to taste so many different foods. All the foods we made were always made with a lot of effort and love, and we always enjoyed sharing with our friends and neighbors. This tradition is one of many that will always stay with me. To this day, I still prepare these foods for Christmas and Lent.

My Love for the Spanish Alabados

Irene-Benavidez-Zamora

My name is Irene Benavidez-Zamora. I was born in 1942, and I was born and raised in Torreón, New Mexico. My parents were Estanislado and Nicolasita Benavidez. They had 17 children, and I'm the eleventh child.

Between the years of 1930 and 2016, eight of the family's children have passed away, and we all miss them greatly!

I have many beautiful memories of my childhood growing up in Torreón. One memory I would like to share with you is my love for the Spanish music, especially the *alabados*. As a child, I attended grade school in Torreón. When I was about 11 years old, I was asked by Mrs. Raquel Herrera, who had been my first-grade teacher, and also by my uncle Demecio Perea, who was also a teacher, to go to Mrs. Herrera's classroom during recess because she wanted to talk to me about my singing. Mrs. Herrera wanted to teach me the Spanish *alabados,* and she wanted me to sing in the church choir. This is what she told me, "*La Cuaresma* is about to begin, and I want you to learn el *Vía Crucis.*" This was a blessing for me, and it opened a door for me to sing, which was something I loved to do. This also gave me the opportunity to learn to sing the Mass in Latin because, at that time, Mass was in Latin. Spanish is and has always been my first language. I learned to sing many Spanish hymns from Mrs. Herrera, who herself was gifted with a beautiful voice. We would sing beautiful hymns to *Nuestra Maria Santísima* and *alabados* about *San Antonio de Padua*, our Patron Saint of the Torreón Catholic Mission Church. According to our ancestry, these *alabados* are very old and go back to the 1800s.

Many of my other activities as a youth revolved around the church. In the month of May, I remember going to church to pray many *Santo Rosarios*. The Rosary was prayed by Maria Chavez, a member of the community, who was a very pious woman. When I was about 12 years old, I was asked to go sing and entertain the other classes in school. This was another great opportunity for me. I also loved to sing in talent shows. Whenever there was a talent show, I signed up. I remember one time when I was in high school, my sister Viola and I won first prize for singing. We then came to Albuquerque and competed, and we won second prize.

The love of Spanish music has always run very deep in my family from way back to the time of my ancestors. My great-grandfather Casimero Lujan from my mother's side of the family was known to be a very talented man in the field of music. He composed many songs and *corridos,* and he was also a poet. One of his *corridos* that was famous in the 1800s was "*La Indita de Siquio Lucero,*" a story written about twin brothers. My uncle Sisto

Lujan was also a composer and played *el violín*. My mother, Nicolasita, would sing with my brothers and sisters and me all the time. She had a beautiful voice, and she always encouraged us to continue singing the *alabados*.

Music is still a big part of my family's life today. My husband, Antonio (Tony), and I have two daughters Ramona and Velma that play the guitar, and Velma also sings. Barbara and Magdalena, my sisters, sing in the choir at St. Bernadettes Catholic Church in Albuquerque. My brother Estanislado Jr. plays the saxophone and has played and sang with many bands in the past, and I have written many hymns that we sing in our church choir today.

In conclusion, I want to say that now in the year 2016, our big choir that we once had in the *San Antonio de Padua* Catholic Church in Torreón has been reduced to only four of us. My sisters Viola and Flora and I are the singers, and my husband, Tony, has provided our music with his guitar for many years. Florelia (Flora) is our choir director and has been for many years. At the age of 76, her dedication and commitment have been our greatest inspiration. My hopes and prayers are that these beautiful Spanish *alabados* that have been handed down from our ancestors will continue to be sung for many generations to come.

Viola Lesperance, Flora Alderete, Tony and Irene Zamora

Serving in WWII and Herding Sheep

Feliciano Chavez and Reginita Garcia-Chavez

I am Feliciano (Chano) Chavez, and I was born February 12, 1914, in Torreón, New Mexico. I am the son of Eduardo Chavez, who was born February 25, 1885, in Torreón and Dolores Lujan-Chavez, who was also born in Torreón. My father's parents were Feliciano Chavez and Candelaria Orona-Chavez, who were both from Tomé, New Mexico.

At one time my grandpa Feliciano Chavez owned a ranch three or four miles south of Willard, New Mexico where he had horses and cattle. The Native Americans and the people in Torreón and the other nearby towns would often fight over the spring water in the area. One day my grandpa Feliciano was kidnapped by Native Americans from Gran Quivera, which is just south of Mountainair. After being held prisoner for some time, my grandpa came up with a plan to escape. Every day he kept an eye on the horses to try and figure out which one would be the fastest to escape on. One night when everyone was asleep, he untied the rope the horse was attached to, jumped on the horse and escaped.

I was about five years old when both my parents died from the influenza epidemic of 1918. My younger brother Herman was six months old, my sister Maggie was eight and my sister Juanita was six years old. From about 1918 to 1924, my brother and sisters and I went to live with our grandma Candelaria Orona-Chavez, who was in her late 50s at the time. Our grandpa Feliciano had already passed away. My grandma died in 1924, and that's when my brother Herman and I had to go live in an orphanage in Albuquerque. My sisters Juanita and Maggie were taken in by my Aunt Ofelia, the sister of my dad. The orphanage, St. Anthony's Home for Boys, was in Albuquerque on 12th street. It was a large orphanage with many kids, and I do remember going to school while I was there. I think the classes were taught in English. My brother and I stayed in the orphanage for about a year and a half. When I was about 11 or 12 years old, my uncle Leopoldo, the brother of my dad, came to pick us up from the orphanage, and he took us to live with our uncle Melcor and his wife, Concecíon Chavez. Uncle Melcor was the brother of my dad, and he had a ranch about three miles east of Torreón. He planted pinto beans and corn, and he was one of the first farmers in the area to have a large crop of beans.

I went to school in Torreón with about 20 other kids, who were all different ages. The school is now the community center. Some of the teachers who taught at the school, at one time or another, were Roberto Perea, Jose

Sanchez, Raquel Herrera and Ignacio Garcia. School was mostly taught in English. My family only spoke Spanish at home, so it was difficult to learn English. In about the 5th grade, I had to quit school to go work. I went to work with Claude Brown on his ranch, which was five miles east of Torreón. I lived there, and I got paid $5.00 to $6.00 a month plus room and board. Claude Brown was very good to me. I remember his wife was a great cook. She made excellent biscuits and gravy that I will never forget. She also made beans and chile that were also very tasty. I also worked with my uncle Melcor on his farm. When there wasn't work with my uncle Melcor, I would work with Claude Brown. I had a cousin Frank (Francisco) Chavez who I was very close to. For about a year, we both worked with Frank's dad, Leopoldo, at a tobacco farm, harvesting plants. My uncle Leopoldo was one of the best uncles I ever had.

When there was time for fun, I liked to play ball or make *zancos*. The *zancos* were very popular in Torreón. They were made from a piece of wood, and a leather strap was nailed across the wood to hold the foot in. In the bottom of the *zancos,* we would drive a nail or screwdriver into the wood so that we could walk in the snow and ice and not slip. The *zancos* were difficult to put on, so we had to lean against a wall and step into one of them with one foot. Then we would step into the other one with the other foot, and we would walk away from the wall.

As a teenager, I spent time working with the Civilian Conservation Corp. The camp was located south of Manzano. I made a dollar a day, meals were included and they gave me a place to sleep. We built fences from Abo to Mountainair because at that time there were a lot of wild horses in the area. For a time, I worked as a sheepherder in the *sierra de* Capitan, New Mexico. When I was about 19 years old, I worked for an Arizona company also herding sheep. I herded the sheep with my cousin Frank Chavez and Remuldo Torrez. Remuldo was my dad's cousin. He was about 35 years old, and he lived in Tomé, New Mexico. We all traveled in a Model T vehicle from Torreón to Winslow, Arizona and then to the Grand Canyon. Along the way, we had to keep stopping because the vehicle would overheat, and the car was very slow, especially going up steep hills. It took about two days to get to the Grand Canyon from Torreón. When we got to the Grand Canyon, we worked as ranch hands.

From the Grand Canyon, we herded the sheep all the way to Needles, California, which took us about six to seven weeks. It wasn't very hard work, and I had a 30-30 rifle with me. Sometimes we ran into a bear or a coyote that would scare the sheep, and I would have to shoot my gun and scare it away. The company we worked for gave us food to take with us like cans of peaches and pears and other canned foods. They also let us slaughter a lamb to eat. We would kill a lamb, wrap it up and cook it in the hot ashes. This was one of the best meals I have ever had. When we finally got to Needles with the sheep, the lambs were separated from the sheep and sold, and I stayed in Needles for about a month working on an alfalfa farm. When my job was over, I came back to Torreón on the train to Mountainair through Phoenix. I remember in Capitan, New Mexico a sheepherder was paid $1.00 a day plus food. In Arizona the pay was double.

I was 25 years old and living and working as a farmer in Torreón when I received a draft notice from the Army. I had to go to Estancia then to Santa Fe, via bus, to be examined for the possibility of being drafted. I was fit for duty, and I was given a week to get all my personal business in order. I assigned my sister Juanita as my legal guardian. My date of induction was September 17, 1942, and my date of entry into active service was October 1, 1942. I was drafted into the Army Infantry. The infantry soldiers were the grunts in the war.

From Estancia, we were taken to Fort Bliss, Texas for two weeks of boot camp. From there we went to Fort Sill, Oklahoma for basic training. There we trained to hike. We started with five miles a day, then 10, then 15 and then 20 and 25-mile hikes. It was exhausting, and some of the boys would pass out from exhaustion. We also trained to shoot our weapons and to crawl long distances under barbwire. I was trained as a sharpshooter. I learned how to fire a rifle sitting up and lying down. I became a fast shooter, and I learned to roll fast. The training was rough, but I believe this is what kept me alive. I was in Oklahoma for three months, and then I went to Louisiana for one month to learn maneuvers. I was given one week of leave to go home before going to San Antonio, Texas. From San Antonio, we were readied to go overseas. We traveled by train to South Carolina, which took about two days. In South Carolina, we boarded a ship and headed to Casa Blanca, Morocco. I never believed that there was more water than ground on earth until I actually saw it for myself.

It was my first time traveling on the ocean. It was dangerous because the ship had to zig zag a lot to avoid mines and because of the bad weather. Being at sea is really rough when it rains or when it's windy. The wind and rain made the ship swing like it was going to go underwater. The first two days I was on the ship, I was seasick. My First Sergeant Felix Chavez saw that I wasn't feeling well, and he asked me if I had ever been on the ocean. I told him the truth. I said, "I've never been on the ocean." He said, "Try to eat even if you're not hungry." I tried that, and it worked. I never got seasick again. It took about four weeks on the Atlantic Ocean to get from the United States to Casa Blanca, Morocco in North Africa.

My battalion was called the Blue Devils. The 88th Blue Devils Division was the first division made up of men who had all been drafted and the first all-draftee division to see combat in the war. I was drafted with many other Hispanic New Mexicans and Native Americans. I remember the Native Americans were very good soldiers. I also met boys from many other places, and It was here while I was in the army that I was able to improve my English.

From Casa Blanca, we fought and chased the Germans, mostly on foot, all the way to Libya. We lost many lives along the way. The Germans then left Libya and went to Italy. We boarded a ship on the Mediterranean Sea, and we headed after the Germans. We got to Naples, Italy and docked there. We landed on the beach just before sunrise, and as we left the large ship to get on small boats, we were immediately being shot at by the Germans. Luckily, the Air Force had come in to add support as we were trying to make the beach, but still many americans lost their lives there. We stayed and fought there for about a week until the Americans were able to take over Naples.

From Naples we traveled on foot to Santa Maria Infante where there was another battle. Then we went to Rome and then to Monte Cassino. Monte Cassino is where I saw General Patton for the first time. We had a very difficult battle there. We had to wait there three days because we needed air and artillery support. On the fourth day, the air support came. As we went up the mountain, we were shot at, but we were able to take over Monte Cassino. We then left Italy and headed towards the Rhine River in the northeastern part of Germany.

We were in constant fear, always watching out for the enemy and always expecting the enemy to attack at any time. We had to always be on the alert, watching out for ourselves and for the unit. There was no time to think about killing, it was either kill or be killed. We were constantly walking and tired. We did not sleep for days, and we had very little food. We had to carry our water, a heavy backpack full of gear and our weapons. We ate army rations that weren't always good. We would have to soak them in water, and they weren't very easy to eat. It was nothing like the beans and chile I was used to back home. I carried a Browning Automatic Rifle (BAR), a rapid fire gun that weighed about 12 pounds, and I carried ammunition. A boy behind me carried more ammunition. Those of us who carried these types of guns were prime targets because they were rapid fire. We were usually the first to be targeted and shot at, so speed and maneuvering were critical. Normally, people of small stature, like myself, were not able to use and carry these type of guns. However, I was trained as a sharpshooter, and I was able to handle it.

In 1945 my division was crossing a bridge near the Rhine River when I was wounded by shrapnel and taken to a military field hospital tent in Italy. I was unconscious for two or three days. When I started to come through there was a nurse and a doctor nearby. The doctor came by and checked me, and he said to the nurse, "Get him some clean water so he can clean himself up and shave. He's going to be fine." While I was in the hospital, my First Sergeant Felix Chavez contacted the hospital to check on me. We had become good friends, and he said that I had saved his life. I remember I saw the enemy, and I could see my first sergeant. I couldn't get up and run because the enemy would see me, but I rolled and rolled, and I got into a good position to shoot. I shot at the Germans, and that is when I was wounded. I spent about a month in the hospital and then the doctors released me to go back and fight. When I returned to my unit and saw my first sergeant, he gave me a big hug. I went back to fight the Germans, and a few months later, they surrendered on May 7, 1945.

We were then needed in Japan, so we crossed the Atlantic Ocean. We passed through the Panama Canal where the Atlantic and the Pacific Ocean divide. From Panama we went to the Philippines. We were told to be careful because there were many Japanese snipers in foxholes. From the Philippines, we went to Japan. While we were there, we were not sure what was going to happen, but we were told to take cover. The atomic bomb was dropped on August 6, 1945, and soon after the Japanese surrendered. We stayed in Japan for another month, and then we were told we were going to Hiroshima.

We went to Hiroshima in a convoy, behind a bulldozer that shoveled the ash aside to get us through. We went four miles from east to west and four miles from north to south, and we saw the destruction of the atomic bomb. All that was left was ash. Everything was completely gone except the railroad tracks which were wrapped around in circles. We then headed back to Tokyo and then back to the Philippines, where we stayed until November 1945. In December of 1945, my division returned to Seattle, Washington by sea. My separation date was December 2, 1945. When we arrived in Seattle, there was a big band waiting for us, and we were given a nice dinner. Soon after, all the guys split up to go home in different directions. I boarded the train, and I was happy and thankful to be returning home. The whole time I was going through these battles, I always thought that I would stay alive and make it back home, and I did. I went to war with about seven other guys from the Manzano area. Not all of them returned. Leonides Garcia, my wife Reginita's brother, did not return. He was killed in the war.

I returned to Torreón mid-December 1945. Reginita and I dated, and we got married a few weeks later on January 4th, 1946. We were married in Manzano because that is where the priest was able to marry us. I continued to farm for a living and raised a few cattle. I loved farming. I worked on my own land, but I also worked on other people's land. I learned to drive a tractor at a very young age, and I had a good tractor of my own. I planted beans, corn, pumpkins and peas. I would haul my beans and corn on a team of horses to Mountainair to sell.

In 1947 Reginita and I bought the house that is located east of Fidel's bar. The house is near Susie Perea's house and across the street from Imelda and Leo Chavez's house. I bought the house from Carlos Chavez. The house is now owned by one of my daughters.

At one time there was a sawmill about four miles from Torreón towards the mountain. Some people from Torreón worked there. There was another sawmill near Ernest Vigil's place. I used to haul lumber from this sawmill to Mountainair with a wagon and a team of horses. Mr. Marbol McKinney owned the sawmill in town and about ten people worked there. It closed because there was not enough timber in the area.

The *fiestas* in Torreón were a great miracle. The people of Mountainair, Willard, Estancia, Tejique and other nearby towns would come to the *fiestas*. There were plenty of games to play and food to eat. One of the games we played was a game where you had to throw a ball at a doll and knock it down, and we also played *ruleta*. There were also a lot of dances during the *fiestas*. *La Sociedad de San Jose* owned one of the buildings where we used to have dances for *fiestas*. *La Sociedad de San Jose* was established in Torreón in 1936. I am the oldest living member of *La Sociedad*. A few years after this organization was established, each member made 500 adobes at the *arroyo* and then pulled them on a team of horses to build the dance hall. Once the hall was built, it was used for meetings and dances. We charged each person to enter the dance, and the money we made was used to help with funerals and other needs of the community. It was Tomas Lucero who gave me a badge, in the shape of a star, to be a deputy, and it was my job to keep order at the dances. I still have the badge today. There were often fights at the dances because the guys from the small towns didn't always get along. There were also dances at Fidel's dance hall, and the men also drank and played cards in Fidel's bar. Reginita has said, jokingly, that I lived in the bar.

One of my friends as a young man was Phil Chavez from Willard. Phil and I used to go riding in his car together. He was the brother of Antonia Chavez-Garcia. Candelaria Montoya-Alderete (la Cande) was my cousin. La Cande's mom, Pablita, and my dad were brother and sister.

In the 1950s, many families moved to Albuquerque, California and Arizona because of the drought. It was very hard to leave Torreón, but I moved my family to Albuquerque in 1950 because of the drought. I could no longer make a living farming. I loved Torreón and still do today. Reginita and I moved our family to the south Barelas area in Albuquerque. We lived right where the Hispanic Cultural Center is now. The house was a small two bedroom house with a bathroom, living room and a kitchen. We were a family of eleven. We came to Albuquerque, and I worked for the Atomic Energy Commission at Sandia Base, installing light fixtures. I worked there for about 22 years, and I retired on January 13, 1975. In the 1990s, we were one of the many families whose property was bought, and we had to move from the Barelas area in order for the city to build the Hispanic Cultural Center. We purchased a house on the westside of Albuquerque where we continue to live. I worked up into my late 80s as a crossing guard for Albuquerque Public Schools. I loved the kids, and they loved me, and they would often bring me small gifts. I loved working, but my eyesight started to fail, and I could no longer drive.

After we moved from Torreón, we continued to visit Torreón often, and we stayed at our house we had there. Reginita and I continued to be part of *La Sociedad de San Jose*. For many years, I was the guide for the yearly pilgrimage from Manzano to Torreón. I walked up in the front carrying a flag, guiding the pilgrimage and directing traffic. I am now 102 years old. My secret to a long and happy life has been to live together as husband and wife and to raise your kids to work hard and to take care of themselves.

I am Reginita Garcia-Chavez. I was born October 24, 1925, in Torreón, New Mexico. I was born in my parent's home, which is still there today. This house is just east of the house Feliciano and I bought after we got married. I lived in this house with my parents until I got married at the age of 19.

My dad Eliseo Garcia was born October 20, 1895, and died November 8, 1977. His parents were Octaviano and Lugardita Garcia.

My mom Matildita Lujan-Garcia was born January 8, 1900, and died August 9, 1983. Her parents were Pedro Lujan and Lupita Fernandez. When Lupita died, Pedro married Ofresna. My great-grandparents were Trinidad Vigil and Manuel Vigil.

I had seven brothers: Leonides, Alfonso, Orlando, Antonio (Tony), Eloy, Rosendo (Rosie) and Ray. All are deceased except for Ray. I had two sisters. Lugardita (Wala) Garcia-Nelson was the youngest and is now deceased. My other sister is Sefe Garcia-Chavez. I was the oldest of the three.

We spoke Spanish at home. I learned a little English before going to school, but I mostly learned it at school. I had many chores to do at home. I had to cook, clean house, feed the chickens, take care of the animals, milk the cows, make cheese, can fruits and vegetables and fetch water from the *arroyo*. We didn't have well water, and we didn't have indoor plumbing, so water had to be carried from the *arroyo*. At that time, the *arroyo* was full of water. Everybody hauled water from the *arroyo*. It was good for everything, including the cows and the horses. In the garden, we grew grapes, pinto beans, pumpkins, corn and squash, and we would sell or trade these items for things we didn't have. There was a store in Torreón. The store sold food, some pots and pans, some clothes and other things people needed. People also went by horse and wagon to Mountainair to buy things because sometimes they could get a better deal there. I remember as a child people also traveled to Albuquerque in their covered wagons to buy things. It would take two days to get to Albuquerque in a horse and wagon.

We didn't have that much time for fun when we were kids. Everyone in the family worked hard, including the kids. When I did have free time, I played with dolls that were made from rags. I spent a lot of time playing with my sisters and reading books. We made toys from things we found like bottles or pieces of wood. The kids at that time also liked walking along the *arroyo*. My family enjoyed going to the *fiestas*, dances and other community activities. I remember I got a marriage proposal from Epifanio Torres, but I didn't want to marry him.

When Feliciano returned from the war, we started dating. I don't remember meeting Feliciano in any particular place, but we were from the same town, so we often saw each other around town. Our courtship consisted of going for walks, going for rides in his truck and double dating. We married within a month of his return, and we got married on January 4, 1946. We got married in the church in Manzano. After the ceremony, we had a small reception also in Manzano. Feliciano's *padrino* was Lamberto Baca, and my *madrina* was Mary Ursodita Vigil. I gave birth to 10 children. Leonides (Leo), Jeanette, Dolores and Lawrence were all born at home in Torreón. Elizabeth, Rita, Mary (who is now deceased) Herman and Martha were born in hospitals in Albuquerque. My last child was a stillborn birth.

Memories of Torreón, New Mexico

Feliciano and Reginita Garcia-Chavez

Feliciano Chavez

Feliciano Chavez

Reginita Garcia-Chavez

Los Garrapatas AKA The Torreón Ticks

Gene Chavez

My name is Gene Chavez, and my family is originally from Torreón, New Mexico. My parents were Francisco A. Chavez and Eloise M. Torrez. My father was born September 21, 1915, at El Rancho de Tule, three miles south of Estancia, which was the home of his maternal grandparents. My mother was born March 6, 1920, in Chilili, New Mexico. I was a middle child of the 12 children born to my parents.

Both my grandparents and parents spent many years living in Torreón and or in close proximity to it. My dad inherited the Los Alamitos Ranch from his mother, Maria (Lupita), which was located three miles due north of Punta de Agua, New Mexico.

My paternal grandfather was Leopoldo (Polo) T. Chavez, who was born in Tomé, New Mexico, February 18, 1887. He was married to Lupita Gonzales, who was born in Willard, New Mexico in 1889. My grandfather Leopoldo lived for many years in a house roughly 100 yards southeast of the present day Torreón Community Center. He lived there until he passed away and is buried at the Torreón cemetery located east of town. When my grandpa was alive, he was a *marcarnoria*. He had the gift of locating wells on people's property.

One of my earliest memories of *el pueblito de* Torreón was when I was eight or nine years old. One winter morning in Albuquerque, it was late November or early December, my dad woke up my two older brothers and me to go to a *matanza* at my grandpa Leopoldo's house in Torreón. I vividly remember the cold dark morning that winter riding in my dad's old Chevy pick-up. Since it was pitch dark, I was thinking we were going to wake-up my grandpa Polo and surprise him. When we arrived, it was still dark and very cold, but Grandpa Polo and my uncles were already outside joking and laughing. Before we knew it, the pig was being cut up, and they were cooking *chicharrones* in a big cast iron pot. For a little boy, this was a very exciting trip and experience. That was the first *matanza* I had ever been to, and I never forgot it.

In the 1950s, New Mexico suffered from a severe drought, usually referred to by the locals as *"la seca."* I grew up in the late 1950s hearing many stories about *"la grande seca."* All the fields were dry. There was dust blowing everywhere that created sand dunes in the ranches. It was impossible for locals to farm, raise crops or sustain livestock. Due to *la seca*, there was a mass exodus of families, ranchers and farmers leaving to bigger communities like Albuquerque to seek work. During this time my father relocated the family from the Los Alamitos Ranch to Estancia. We then moved to Grants and finally to Albuquerque where my dad worked in construction for many years. Although we moved to Albuquerque out of necessity, my family never forgot their ties and connections to the town of Torreón.

My dad kept his Los Alamitos Ranch, and over the years as climate conditions improved, he raised livestock, sheep and even tried planting wheat. During my high school and college years, it was not unusual for my dad to take my brothers and me to brand cattle, repair barb-wire fences, plant crops or do other chores that needed to be done on the ranch. My dad ran cattle at the ranch up until the mid-1990s, when his age and my mom's health told him it was time to stop.

I remember many times on trips to my dad's ranch, we would stop in Torreón at my grandpa Leopoldo's house to visit or to eat some New Mexican home-cooking. My grandpa died June 6, 1966. I remember attending the funeral mass at the *Iglesia de San Antonio* in Torreón. The graveside services and burial were at the Torreón cemetery. I remember the burial plot and how hard, rocky and unforgiving the barren ground seemed. Sadly, as the pallbearers lowered the coffin with ropes, how sad and final the burial of my *abuelo*. My grandmother Lupita had died many years earlier on April 2, 1924, at the age of 35. She is buried adjacent to the *Iglesia de San Antonio* in Torreón.

Aside from my grandfather Leopoldo's and my father, Francisco's, long association with the *pueblito* of Torreón, the family's other legacy, or if you will, claim to fame, is that the Hermanos Chavez, my brothers Leo, Frank, James and I, were original and longtime members of a New Mexico band known as *Los Garrapatas*.

My two older brothers Leo and Frank started playing in bands during the mid-1960s. Later on, Leo joined a riding club known as the *Escobosa Riders*. This club would sponsor rodeos during the summer months in Escobosa, which was just a few miles north of Torreón. Leo began bringing my brother James and me to the rodeos and having us sit in with the rodeo musicians. Eventually, with Leo playing the accordion and with my brothers and I playing the guitar and drums, we became part of the official rodeo club band. One day at one of the rodeos, the master of ceremonies Mr. Ben Torrez, our uncle, said,

"Ahhhoooeeh, estos hermanos Chavez son como los garrapatas, se te meten en la oreja, y no puedes quitar el sonido."

"These Chavez brothers are like ticks, they get in your ears, and then you can't get rid of the sound."

That's how *Los Hermanos Chavez*, as we became more proficient and popular, became known simply as *Los Garrapatas*. We played primarily traditional New Mexican *rancheras* and *corridos*, and we made a sincere effort to keep the lyrics and melodies true to the traditions of New Mexico Music. This is the type of music that has been played in New Mexico for generations. You can hear this music played at weddings, traditional church *fiestas* and many other occasions such as birthdays, anniversaries and *matanzas*. Our hope as a band has always been to keep the New Mexico music tradition alive as a vibrant, exciting part of our culture. Many of our original lyrics and compositions relate stories, sayings and anecdotes that we all grew up with and are so ingrained in our Hispanic culture. For example, the inspiration for one of our original songs *La Matanza Jam* came from boyhood experiences of attending *matanzas*. In the lyrics of this song, we tried to describe and capture the essence and rich tradition of *matanzas* in New Mexico.

As a traditional New Mexican band, we have been very fortunate to have played at many different venues. We played at traditional *fiestas* all over New Mexico, the New Mexico State Fair, the annual KANW *Quince Grandes* Awards Show and at the Sandia Casino Amphitheater. We have recorded several CDs, and our music can be heard on radio stations throughout New Mexico, including the famous 89.1 KANW FM, APS Station in Albuquerque. We have also been very fortunate to have been recognized and to have received numerous music awards from both the New Mexico Hispano Music Association (NMHMA) and the New Mexico Hispanic Entertainers Association (NMHEA). The band initially consisted of the four Chavez brothers, but at various times, the band also included three nephews: Frank Jr., Marcos and Raul Chavez. Although we have been known as *Los Garrapatas* for several years, some people refer affectionately to us as the "*Torreón Ticks.*"

Lastly, I would like to mention that we (as a band) were honored to write and record a *corrido* for one of Torreón's most decorated heroes of World War II and New Mexico's native son, our *primo* Feliciano (Chano) Chavez. *El Corrido de Chano* is a tribute honoring his life, his war record and his family history. Moreover, this humble man celebrated his 102nd birthday on February 12, 2016.

Presently, I have two brothers that live in Torreón. My younger brother James lives in a two-story house on the westside of the highway as you enter Torreón. My other brother Frank lives a couple of miles southeast of Torreón in a house he built himself in the 1970s.

In closing, *Que viva el pueblo de* Torreón, *su amable gente, música, cultura y muchas gracias por su apoyo y amistad sobre todos estos años.*

In closing, long live Torreón, its kind people, its music, and culture and thank you very much for your support and friendship over all these years.

Los Garrapatas AKA The Torreón Ticks

LA MATANZA JAM
Written/arranged by G.S. Chavez

Vamos todos a la matanza de mi tío
El marrano ya encuentro el cuchillo
Mi suegro lo mató, muy temprano
¡Hay que hacer fiesta, con el marrano!

Mi suegra y mis tías, traen tortillas
Y la comida, para celebrar el día
Mi Cunado, conseguio la cerveza
¡Al marrano, ya le faltan las orejas!

"coro"
Pues vamos todos a comer chicharrones
A bailar y cantar muchas canciones
Las mujeres se divertien platicando
¡Doña Lola grita – y sale bailando!

El amor de mi alma, anda conmigo
Los parientes la saluden con cariño
Tan bonito y morenita, mi querida
¡Es la luz y pasión, de mi vida!

Los primos, como grillos hacen ruido
Con guitarra, cantan cumbias y corridos
Las hermanas, con sus niños recogidos
¡Hey que alegre, la fiesta - de mi tío!

"coro"
Pues vamos todos a comer chicharrones
A bailar y cantar muchas canciones
Las mujeres se divertien platicando
¡Que bonito – pues todos gozando!!!

The Torreón Acequia

Gilbert Chavez

My name is Gilbert Chavez. I was born in 1949 and raised in Torreón, New Mexico. My parents were Fidel Chavez and Lourdes Chavez y Chavez. My wife is Maxine Anaya, and her parents are Leverato Anaya and Estella Anaya-King. My wife and I got married in 1976 in Tajique, New Mexico, which is just two miles north of Torreón. We have been married 38 years, and we have two sons. Both of our sons moved to Albuquerque after graduating from Estancia High School, which is about 15 miles north of Torreón.

I am a member of the Torreón Water Association. We have about 27 members and about 15 people are active members. Every spring we get together to clean the *acequia*. The *acequia* is very important to the people of Torreón, and we work together to maintain it. How we do things now has changed from the past. Now there are more rules and regulations to follow.

The land is very important to the people of Torreón. On our land we grow beans, blue corn, green pumpkins, tomatoes, cucumbers, peas, strawberries, and we have fruit trees.

I graduated from Estancia High School in 1967, and I served in Vietnam in 1969. I was wounded in Vietnam, and I spent several months in a hospital recuperating. There were other guys my age from Torreón who also served during Vietnam. Thankfully, we all returned home.

Mis Recuerdos de Torreón

Frank Ruben Chavez

I am Frank Ruben Chavez, and I was born in Albuquerque, New Mexico in 1931. I am the son of Frank Torres Chavez, who was born in Torreón, New Mexico in 1909 and Jesucita (Jesse) Garcia, who was born in Manzano, New Mexico in 1910.

My father's dad was Elfego Chavez, who was born in Torreón in 1883, and his mother was Maria Juanita (San Juan) Torres born in 1884. Elfego's parents were Maria Lucero, who was born in 1865 and Miguel Antonio Chavez, who was born in Torreón in 1840.

My mother's father was Jose Angel Garcia, who was born in 1875. He was the brother of Ross Garcia, who owned the Ross Mercantile in Torreón. Jose Angel was often remembered as a stern man who slept or was bedridden for several years. However, there were many days when he would get up and walk around all night. He loved dancing and would periodically be seen selling piñón and playfully distracting the workforce. Some say he was *embrujado* by a woman who had wanted to marry him. Instead, he married my great and holy grandma Soledad Vigil, who was born in Torreón in 1884. My grandma Soledad was sharp, hardworking, was very faithfull and she read and wrote with a very fresh and progressive mind.

My first wife, Irene Sanchez, was born in Torreón in 1936. Her father was Ubaldo Sanchez, who was born in Torreón in 1915, and her mother was Sofia Lovato, who was born in Tajique in 1916. Ubaldo's parents were Benigno Sanchez, who was born in Torreón in 1885 and Lucia C. Candelaria, who was born in Torreón in 1893. Between the years of 1934 and 1938, Ubaldo Sanchez worked for the railroad in the Mountainair/Willard area. He also worked with the Civilian Conservation Corps (CCC Camp).

In 1922 my parents moved from Torreón to Albuquerque for better employment opportunities. All of us children were born in Albuquerque, except for the youngest, Ramon, who was born in San Pedro, California. Although I went to school in Albuquerque, I would return to Torreón periodically. I would return to help farm, to visit family and to attend events. I loved life in Torreón, and I always looked forward to my visits there. The following are some of my memories.

As a child, I went to Torreón every few months to visit my great-grandma Maria Lucero (Mariita). At about the age of four, I spent a summer in Torreón. I remember visiting my great-grandma Mariita's brother Pablo Lucero, who was born in 1867 in Torreón. My *Tata* (uncle Pablo) would get out his favorite horse and saddle it and give me a ride. I loved riding this horse. It made me feel special. I also attended the *Día de San Juan* festivities in Torreón, where gunny sack races and horse races took place.

Memories of Torreón, New Mexico

After World War I, Torreón was hit hard by the influenza virus. Families would lose three to four family members at once. Some thought it was caused by gasses spread during the war in Europe.

My father used to tell me stories of how it would take two full days to travel by horse and wagon from Torreón to Albuquerque, and in the 1930s, people were still selling wood on the side of the road from their wagons pulled by horses.

One year in the mid-1930s, a *creciente*, a big water runoff, flowed from the *arroyo*. The water ran so high and fast that Jose Tomas Lujan's beautiful 1932 Chevy was swept away.

Dances were a big part of the entertainment in Torreón. In fact, my parents met at a dance in Torreón. There were dances for *fiestas* and weddings. There were dances for *prendorios*, which were celebrations to announce an engagement. Maclovio Perea and Jose Zamora were *deputados*. These guys maintained order during dances when fights would break out. In the 1930s and early 1940s, there were a couple of bars where the guys got together to drink and play pool.

Esque, in the 1930s and 1940s, many stories were told at the *resolana*, the side of town where the sun would hit a wall and create warmth during the colder days. The *hombres* would stand around this area and exchange notes.

Treasures were said to be buried in a well, where my grandpa Elfego Chavez had a ranch. To find it, conditions had to be just so. For example, you had to be alone. It had to be a certain time of day and certain appearances would make themselves known.

I was an Army soldier, and I fought in the Korean War. I almost died during the war and gave much blood for our country. Other veterans from Torreón who lost their lives were Leonides (Lone) Garcia and Samuel Vigil. Leonides died during World War ll. He was the son of Eliseo and Matildita Garcia. Samuel also lost his life during World War ll. He was the brother of Dolorita Vigil.

Here are some *dichos* that I have remembered:

(*dichos* to accept life as it comes)
Antes como antes, ahora como ahora
Cada mente es un mundo
Cada quien (chango) tiene su columpio

Out of the roots of Torreón came many who have pursued higher education and some are as follows:

Ramón Chavez, my younger brother, joined the army and obtained a Master's of Science Degree in Languages. He traveled and taught and lived in many places around the world.

William Chavez, my brother, joined the Navy. He then received a bachelor's degree from UNM. He taught at Santo Domingo Pueblo until he retired.

Carolyn Sandoval, my sister Cathy's daughter, obtained a Bachelor's Degree in English and a Ph.D. in Women's Studies.

Theresa Chavez, my daughter, has a Master's Degree in Counseling from the University of Southern California.

Debbie Chavez, my daughter, has a Bachelor's Degree in Social Welfare.

David Chavez, my son, received a Bachelor's Degree in Mechanical Engineering from the University of New Mexico.

My grandson Mario Chavez, the son of my son Benny, has a Bachelor's Degree in Education.

My granddaughter Irene Chavez, the daughter of my son Ruben, has a Bachelor's Degree in Education.

My granddaughters Eva, Elisa and Erika, the daughters of my daughter Theresa, each have their bachelor's degrees and are currently attending graduate school.

My grandchildren Lauren and Jonathan, the children of my daughter Debbie, each have their bachelor's degrees and currently work and live in northern California.

My granddaughter Alicia Sofia Chavez, the daughter of my son David, received a Bachelor's Degree in Marketing and Advertisement from the University of New Mexico, and she is currently working on a Master's Degree in Community Organizing.

My granddaughter Olivia Merceded Chavez, the daughter of my son David, received a Bachelor's of Science Degree in Nutrition from the University of New Mexico and has just had her first child named Toribio.

Memories of Torreón, New Mexico

Iglesia de San Antonio en Torreón

Wildfires and Working for the United States Government

Susie Chavez-Perea

My name is Susie-Chavez-Perea. I was born in the 1940s in Torreón, New Mexico. My husband, Joe Perea, was also born in Torreón. We were both raised here and have lived here all our lives. I came from a family of 12 children, six boys and six girls. Joe came from a family of six children with four girls and two boys, and we both came from very devout Catholic families.

God always came first in our family and in our town, and many of our traditions in Torreón have been handed down from our ancestors. We only have one church in Torreón, and that is the Catholic Church. The majority of the people here are Catholic, and our church sits right in the middle of town. Its bell can be heard throughout the town when it rings. The bell rings to let people know it's time for mass or various church activities, but probably the most unique reason the bell rings is to let people know of a death in the community. When it is rung really slowly, that means someone from town or someone related to someone in town has passed away. You can then go to the church to find out who has died. Even if we don't go to the church to see who has passed, we will stop and say a prayer for them. We pray the Stations of the Cross on Fridays during Lent, the Rosary for the month of May and October and Novena for the month of June. We have mass on Wednesdays and every Sunday.

My parents had a ranch in the mountains near Torreón. When I was a child, we lived in Torreón seven months out of the year, and the other months were spent up at the ranch. We had a school in Torreón until 1959, and then it was consolidated with Estancia. That was the year I graduated from the eighth grade. My graduation, like all of our programs and teachings, was held at the Cibola Hall, which belonged to the St. Joseph Society. The St. Joseph Society was a league of the church in Torreón that came together to help with the spiritual and physical needs of the community. My dad was one of the society members who helped build the hall, and a lot of the lumber used to build the hall came from my parent's ranch. At that time, everyone shared what they had for the good of the community, and we always came together to help each other. Years later the Cibola Hall was sold to a private owner.

Other than houses, the church and the post office, our little town used to have a couple of bars/dance halls and stores up until about the early 1980s. One of the dance halls was next to our house. When Joe and I got married and bought our house, we soon learned that we didn't have to go to the dance hall to hear the music or to dance. We could dance in our house because the stage where the band played was next to our bedroom, and the music was so loud. During the day, my oldest kids would go out to play in the front yard, and before I knew it, they'd come inside with pockets full of candy and gum. Mr. Garcia, the owner of the dance hall and bar next to our house, would call them over and fill their pockets with treats. The Garcias were our closest neighbors and a beautiful couple.

    We have always had a post office here in Torreón. I had the privilege of being the postmaster for 25 years, and I enjoyed my job very much. The joke in Torreón was that I had the only job in town. I guess you could say, I was the only person who didn't have to drive anywhere to work. Many of my family members were or are in public service through employment with the United States Government. My dad, three of my brothers, my sister-in-law and my husband all worked for the forest service, and now my daughter Arlene works for the forest service. My son Johnny also volunteers as the chief of the Torreón Fire Department, a position handed down to him by his dad a couple of years ago. This brings me to the fires that almost burned our precious town.

    First in November 2007, there was the Ojo Peak Fire in the Manzano Mountains. It burned almost 7,000 acres and three homes in the Manzano and Punta de Agua area. That fire didn't come as close to Torreón, but it was a scary site to see. Then just a few months later, in April 2008, the Trigo Fire started on the westside of the Manzano Mountains. Nobody could have imagined when it was first reported on the other side of the mountain that the winds would quickly carry it over to the eastside. It moved so fast. In fact, about 13,000 acres of our beautiful mountain burned within a couple of days. It was really sad and scary. We had to evacuate the area. Most of us left, except our brave volunteer firefighters, including Johnny and Joe, who stayed behind with our fire trucks to help the forest service protect our homes and buildings. Arlene worked around the clock to keep the public and media informed as to what was happening. The Priest had us remove the saints and crucifix from the church for their protection. As the postmaster, I had to pack up all the mail and important documents and equipment and relocate to Estancia. I worked out of the Estancia Post Office during the week we were evacuated. Joe has fought fires all over the United States for many years in his career with the forest service, but he said it was so hard and sad to watch the mountain where we had spent our lives go up in flames. More than 50 of our friends and neighbors in the mountains lost their homes. While some rebuilt, many never returned. We are grateful that God protected the town of Torreón, all of its resident's homes and especially our church.

    As I close my story, Joe and I will just say we feel like we are some of the lucky ones who were able to stay and make our living and now retire in Torreón. When asked what we do in Torreón, we just laugh and say, "There's never a dull moment here." I often call my daughters, and when they ask, "What's going on?" I usually have a story to tell them about how someone came to visit, or one of my grandchildren won grand champion with one of their animals, or someone in the community is sick, or someone is missing a cow. This isn't a life for everybody, but it's the perfect life for us. We are still here and are proud to welcome you all back whenever you come home to Torreón, even if it's just for a quick visit.

Susie Chavez-Perea

Well-Wishing, Making Butter and Aguinaldos

Lupe Chavez-Vigil

My name is Guadalupe (Lupe) Chavez-Vigil. I was born in the late 1950s and raised in the small town of Torreón, New Mexico. My parents are Reina and Elfego Chavez, and they had seven children, five daughters and two sons.

My dad Elfego is a m*arcarnoria*, a well-wisher, not a well-witcher, and he has been wishing wells for almost 50 years. My dad's uncle Leopoldo Chavez was a well-wisher, and he thought my dad had the gift of well-wishing, so he encouraged my dad to try it. Manuel Brown, the blacksmith in Torreón, also believed my dad had the gift of well-wishing, so he encouraged my father as well. The first well my dad wished was when he was about 37 years old, and it was for Richard Chavez in Torreón. Since then he has been wishing wells for others.

The process goes something like this. My dad will meet with someone on their land and ask the property owner where they hope to find a well. This gives my dad an idea where to start looking. My dad uses a shaved juniper branch that has a shape of a wishbone to help him locate a well. He walks the property with his arms straight out in front of him with each hand holding one side of the branch. He walks until the branch starts to spin. Once it starts to spin, he has located a well. The branch will then start to move up and down, and depending on how many times the branch moves up and down, determines how much water is in the well. My dad is 84 years old now and still active wishing wells. He has wished 147 wells, all accurate with high water pressure. My dad was also a rancher who had many cows and horses. Every year he has a vegetable garden. The summer of 2015, he had a beautiful bean garden.

My mom Reina is a great seamstress. She sews beautiful clothes, curtains, bedspreads, blankets and other items. She also crochets afghan blankets, dresses, ponchos, hats and scarfs. I didn't take after her, but my daughter Tiffany Vigil did. When Tiffany has down time from school, she spends hours crocheting. My mother has also spent many summers making *capulin* and apple jelly.

In the past, the people of Torreón had to work very hard to maintain their land and their homes. Everyone had big families back then, so there were a lot of challenging moments growing up in a large family. My family didn't have a lot of material things, but we enjoyed the little we had. We learned how to take care of each other and how to share. We were very humble and content, and we had God in our lives. Every night before bed, my

Well-Wishing, Making Butter and Aguinaldos

family and I would all kneel down together and pray the Rosary. We went to church every Sunday, and we went to church for the Holy Days of Obligation, Novenas and just to visit the Lord. What an honor and pleasure it was growing up knowing God. I thank my parents for that.

One of my favorite times being at home with my family was when the electricity would go out. There was No TV! My dad would pull out the lantern and place it on the table. We would all gather around the table, and my dad would tell us *cuentos!* He would tell us really good stories. This was great **quality time with my family.**

Another great memory was when my family and I would all get together to make fresh butter. My dad would gather us children in a big circle, and he would hand us a big jar full of cream. That jar needed a lot of shaking to form into a ball of butter, so we each took turns shaking the jar. When we were tired of shaking, we would pass the jar on to the next person. We made this activity into a fun game. Finally, after a lot of shaking, the cream turned into butter. Once the butter was formed, we took it out of the jar, added salt and shaped it. Yum!!!! Yum!!!! It was delicious, real homemade butter. My family had a milking cow that produced a lot of milk, so we always had fresh milk, cream, cheese and butter.

Growing up in Torreón was so much fun! It was "clean fun." All the kids in town played outside until it got dark. We would play hide-and-seek or jump rope, and we rode our bikes. We also played in a barrel. The barrel roll was my favorite. I would get inside a barrel, and one of my sisters or brothers would push me down a hill. Then we would switch. Someone else would get in the barrel, and I would push them down the hill. It was fun, fun! My dad enjoyed playing softball with us, and in our family, we had enough siblings to form a baseball team. My family never had a summer vacation, but boy did we have a fun summer with family and friends. In those days everyone would visit each other. The parents would visit with each other and drink coffee and eat *biscochitos* while the children played. At this time, all the children had great respect for their elders. The time was precious.

I spent a lot of time with my friends Angela (Bongie) Chavez, Cathy Garcia and Donna Salas, who were all from Torreón. Cathy was the daughter of Fidel and Antonia Garcia, and it was fun at their house because they had this huge water tower with a ladder. We liked to climb up the water tower, and we called it "Petticoat Junction!" We played dress-up with old formal dresses and high heels, and we pretended that we were Diana Ross and the Supremes. I was Diana Ross. "Stop! In the Name of Love," I used to sing. Oh, it was so much fun. Every chance we got, we would ride our bikes inside the *Sala de Fidel*. We built ramps with boards and blocks, and we would "pop wheelies." For Halloween we would set up a haunted house in the dance hall. We thought it was pretty scary. We liked to scare the town drunk that walked the streets drunk. I would take him by the hand and bring him into the *sala*. We had a field day watching him get scared and cry. He would say, "¡Quiero ir a mi casa! ¡No voy a beber más!"

While we were playing at Cathy's house, Cathy's mom would come and check up on us, from time to time, to make sure we were okay. She would bring us lemonade and homemade cookies. She would ask, "Are you hungry, Honey?" She always addressed us by "Honey."

I went to school in Estancia, and I was very active and involved in sports, cheerleading, drill team and track. It was easy to be involved because it was a small school with not that many students. My high school years were the best years of my life. It was so much fun. Today's generations drop out of school or want to rush through it. When school was out at the end of the day, I would get off the bus and make time for God and the elderly in the area. It would be church and God and then my grandparents Carlota and Jose Maria Perea. I would visit them twice a week. When my grandpa would see me coming, he would say, *"¡Tranca el refrijador, ya viene la Lupe!"* I would eat like no other! The other days would be spent visiting my *tía* Candelaria and my *tío* Pedro Alderete. I would help my *tío* Pedro bring in wood. My auntie Candelaria and I would spend time talking and enjoying each other's company. She loved the way I combed her hair. I remember my *tía* Candelaria always had a dish of butter on the table, and it was the real butter. Yum!! I would stick my finger in the butter and eat it, and Hilda and Christella, my cousins, would get mad at me. I remember Hilda would say, "Hide the butter! Here comes Lupe!" My visits to see my *tía* Leonela and *tío* Melcor Lujan were also a great memory. The moment my aunt saw me, she would say, *"Tarre bonita la Lupe, lavame los trastes."* I would honestly wash the dishes out of respect.

After school my brothers and sisters and I would come home and get started with our chores. Each one of us had our chores to do. My parents did not have to tell us; it was our responsibility to know what we had to do. I did the cooking. I learned how to cook when I was 10 years old. Pretty much my menu was **beans, potatoes, red or green chili and tortillas or potatoes, beans, tortillas and chili...** I made many dozens of *tortillas* every day. We did not have the processed foods and the fast foods that we have today. On Saturday mornings, my mom and my sisters and I would get up and start cleaning the house. It was fun because we watched American Bandstand with Dick Clark on TV while we cleaned, and I danced while I vacuumed, dusted, mopped floors and did other chores. In the summer we always had a garden, and we worked hard in the garden and at the ranch. At the ranch, we had to round up the cattle. As hard as it was, I always made it fun. I was a little mischievous, so I always found a reason to laugh, sing and be silly. After all, the saying is **"Live, Laugh and Love."**

I was also in the church choir in Torreón. It was a great pleasure to sing with the Benavidez sisters. Flora and Barbara Benavidez were my inspiration and my role models. We had a lot of fun during choir practice. Again, I always made the best of everything.

The church *fiestas* in Torreón were an exciting event we always looked forward to. The celebration began Friday evening with Holy Mass in the church and usually followed by a dance at Fidel's dance hall. On Saturday the *fiesta* lasted all day and ended that night with a dance. All the people

Well-Wishing, Making Butter and Aguinaldos

from the small towns around Torreón would come to join the fun. The dancing was a great joy. My mom would start early in the year making our new outfits for the *fiestas*. I was blessed with two new outfits. The *Fiestas de San Antonio* are still held every year in June.

When I was a kid, the winters in Torreón were very cold and long. We used to get a lot of snow, past my knees, but we still had to go to school. Sometimes there was so much snow, my dad would take us on the tractor to catch the bus near the community center. The school never shut down. The water pipes would freeze in our house. No Water... I would gather clean snow and melt it to wash up, and we had a *platón* on the woodstove for washing our hands.

Winters were for *Matanzas!* Yum! We made *chicharrones* and had good times with many family and friends. The women in the kitchen made corn *tortillas* and baked blood with raisins and *piñón* nuts. The men cooked the meat outside and drank *sangria* and beer. They cooked everything from the pig, and I mean **everything!** The ears, the tail, the feet, the tongue, the intestines, everything was cooked. In those days, we did not waste anything. It was food.

Christmas was another great memory. *Las Posadas* was Christmas for me as we prepared for the birth of Baby Jesus. The community gathered in different homes each night for *Las Posadas,* and there was great music and great food. The church choir sang and played their guitars, and Father Olona, who was the priest in Torreón in the early 1970s, sang with us. Christmas was about God, Baby Jesus, good food and family. We ate the traditional foods: *posole*, red chile, *tamales* and *biscochitos*. Up until I was about the age of 12, the kids celebrated *Aguinaldos*. We would walk to all the houses in town, and at the door, we would say, "¡Mis Christmas! ¡Aguinaldos! ¡Aguinaldos!" They would open the door and hand us an apple or an orange, nuts or hard candy. Then we moved on to the next house, and we did it again. It was fun! Christmas Eve, we went to Mid-Night Mass, and I got to wear a new outfit. I was so proud and happy. After all, it had been six months since my last new outfit. Christmas Day was fun and simple with the **ONE** item we received. We were content.

My friends and I all graduated from Estancia High School, and we all went our separate ways, got married and had children. I moved to Albuquerque to pursue my education and to work. I married Irvin Vigil, and we had two daughters, Tanya and Tiffany Vigil. Our children will never know or understand the simplicity of clean fun, the creative games we played and what a wonderful time it was growing up in the small town of Torreón, New Mexico.

Elfego Chavez wishing for a well

Elfego Chavez working in his garden

Fidel's Bar and Playing Sports

Eloy Garcia

My name is Eloy Garcia. I was born September 3rd, 1941, in Torreón, New Mexico, three months before Pearl Harbor was attacked. I am the third child of Fidel Garcia and Antonia Chavez-Garcia. I was baptized by my mom's brother Santiago (Jimmy) Chavez and his wife, Julia Martinez-Chavez. Nicolas Maez, my mom's cousin, confirmed me.

I'll start my story when I was about six years old, and I was learning to ride my two-wheel bike in front of my dad's bar which was right next to our home. Across the street from the bar was a building where some of the men from town would sit to talk and pass the time. Anyway, I would get on my bike and try to ride it, and I would fall. The men would yell, "¡Se cayó! ¡Se cayó!" Of course, I would get back on my bike, get nervous and fall, and they would not leave me alone. When I was a few years older, one of my chores after school was to take wood to the bar. I would walk into the bar pulling my red wagon full of wood. I would have to walk across the room to the woodstove, and the men sitting near the stove would say to me, "*Esta cantina es mia.*" I would say, "*No, es mia,*" and we would go back and forth. The men always enjoyed teasing me.

I made my First Holy Communion in the church of San Antonio in Torreón when I was about eight years old. The priest at the time was Father Mckniff. The other kids who made their First Holy Communion with me were Christina Lujan-Zamora, Lita Salas, Tercilia Chavez, Jose Chavez, Maurilio Sanchez and Billy Lujan. I later became an altar boy, and I served as an altar boy until I went to high school. At that time most of the Mass was in Latin, so we had to learn the prayers in Latin. Mr. Sanchez, a school teacher from Torreón, would help us learn our prayers.

The church and the Catholic religion meant a lot to the people of Torreón, and it still does. During Lent we made many sacrifices, we did penance, and we fasted. We didn't listen to music, and we didn't dance or go to the movies during Lent. On Fridays we didn't eat meat, and we went to the Stations of the Cross at church. During Holy Week, we had services in the church all week. On Holy Thursday we made our lenten foods, and we ate them on Good Friday. The lenten foods were salmon cakes, *quelites, torta con juevo, sopa* and *tortillas.* Saturday was *El Sabado de Gloria,* and Lent was over at noon. That evening we had a dance that we all looked forward to.

People didn't get married during Lent. However, when someone did get married, they always had a wedding dance with *ranchera* music and polkas. Two other dances that were very popular were *La Marcha* and the *Dollar Dance*. During the *Dollar Dance*, people had to pay the bride or groom a dollar to dance with them. It was also common for the bride to be kidnapped before the wedding and held for ransom. Of course, the bride was always found, and it was all done in fun.

      Dances were a big deal in Torreón and a big part of our entertainment. People from all the nearby small towns would come to the dances. They didn't have to be invited. Everybody was invited! The people from Torreón also attended dances in the other nearby towns like Willard, Mountainair, Manzano and Moriarty. One of the bands that came to play in my dad's dance hall was *The Happy Owls* with Ross Salas on the saxophone, Teodoso on the drums, Amadeo Sanchez on the banjo, Macario Chavez on the cornet and one of the Luceros from Mountainair on the guitar. Agapito Garcia from Willard with his son's Salomon and el Sidro was another band that played at my dad's bar, and another band from Willard was the Chavez family with Antonio and Bobby Chavez. A band that came much later was Melcorcito and the Moonlighters. Melcor was the son of Melcor and Leonela Lujan from Torreón.

      As a child, I had a lot of friends and cousins living nearby, and everyone in town knew each other. We would all play together before and after school. At night we would hang out in front of my dad's bar because my dad had a huge outdoor light in front. The kids would get together to talk and play. Everywhere else in town it was dark.

      A *maromero* named Tamborin would come to town and put on a show in my dad's dance hall during the summer. Tamborin would drive into town announcing the show with his big speaker attached to the roof of his car. The show was about 10 cents, and about 20 or 30 people would show up to watch the show. The show consisted of a magic show, a clown who did tricks and a couple who played the guitar and sang songs in Spanish.

      On Sunday nights, my dad used to take my family to the movie theater in Mountainair. It cost about 10 cents for kids and 35 cents for adults. We enjoyed watching the western movies with Roy Rogers, Dale Evans and Trigger, the horse. We also liked movies with Gene Autry and the comedies with Bud Abbott and Lou Costello and Dean Martin and Jerry Lewis. Cisco Kid and Pancho, Superman and Tarzan were other movies we enjoyed.

      During the winter months, we liked to make a small fire in the *montecito* to stay warm. Sometimes we brought potatoes from home, and we made a fire and cooked the potatoes.

      One of my favorite things to do as a youth was to play and watch sports. The first year we got a TV in our house, I remember coming home from school, and the Brooklyn Dodgers were playing the New York Yankees in the World Series. I knew all the names of all the players for the Brooklyn Dodgers by heart. The Catcher was Roy Campanella. The other players were Don Drysdale, Johnny Podres, Sandy Koufax, Gil Hodges, Jr. Williams, Jackie Robinson, Pee Wee Reese and others, but my favorite was Duke Snider.

Fidel's Bar and Playing Sports

When I was about 7 or 8 years old, there were enough kids in town to make two baseball teams. I was still a little young, so I wasn't on a team, but there was a team on the westside of town and a team on the eastside of town. The team on the westside would practice at Manuel Archuleta's place, and the team on the eastside would practice near Prudencio Hulbina's place, east of my home. The players on the eastside team were Rossie Garcia, Ray Garcia and his brother Eloy Garcia, Desiderio Salas, Riche Chavez, Leo Chavez, Gabriel Chavez, Antonio Maldonado, Rudy Garcia, Tony Garcia, Chris Sanchez and my brother's Fidel Jr. and Abie. Players for the westside team were Jose Maria Perea, Santiago Perea, Jesus Chavez, Levie Luján, Fermín Lujan, Valentin Sanchez, Junior Candelaria, Luis Benavidez, Lorenzo Zamora and Carlos Sanchez. The two teams would play against each other, and they were competitive. Sometimes someone would get hurt or upset, but in the end, they always made up, and they had a great time.

Around the late 1940s and early 1950s, every small town in the area had its own baseball team that played against the other nearby towns. Some of the guys who played on this team were Teodosio Herrera, Ross Salas, Amadeo Sánchez, Polonio Sanchez, Franke Herrera, Hernán Perea, Ignacio Garcia, Tony Galento Garcia, Charlie Chavez, Russito Garcia, Willie Garley, Demecio Perea, Bolesleo Perea, Alonso Chavez and a few others. I remember watching them play here in town, and I would watch them as they all piled up in the back of Ross Salas's big truck to go play in Manzano or Mountainair. I remember one incident that happened while they were playing the town of Vaughn. A player by the name of Landro Abeyta had a hit and was running to second base when one of the Torreón players Ernesto Gallegos, who was playing second, tried to tag Landro out. Ernesto got hit in the jaw, and he got his front teeth knocked out. From then on, everybody started calling him *molacho*.

I went to school in Torreón up until the eighth grade. In grade school, I played on the basketball team. We played against Tajique, Manzano, Punta de Agua, Abo and Ewing, all towns in the Manzano Mountains. The coaches in Torreón were Mr. Jose Sanchez and Mr. Demecio Perea. The coach in Tajique was Mr. Secundino Padilla. The coaches in Manzano were Mr. Nick Candelaria, Mr. Jose Padilla and Mr. Julio Chavez. The coach in Punta De Agua was Mr. Ignacio Salas, and the coaches in Abo were Mr. Cisneros and Mr. Esquivel. I can't remember who the coach was for Ewing del Llano. Sometimes our tournaments were held in La Cibola Hall in Torreón, or sometimes they were held in the Mountainair community building. We liked playing in Mountainair because we got to spend the whole day in town. Every team played at least two games. Either you went to the winner's bracket or to the loser's bracket. The team to beat was Manzano. They always had the best players and coaches, but Punta de Agua and Abo had good teams too. It seemed like Torreón and Manzano usually played for the championship.

In about 1958, I was old enough to play on one of the Torreón baseball teams that played against the other towns in the area. The players on our team were Orlando Lujan, Chrisobalo (Chris) Sanchez, Jose Maria Perea, Desiderio Salas, Fermin Lujan, Ricardo Chavez, Leo Chavez, Jacobo Chavez, Manuel Silva, my brother Fidel and me. We played in a league against Mountainair, Willard, Vaughn and Santa Rosa. During the summer we had a game every Sunday. We didn't win many games, but we had a good time.

One of the games I will never forget is when some of the older guys from these teams had moved to Albuquerque to go work. They were now playing baseball in the big city. Anyway, they wanted to come back and play a game against us. Some of the players on the team from Albuquerque were Ray Garcia, Willie Garley, Guillermo (Gordy) Chavez, Ernesto Gallegos, Moises Chavez, Eduardo Chavez, Frank Herrera, Jose Perea and some guys from Kinney Brick in Albuquerque.

A time was set for a Sunday afternoon, and everybody had been looking forward to this game. Finally, it was time to play. The pitchers for the Albuquerque team were Willie Garley and a lefty from Kinney Brick. Nobody was supposed to hit against Willie Garley. He was a good pitcher. Our pitchers were Jose Maria Perea, Chris Sanchez and Desidero Salas. Anyway, it was the first or second inning, the score was zero to zero, and I went up to bat. I got a hit and made it to second base, and then somebody drove me in for a score. We were ahead about three nothing. Then all of a sudden, it started to rain, and the game was called off. We were disappointed to see the game called off, but we all decided to go party at Ray's house. We had a good time drinking and talking about the game. Who knows who would have won the game that day.

In high school, I played baseball for Estancia High School. I remember one game we played against Mountainair High School in the old Mountainair rodeo grounds. Manuel Gutierrez from Manzano was the catcher for Mountainair at the time. During one inning, I was running, trying to steal home base and Manuel blocked me as I tried to touch home plate. As I skid onto base, I stretched out my arm, and Manuel stepped on my hand with his cleats. I must not have been hurt too bad because I was able to continue to play. I also enjoyed going to the Estancia High School basketball games. Estancia at the time had a class B basketball team which was one of the best teams in the state. It was led by four Chicanos from Willard: Sidro Garcia, Arturo Garley, Julian Velasquez and Chris Garcia.

Besides playing sports, I also had a lot of jobs and chores to do as a kid, and my brother's Fidel and Abie and I would share the chores. My dad had a ranch, and there was always a lot of work to do on the ranch. There were fences to mend and cows and horses to feed. At home next to the house and bar, we had a corral. In the corral we always had a cow to milk and pigs to feed. We would also chop wood for my grandma Nemecia, my dad's mom.

When I was a teenager between the ages of 14 and 17, I worked in the grocery store and gas station that my uncle Pedro and auntie Gricelda Zamora owned. Auntie Gricelda was my dad's older sister by about four years. I worked at the counter helping people, and I stocked things such as candy, bread and canned foods. We had fresh meat in the store, and we sold

Fidel's Bar and Playing Sports

about two lambs a week. There was a telephone in the store, so this is where everyone came to make their phone calls or receive their phone calls.

My uncle Pedro (Pete) was born in Torreón. He was a World War 1 Veteran, and he was one of the first to serve in the war from Torrance county. He was a big man with a good sense of humor. I remember when the girls came to buy something in the store, he would grab them by their hands and do a dance with them. He drove a 1947 Chevy, and when it was too cold or when there was a lot of snow in town, he would often drive the kids to the school house in Torreón. Uncle Pedro planted beans in El Cuervo which was south of Torreón. He would often take the boys to help him work the land. One time when I was a young boy, he took my brothers Fidel (sonny) and Abie, some friends Dicke, Tony and Luis Benavidez and me to go work in the bean field with him. When it was time to pay us, he paid everyone except Luis and me. We asked him to pay us, and he said he wasn't going to pay us because we weren't good enough to throw the *perrodos* over the fence. I think I cried, and he finally paid us about 15 cents each.

Uncle Pete died in 1956. My auntie Gricelda kept running the store until business started to slow down, and in about 1962, she moved to Albuquerque. She died at about the age of 98. My auntie Gricelda was a very smart woman and a very talented piano player. At one time she ran the post office in Torreón, and in her youth, she attended school at St Vincents Academy in Albuquerque. Both her and my uncle Pedro attended Highlands University. Auntie Gricelda and uncle Pedro had four kids: Maria, Juanita, Frank and Christina.

I also worked in my dad's bar. I served drinks, I brought in wood and I kept the fire in the woodstove going. A few things I remember about the bar is that at one time my dad had slot machines in the back room, and on Sundays it was illegal to sell liquor, so the bar was closed. However, on Sundays men would still come and want to buy beer. My dad was very interested in politics, and I remember when Senator Dennis Chavez was campaigning, he came to my dad's bar to campaign. As follows are some of the memories of the men that spent time in my dad's bar.

Cuando yo estaba creciendo en Torreón, mi papá tenía una cantina. Ahí se juntaban todos los hombres a platicar y echarse una cervecita. Los hombres que se juntaban eran gente ya grande de edad y eran muy buenos conmigo. Uno de los señores era Antonio Maldonado. Él vivía al lado de la cantina y era muy amigable. Todos lo querían por sus dichos y cuentos. Era bueno para construir casas de adobe y también era bueno para cazar venado. Mi papá siempre lo llamaba para que los ayudara a matar un cochino o un marano, como quieran decirle.

Manuel Brown llegaba con sus amigos gringos a tomar una cerveza o dos después de hacerles un trabajo en la fragua que el tenía. Era Manuel que componía las norias y los papalotes en los ranchos.

José Torres era un hombre muy inteligente no mas que no pudiera andar sin muletas. A él le dio polio de niño. Él podía componer los relojes, mantenía su yarda bien limpia, y era un hombre muy organizado. Era Jose quien le ayudaba a mi papá en la cantina cuando mi papá tenía otro negocio que hacer. Después de trabajar en la cantina, mi mamá le preparaba comida para que viniera a cenar con nosotros. Ya, él tenía su lugar donde se sentaba en la mesa.

Don Onofre Montoya era borreguero, y él se iba por meses a quedar borregas en los campos. A veces, él le ayudaba a mi papá en el rancho. Me acuerdo que este hombre entraba a la cantina y se hacía su cigarrito de Velvet. Él se paraba en un rincón y no decía nada, no mas lo que le preguntaban. Él tomaba una cerveza muy a lo lejos con ciertos amigos.

Otro señor era Don Vicente Montoya, él abuelo de mi esposa Christella. Él era muy amigo de mi papá, y él se juntaba con otros señores a jugar a las barajas en la cantina. A veces estos hombres jugaban hasta el amanecer. El señor Vicente era él que llevaba a los niños a la escuela en Estancia en su school bus. Él y mi papá hicieron mucho por la comunidad de Torreón con la asociación del agua y cuando enderezaron y enpavonaron el camino. A don Vicente le decían la plebe "mi primo."

Luego en septembre, el tiempo de la cosecha y las fiestas, llegaba un hombre. Él venía a trabajar cuando lo necesitaba, but once he got his first pay he would go on una borrachera, and all the young boys and girls were afraid of him, but he was harmless.

Otro señor que jugaba mucha las barajas en la cantina era un hombre de Mexico. Este señor pasaba mucho tiempo en la cantina con mi papá y sus amigos. No se como llegó a Torreón pero él tenía su familia en Torreón. En el año 1950, más o menos, alguien lo reportaron con la inmigración, y se lo llevaron pa tras a México. Me acuerdo que mi papá fue con un abogado a Juárez y El Paso para que lo dejaran quedarse en los Estados Unidos. Después de dos o tres años volvio.

When I was growing up in Torreón, my dad owned a bar, and the men would get together there to talk and drink. As time went by, I got to know these men well, and they were good to me. One of the men who came to the bar was Antonio Maldonado, who lived next to the bar. Mr. Maldonado was very friendly, and everyone liked him for his sayings and his stories. He built really nice adobe houses. He was also a good deer hunter. My dad always called him when he needed help to kill a pig.

Another man who spent time in the bar was Manuel Brown, who owned a blacksmith shop. After work, he would arrive with his gringo friends to drink a beer or two. Manuel was the one that fixed all of the wells and the windmills in Torreón, and he often hired guys from Torreón to work with him. He and my dad were good friends.

Jose Torres was another man who came to have a drink at the bar. He was diagnosed with polio as a child, so he walked with crutches, but he was able to get along just fine. Jose was a very smart man. He fixed clocks, he always kept his yard very nice, and he was very organized. My dad would call Jose to come and help him in the bar when he had other business to attend. After he worked in the bar, my mom would invite him to have dinner with us. He already had his regular place at the table.

Mr. Onofre Montoya was a sheepherder. He would be gone for months at a time herding sheep in the fields. When he wasn't herding sheep, he would sometimes help my dad at the ranch. I remember he would enter the bar and make his Velvet cigarettes. He would then stand in a corner not saying anything. He would only answer what you asked him. Sometimes he would drink a beer off to the side with some friends.

Mr. Vicente Montoya, the grandfather of my wife Christella, was another man who would come to the bar. He would get together with other men to play cards, and sometimes they played until early morning. Mr. Vicente was the school bus driver. The school in Torreón only went up to the eighth grade, so Mr. Vicente drove the high school kids to high school in Estancia. My father and Mr. Vicente were very good friends, and they both did a lot for the community. They were both involved with the Torreón Water Association, and they helped to get some of the roads straightened and paved in Torreón. Everyone in town called Mr. Montoya "mi primo."

There was another man who came and spent time in the bar and played cards with his friends, and he and my dad were also good friends. He came from Mexico. I don't know how he came to live in Torreón, but he and his family lived there. In the year 1950, more or less, someone reported him to immigration, and they came and took him back to Mexico. I remember my dad went with an attorney to Juarez and to El Paso to see if he could help him return to the United States. After a few years, he did return.

Later in September, came harvest time, the *fiestas* and a certain man from town would come around. He went to work when he needed to, but once he got his first paycheck, he would get drunk. All the boys and girls were afraid of him, but he was harmless.

In the late 1940s and early 1950s, a lot of people left Torreón because of the drought. Some people left to Albuquerque, Los Alamos and some as far as California. It was sad to see them go. Some of these people we never saw again, some we kept in touch with, and some continued to visit Torreón.

Here is a brief history of my family:

Jose Andres Garcia y Guadalupe Baca eran los padres de Rafael Garcia. Rafael Garcia era el padre de don Ignacio Garcia.

Ignacio Garcia was my great-great-grandpa, he was my dad's grandfather. He was born in La Plaza de Santa Fe in 1835 during the Mexican revolt. He and his wife Dolores Padilla lived in el Sausal by the Rio Grande River north of Belen, west of the Manzano Mountains. Around 1855 they moved to Manzano and started a family. They had five sons and three daughters. Cesario era el mayor y luego nació Celedonia, Ross, Vicenta, Andrea, Eutimio, Juanita y el más joven era José.

Cesario se casó con la señorita Carlota Garcia y tuvieron cinco hijos: Dolores,

Eusebio, Rafael, Manuelita y Roman.

Celedonia se casó con Jose Sanchez y tuvieron hijos.

Mi abuelo Ross se casó con Nemesia Romero y tuvieron siete hijos: Juanita, Eutimio, Gricelda, Fidel (mi papá), Ross Jr., Antonio y Jose Ignacio.

Vicenta se casó con Eleno Zamora y tuvieron nueve hijos: Manuel, Franscisquita, Mercedes, Anita, Ignacio, Casimiro, Santiago, Antonio y Ramona.

Andrea se casó con don Valentin Lujan y tuvieron ocho hijos, solo tres sobrevivieron, quienes fueron Trinidad, Sofia y Jose Leon.

Eutimio se casó con Guadalupe Sanchez y tuvieron sies hijos: Pedro, Rosa, Josefa, Fidela, Ignacio y Luis.

Juanita se casó con Jesus Lujan y tuvieron cinco hijos: Francisco, Maria, Maximiliano, Anita y Juan (Juanito).

Jose se casó con Soledad Vigil y tuvieron nueve hijos: Placido, Felicita, Anita, Salomon, Alberto, Carlota, Jesuscita, Ricardo y Leonor.

Eloy's First Holy Communion. Front row Eloy, Billy Lujan, Madrilio Sanchez, Josesito Chavez

Fidel, Abie, Eloy, Nancy, Carmela Garcia

Eloy Garcia

Fidel Garcia in his bar with Valentino de la O, who was the host of the Val de la O show

Fidel Garcia Sr.

Eloy Garcia

Ross Garcia
and
Fidel Garcia Sr.

Fidel Garcia Jr.

I am Fidel Garcia Jr., and I was born in Torreón, New Mexico in 1937. My parents were Fidel Garcia and Antonia Chavez-Garcia. My dad was born in Torreón, New Mexico in 1900, and my mom was born in Willard, New Mexico in 1915. My dad's father was Ross Garcia, who was born in Torreón in 1865, and his mother was Nemesia Romero-Garcia, who was born in 1869. Their children were Juanita, Gricelda, Eutimio, Fidel, Ross Jr, Jose Ignacio and Antonio.

My grandparents lived in Torreón, and they had a large cattle and sheep ranch. My grandfather also owned Ross Mercantile in Torreón. I never met my grandfather Ross because he was killed when my dad was still a young boy. I know only a few things about my grandfather from stories my dad told me. My dad was about ten years old when he and his father traveled to Juarez, Mexico on the train. While they were in Juarez, they went to the bullfights, as a kid that sounded very exciting to me.

In the year 1914, my grandpa Ross was killed by his son-in-law Enrique. Enrique was married to Juanita, Ross's daughter. The story is that Enrique was harming his pregnant wife, Juanita, at their home in Torreón. Somebody went and told my grandpa Ross what was happening, and my grandpa Ross went to Enrique and Juanita's home to see what was going on. When my grandpa walked into the house, Enrique, who was hiding behind the door, hit my grandpa on the side of the head with an ax and killed him. Enrique was sentenced to life in prison on March 15, 1915. After this tragedy, Juanita went to live in California, and years later my grandma Nemecia married Valentin Lujan. On December 20, 1929, Jose Garcia, the brother of my grandpa Ross, wrote to Governor R.C. Dillon requesting a pardon of Enrique's prison sentence. The letter stated that he and his family felt that justice had been served, and Enrique should be set free. On December 29, 1931, Enrique was granted a pardon and restored to citizenship.

My dad was fourteen years old when his father was killed, and at the time he was attending St. Michael's boarding school in Santa Fe, New Mexico. That was the end of my father's education. He had to return home and help take care of the ranch, store and family. I can just imagine how the death of his father changed his life forever and what his life may have been like if his dad had not been killed.

When my dad was about 17 years old, he went to work for the

railroad on his way to Los Angeles, California. While working for the railroad, he worked with horses that handled material like dirt and gravel, and he drove spikes into the ground using a sledgehammer. My dad said it was very hard work, but he made it to California where he spent about 15 years. While he was there, I believe he spent most of those years working in a drugstore.

In 1935 during the Great Depression, my dad returned to New Mexico and opened up a bar. Prohibition had just ended. My dad had inherited land from his father, so he was also a cattle rancher. The bar was called the Golden View Bar, and later my dad changed the name to Fidel's Bar. The bar had a small dance hall attached to it. Years later my dad doubled the size of the hall. There used to be really fun dances in the hall, but sometimes there were a lot of fights. People from the other nearby towns would come to the dances, and the guys didn't always get along. The dance hall was also used for other activities besides dancing. A *maromero* would come and do some circus and magic tricks for the kids. Other times someone would come with *títeres* and put on a puppet show. Movies were also shown in the hall for the community to watch.

My grandma Nemesia had said when she died, she wanted to be buried in the same grave as my grandpa Ross. After she died in 1951, some men from the community went to dig up my grandpa's grave. They dug up the grave, and when they got to the box that the coffin was in, nobody wanted to open up the box. Somebody went to get my dad, and he came and opened the box and the coffin. I remember when he opened up the coffin, my grandfather was mummified. His hair and clothes were just like the day they buried him, 37 years earlier. My grandmother was then buried in the same grave as my grandpa.

In the early 1950s, there was a really bad drought in New Mexico. The whole Estancia valley that had once been cultivated for planting beans was now dry. The ground was so loose that the wind would pick up the dirt and blow dust everywhere. The dust was so thick, we couldn't even see the sun. The wind would pick up the tumbleweeds, and they would get caught in the fences, which made huge sand drifts. At times the roads were covered with so much dirt, we couldn't drive through them. The cattle at the ranch didn't have anything to graze on, so we had to feed them cactus. We would burn the needles off the cactus then feed it to the cattle. At this time many folks left their farms and ranches and moved to California or Albuquerque, never to return. Eventually, some of the sons and daughters or grandchildren of these families did return home.

Fidel Garcia Jr.

Fidel's bar

Ross Mercantile in Torreon, New Mexico

Early scenes recaptured- Taken around 1906, this early photography shows Ross Garcia's General Merchandise Store in Torreon, N.M. The store, now a residence, was owned by the father of Fidel Garcia, of Torreon. Mrs. Garcia's grandfather carved the lattice along the roof and posts on the porch before she met and married Fidel. (Photo contributed by the Fidel Garcia family)

Fidel's bar

Fidel and Antonia Garcia on their honeymoon.

Fidel Garcia Sr.

L-R Valentin Lujan, Nemecia Garcia, Fidel Garcia, Antonia Garcia, Barbarita Campos

Philip Hubbell

Insurance — Surety Bonds — Real Estate

Albuquerque — 111 West Gold Avenue — New Mexico
Phone 356

Fire, Automobile, Tornado, Windstorm, Rent, Rental Value, Use & Occupancy, Tourist Baggage, Sprinkler Leakage, Explosion, Riot, Parcels Post, Registered Mail, Inland Marine

Dec. 20, 1929.

Hon. R. C. Dillon, Governor,
Santa Fe, N. Mex.

Dear Sir:

I am the brother of Ross Garcia, who was killed about fifteen years ago, and at that time Enrique Salas was sentenced to the penitentiary for the crime.

I most sincerely believe that Salas has suffered more than enough for the act, and I hereby wish to respectfully request that you pardon the said Enrique Salas. I believe that as the brother of the deceased I am the one who should be most vitally interested in the case. I feel that the ends of justice have been served, and that Salas should now be given his liberty. I submit this to you in all sincerity, and will appreciate it very much if you will pardon Salas.

With best wishes and thanking you, I am

Very respectfully,

Jose Garcia

Growing up in New Mexico in the 1950s and 1960s

Milton Garcia

I am Milton Garcia, and I was born in 1952. I am the son of Fidel Garcia Sr. and Antonia (Tonie) Garcia. My older brothers are Fidel Jr., Abie (now deceased), Eloy and Jimmy. My two older sisters are Nancy and Carmela, and my younger sister is Cathy.

As a young child, I enjoyed playing in the dirt with my Donald Duck car. It was a yellow car with white tires that was made of rubber, and it had the head of Donald Duck sticking out of the roof of the car. That car was my most favorite possession at the time. I think I finally gave it up when I started school. During my younger years, I played with my neighborhood friends. I played with Marcario Salas, who lived next door to my family. Marcario had an older brother Jimmy and a younger brother Herman who I also played with. Sometimes I played with Nazareno Chavez, who lived across the street with his aunt Rafelita. We enjoyed playing in the dirt. We built dams, creeks, lakes, roads and mountains. We carved canoes from tree bark and made slingshots from tree branches and old bike tubes. These were the best years of my life. I had no worries, good health, great friends and I always felt good and happy. Everything was okay.

Before starting school in Torreón at the age of six, I only spoke English. My mother was a high school graduate and was a substitute teacher at the school in Torreón. She felt that the English language was very valuable, and this was the language I learned at home. When I first started school, I made a lot of acquaintances and friends who spoke primarily Spanish. Some of these kids would make fun of me because I only spoke English. I quickly learned how to speak Spanish in order to fit in. Spanish then became my primary language for the next few years, but when I was in the classroom, I spoke English.

Once I started school, my network of friends and acquaintances grew. The kids in my grade were Nazareno (Fidel Jr.) Chavez, Marcario Salas, Juanito Lujan, Isabel Zamora, Dennis Alderete and Tony Sedillo. My circle of friends also expanded into the other grades. These kids were Joe Manual Zamora, Norbert Sanchez, Frank Sanchez, Eloy Sanchez, Gilbert Chavez, Jimmy Salas, Leroy Alderete, Herman Salas, Peté Alderete, Clemente Perea, Joseph Sanchez, Agnes Sanchez, Bernadette Sanchez, Pablo Perea, Ignacio Lujan, Concha Chavez, Rosemary Chavez and Erineo and Luis Salas. As I grew older, my friendships expanded even more.

The first teacher I had in school, I had an extreme fear of. Bless her heart, but her tactics in dealing with children would not be acceptable in

Growing up in New Mexico in the 1950s and 1960s

today's world. May she rest in peace! Unfortunately, she was my teacher during my first three years of school. I then had Mrs. Aragon for two years and have only good memories of her. I then had Mr. Perea for the fifth and sixth grade. Mr. Perea was also the principal of the School. At this age, the students were a bit more rebellious and liked pushing Mr. Perea's buttons. Mr. Perea was a good teacher, but he had to deal with a bunch of rowdy kids.

I went to school in Torreón up to the sixth grade. During my last year of school there, I played on the school's basketball and baseball teams. We had an A team and a B team for basketball, and our mascot was a tiger. The B team uniforms were green and white, and the A team uniforms were orange and black, the color of a tiger. The A team didn't have enough older kids to form a team, so our coach Mr. Perea recruited some older kids from Torreón who were already in high school to be part of our team. I recall going to two tournaments, one was in Morarity, and the other one was in Los Lunas. We played in one tournament and got eliminated during our first game. That was the highlight of my basketball career in Torreón.

Besides going to school and doing a lot of daydreaming, I played a lot of basketball just for fun as a kid. My brothers and I had a basketball goal mounted outside my dad's garage. My friends and I also played football and baseball, and we went ice skating in the creek by the bridge when the water froze over. That creek always had water. I remember one summer the creek was stocked with trout, and we fished the whole summer. We also swam in the creek. We had several favorite swimming holes where the water would accumulate, and the water would get up to about four or five feet deep. We used to walk along the creek west of Torreon up to what used to be my padrino Alejandro's ranch. (It may have been Eutimo, I don't remember for sure anymore.) The ranch was approximately five miles west of Torreón. Anyway, when my *padrino* and my *madrina* sold the ranch, the new owner built a lake on the ranch, and we also went swimming there.

During piñón season my friends and I would go out and look for pinecones that still had piñón inside them. We would build a fire and heat the pinecones in a can over the fire. This caused the pinecone to open up and drop the piñón, and then we ate the piñón. I recall that by the time we got home from our campfire, our hands were so full of turpentine sap that we would have to take it off with either grease or gasoline. We also got that sap all over our pants. I'm sure, I was a pain in the neck to my mother back then.

Many of my other activities in my youth were religious activites or family gatherings. During the late fall or early winter, my aunt Maria and uncle Ross Garcia would have gatherings at their place. They would build a bonfire outside and food was served. We also had a lot of dances in town at my dad's dance hall that was next to our house and attached to my dad's bar. The dance hall was also used for other events. Every year a guy came to town, and he would put on a magic show and a circus in the hall. This guy also did impersonations of Cantinflas, the Mexican comedian. Before the show, this guy would drive from one end of town to the other announcing the show. He had these large speakers on the top of his car that he would speak through.

Sometimes small carnivals came to town and were held just south of my dad's bar.

My father operated a bar which provided me the opportunity to be around men that drank and to be of service as a bartender. I spent a lot of time at the bar with my father. It seemed like the bar never closed. Men consistently came to the bar or to my parent's house during off-hours and on Sundays requesting that they be sold some liquor. Some men could not be without their liquor. There were two bars in town at the time, and the bar signs would light up the entire town at night. It gave us kids the opportunity to ride our bikes at night because we could see where we were going. The bike was the main form of transportation for us kids. Having so many older siblings, I never had the opportunity to have a new bike. My bikes were always hand-me-downs with big fat tires. Occasionally, I would have to take one of my bikes to Manual Brown, the town's blacksmith, so he could weld my petals back on the bike that would break off. We had two blacksmiths in town; the other one was Sam Rymer. Both he and Manual Brown were great friends of my father.

Growing up in Torreón also gave me the opportunity to work on my dad's ranch with my father and my brothers. Sometimes it took us two days to complete the entire process of branding calves because we had to deal with some crazy cows. The cows back then were wild. As soon as they saw us driving into the ranch, they would run away like wild deer. It was a real chore to get them into the corral. We had to get on the horses and round them up. Once we finally got the cows in the corral, we were able to start branding, and everything, usually, went well. Sometimes I went with my dad to take the cows to be sold which wasn't an easy task. Some of these cows were so mean they would kill you if you let them. We had to be very careful with them. They would try to break through the truck rails when we were transporting them to be sold, and sometimes they even tore up the fences in the ranch and then we had fences to repair. We always had plenty of work to do on the ranch. During the summer, we had to fill barrels of water on a daily basis to take to the ranch because there wasn't enough water for the cows to drink. My dad's friends Manuel Brown, Antonio Maldonado and Manuel Antonio always came to help us at the ranch. My dad was lucky to have had such good friends that came to help.

We rode horses at the ranch, but it really wasn't one of my passions. I did it out of necessity like when I had to round up the cattle, but sometimes I did ride for pleasure with my friends. I didn't always trust the horses because sometimes they too could be wild. I remember an incident that my brother Abie had when he was transporting one of his horses in the back of his truck. The horse jumped over the rails of the cab and onto the front hood of the truck while he was driving. Luckily, Abie was not hurt.

I didn't care too much for riding horses, but I did love dogs and my family always had a dog when I was a kid. Since we lived out in the country, sometimes our dogs would get into fights with porcupines and come home full of porcupine quills. Sometimes they would come home smelling really

Growing up in New Mexico in the 1950s and 1960s

bad because they went after a skunk.

Besides working in the bar and at the ranch, I had other chores to do at home. During the summer, my brothers and I had to go chop wood in the mountains and bring it home. In the winter I had to chop wood and bring it inside the house and the bar to keep the woodstoves going. The woodstove was our only means of heat.

When I left school in Torreón, I went to school in Estancia for junior high and high school. Unfortunately, during junior high, I was exposed to some of the prejudice towards us Spanish kids. Some of the kids in the school did not like us, and I found it very hard to see how mean some people could be. That being said, I also found that many of the kids I met in junior high school were good people and a lot of them became friends of mine. Not everyone was prejudiced against us.

In high school, I had the opportunity to be a starter on my basketball, football and track teams. My senior year, I was appointed as one of the captains of my football team because of my good work ethic. I was also an officer in the Future Farmers of America Club for several years and was part of the crop judging teams that represented the school at the state judging contests in Las Cruces. In high school, Fidel Chavez Jr. (Nazareno, Neno) and I were involved in a lot of the same activities, and we got to be good friends. We stayed after school together to practice or to do other activities, and we would ride together to and from Estancia

One year during high school my friends Ignacio Perea, Dennis Alderete, Boy Perea from Estancia and I formed a band called "The Parrot and the Parrot Kids." Ignacio was the band leader, singer and organ player. Dennis played the base guitar, Boy was the drummer and I played the trumpet. We used to drink wine and practice every night at what we called the "Little House" which was a house just south of my parent's home. We had one gig which was for the Homecoming Dance at Mountainair High School. It actually went very well. Later we had planned on playing at my father's dance hall, but there had been rumors going around that some of the guys from Mountainair were planning on coming to the dance to make trouble. We had to cancel the dance, and we never played together again. That was the end of my fabulous music career.

When I was a teenager, my friends and I used to drive to Estancia, Willard and Mountainair to meet and date girls. I met several girls and made some good friends. One night while Clemente Perea (Blues), Joe Manual Zamora and I were in Willard, we got our rear windshield busted by some of the guys from Willard. The guys from Willard and Mountainair didn't have a favorable liking to some of us, and we were involved in a few fights with them.

The year I graduated from high school, some of us would drive to Albuquerque to attend high school graduation parties at the Post 49 on Central between Juan Tabo and Eubank. I remember one night, one of my friends was chased and tackled by the security guard, but I can't remember for what reason. A week or so later, Jimmy Salas, Erineo Salas and I went

Memories of Torreón, New Mexico

back to Albuquerque. We met some girls from the village of Sedillo, and after the party, we drove them home. On the way back home, we were driving between Chilili and Tajique when one of us fell asleep at the wheel, and we flipped over and rolled the truck. After the crash, we got out of the vehicle, and we were all okay. We walked to Ray Barela's place just west of the T. We woke him up at about 2 o'clock in the morning, and he gave us a ride home to Torreón. We were lucky to still be alive.

One time my friends and I were pulled over by the town sheriff near Estancia. He pulled us over and asked if we were drinking. I still remember him flashing his flashlight into the car and he grabbed one of our beers and poured it out. For some reason, two of my friends (names withheld to protect the innocent) ended up spending the night in jail.

Immediately after graduating from high school, I went to work with the United States Forest Service for a while. I scouted campgrounds and fought forest fires. I was sent to California and Washington for most of the summer and experienced extreme fires, friendships and team losses that occurred when a helicopter went down with some firefighters.

As of today, I'm still a cattle rancher. So I guess working on the ranch with those crazy cows as a youth wasn't all that bad. When my son Matthew was growing up, he loved going to the ranch. Now he works with cattle. He was recently Assistant Professor at Louisiana University where he did research, taught cattle breeding classes and worked with cattle breeders. He is now an Assistant Professor at Utah State University where he works with cattle breeders and is involved in research to improve cattle breeding.

Growing up in Torreón taught me to be responsible. It taught me how to do an honest day's work, and it provided good moral values for me to follow. I learned to be good, kind and honest. Torreón made me what I am today. What I will always remember are the friends that I made in Torreón. Although, I do not see my old friends very often, I do consider them friends for life.

Clemente (Blues) Perea

Jimmy Salas

Maggie Benavidez and Milton Garcia

Eloy Sanchez

Johnny Lujan

Norbert (liberty) Sanchez

Fidel (Neno) Chavez Jr.

Erineo Salas

Joseph Sanchez

Marcario Salas

Jose Manuel Zamora

Gilbert Chavez

Baseball and Serving our Country

Raymundo Garcia

My name is Raymundo (Ray) Garcia. I was born in 1934, and I was born and raised in Torreón, New Mexico. I am a retired New Mexico professional land surveyor. My parents were Eliseo Garcia and Matildita Lujan-Garcia. My dad was born in Torreón in 1895, and my mom was born in 1900. My parents had ten children. There were seven sons and three daughters.

My dad's father was Octaviano Garcia from northern New Mexico and his mother was Lugardita Garcia. Their children were my dad, Eliseo, and Delfina and Juanita.

My mom's parents were Pedro Lujan from Tomé, New Mexico and Lupita Fernandez from Las Vegas, New Mexico. Their children were Jose, Leandro, Eulogio, Roman, Rosarito, Aurora, Trenidad, Lina and my mother, Matildita.

My grandfather Pedro Lujan had four brothers. They were Abran, Jesus, Valentin and Andres. Everybody had big families in those days.

My oldest brother Leonides Garcia was a carpenter for the Civilian Conservation Corp, a government outfit. He then went into the military and served with the 200th Coast Artillery during WWII. He survived the Bataan Death March and was a prisoner of war from 1943 to 1944. He died during the war on October 24, 1944. Around that time, the American Legion Post in Torreón was named the Garcia-Luna American Legion Post (now the community center). It was named in honor of my brother Leonides and Candido Luna, who was also from Torreón. Candido was also a prisoner of the Bataan Death March and died during the war.

In around the year 1947, Torreón had three softball teams consisting of young boys from Torreón. On the southwest part of town, there was the team called the Lucky Strikes. The players were Orlando Lujan, Edwardo Chavez, Levi Lujan, Jesus Chavez, Melcor Lujan, Benjamin Sanchez, Margarito Tapia, Reuben Chavez, Fermin Chavez, Johnny Perea, Eloy Perea, Jose Maria Perea and others. The Lucky Strikes practiced near the church. On the northwest part of town, there was the team called the *Sapos*. The players were Rojerio Montoya, Benjamin Montoya, Rudy Montoya, Manuel Vigil, Gabriel Chavez and others. On the east part of town was the team called the *Mentolatos*. The players were Antonio Maldonado, Eloy Garcia, Fidel Garcia, Abie Garcia, Dick Salas, Lino Salas, Rudy Garcia, Richard Chavez, Leo Chavez, me and others. The three teams played against each other. It was all for fun, and we really enjoyed playing together.

My dad made a living as a farmer, and in 1951 because of the drought

Memories of Torreón, New Mexico

my dad moved the family to Albuquerque. We continued to visit family and friends and attend *fiestas* in Torreón. When the drought ended, we continued to farm and ranch. To this day I still enjoy attending *fiestas* and spending time in Torreón.

Beans! Beans! Beans!

Carmela Garcia-Anaya

When I was a young girl growing up in Torreón, New Mexico, a small village between Estancia and Mountainair and just east of Albuquerque, my brothers and sisters and I would often say, "No more *frijoles!*"

Frijoles were all we had almost every day for lunch and dinner. "Why can't we have something different?" We would often complain. In a family of eight children ranging from two years old to eighteen years old, how do you stretch the food supply? We were not poor, but we were not rich. So mama had to make beans often. Beans were an excellent source of protein that went well with potatoes, red or green chile or meat, when we had meat. And of course, we had good ol' home-made *tortillas* that went well with anything sweet or salty. That was our bread.

My brothers and sisters and I would try to think of things we could do or reasons why we shouldn't have to eat beans. We would pretend, we weren't hungry, or we would say, we were sick. We thought about giving the beans to our dog Mikey, or we even thought about running away from home.

However, the best meals were when we would butcher a pig. A *matanza* is no easy task. There is a great deal of work to be done. We would get up at the crack of dawn to start a huge fire outside to get the water boiling. This water was necessary to skin the pig. We would boil the water in those large black pots. The kind of pots that witches use in story books. I remember the sound of fire crackling and the smell of pine and cedar burning and the warmth the fire gave out. Everyone rushing together to get things done gave me the feeling of a festive atmosphere. There were knives to sharpen, tables to set up outside, pots and pans to gather and many other tasks to complete. Relatives, neighbors, and friends would come to help share the work and share all the food.

When the hog was killed, cleaned up and stripped of all the hair on its body, it was time to strip the layers of fat from the pig and make *chicharrones,* yum! The smell was heavenly. The men cut the pig, and every inch of the pig was used, nothing went to waste. The pig's ears were scraped clean and cooked in the red-hot embers. The pig's feet were scraped clean and boiled and added to *posole* which made a delicious meal for Christmas. Even the insides of the pig were used to make *menudo,* a delicacy. I was too squeamish to eat the *menudo.* However, the grown-ups loved it. The whole head of the pig was cleaned and baked in the oven with an apple in its mouth (no kidding). Some folks loved it. Some things we never forget. I remember mama would send us kids to take *chicharrones,* red chile and fresh home-made *tortillas* to neighbors and relatives who weren't able to make it to the *matanza.*

Memories of Torreón, New Mexico

    For a few weeks after the *matanza*, my mother would make delicious pork ribs and sometimes if the chile wasn't too hot for us kids, she would make *carne adovada*.

    However, when the pig was almost gone, we would start eating beans again. I do have to admit, the fat of the pig made the best lard in all the land, and that lard is what made those *frijoles* taste so good. We just didn't want to eat them every day. When my brothers and sisters and I would start complaining about eating so many beans, our mother would tell us a story about boys and girls in a faraway land that didn't have enough rice to eat to keep them alive and healthy. She would say, "Sometimes these boys and girls would have to go for days without eating." I would think to myself, *I'm glad I don't have to go for days and days to have my next meal, and maybe these beans aren't so bad after all. Maybe if I add a little ketchup one day and a little butter the next day, it would give them a different taste.* Sometimes it helped and sometimes it didn't. Now that I'm older and I can eat anything I want to eat, guess what I want to eat? *Frijoles*! Beans! Beans! Beans!

Carmela Garcia and Cathy Garcia

Abie, Fidel, Carmela, Nancy and Eloy Garcia

Growing up a Cowgirl

Carmela Garcia-Anaya

Nestled between the mountains to the east and the prairie to the west is a small New Mexican village called Torreón. This town is where I grew up. I loved growing up in this small mountain village and wouldn't have changed that for anything. I am Carmela (Mela) Garcia-Anaya, and I was born in the 1940s in Torreón. I am the daughter of Fidel Garcia, who was born in Torreón in 1900 and Antonia Chavez-Garcia, who was born in Willard in 1915.

The days were bright and secure. Life was not easy, but it was exciting. As a kid, I was always curious, and anything I found could be turned into a toy. I would hunt for metal. (My dad would hunt for metal to sell.) I would also look for pretty rocks and anthills to study. One time I dug an anthill so deep, I found the queen ant. I remember she didn't have any color. She was white, and she never had to get out to work. I found that very fascinating. Of course, there were times when I would get bit by an ant.

I was such a tomboy when I was young. I was never bored. Across the street just north of our house, we had a corral where we kept sheep. I wore a cowgirl vest, and I had my own rope that went along with it. I would rope the sheep just for fun, and I was good at it until I caught the wrong sheep. This sheep was not gentle, and she plowed after me. I never wanted to rope the sheep again.

I loved shooting my BB gun. I especially liked shooting at the windmill as it turned to pump water. I liked hearing the *ting, ting, ting* sound as the BBs hit the windmill. My brothers and I also liked to shoot at cans and bottles.

At the age of ten, I would walk to the *arroyo* which was about 300 feet from my parent's house. I was never afraid just curious and always eager to find something different. I loved the *arroyo* when I was young. I would stick my feet in the water and throw rocks into it. As I got older, I would walk along the *arroyo* and just think. I loved being there. This was a time when there was no fear of anyone we didn't know or danger of rushing water. The water was still, clean and clear, but during times of a big storm, we stayed away.

Sometimes we would get a huge rain storm. After the storm, the whole town would gather together outside to watch the raging water come down from the mountain. My family and our neighbors Mr. Salas and his children Dick and Mary would all gather to watch the water and listen to the loud sound of nature's force. Sometimes the water would run into town flooding a few houses in its path.

My friend Viola Benavidez and I spent a lot of time together when we were kids. Viola lived on a street we all called Rocky Road because it was very rocky. At that time there were no street names in town, so everyone just called this street Rocky Road. A few years ago the county came in and named the streets. It is now officially called Rocky Road. Viola and I spent a lot of time together walking back and forth to each other's house on this street. I didn't always like walking on this street because sometimes we would walk late at night and one of the boys from town would jump out of an old abandoned house and scare us. Luckily, my house was next to the bar that my dad owned, and there was always a bright light that lit up the area near the bar and my house.

When I was growing up in Torreón, there were always church celebrations to attend. Corpus Christi was celebrated every year in June. Neighbors got ready for this tradition by setting up beautiful altars outside their homes. Then there was a Mass and a procession around the church.

For the annual church *fiesta,* there was also a Mass and a procession. There was a lot of singing, and I loved it. It was a great way to honor the Patron Saint of the Church, San Antonio de Padua.

After the church services on Saturday evening, there was a dance. It was exciting because the dances were held in the hall that my dad owned. We would decorate the inside of the hall with crepe paper streamers. We would wrap the crepe paper around the tall, beautiful, spiral wood columns that my uncle Phil carved. Sometimes my mom would set up a stand and sell hamburgers during the festivities. Before and after the dance my brothers and sisters and I had to sweep and clean the hardwood floors in the hall. It was a lot of work, but it was fun.

When I got married, my husband and I moved to Utah because my husband was in the military. When we came back to New Mexico, we made our home in Albuquerque. When my children were young, we always went back home to Torreón on weekends to visit my parents. My parent's home would be full of family, and all my nieces and nephews got to spend time playing together. I had a wonderful time growing up in Torreón. I have wonderful memories of friends and family that I will never forget.

Spending Time with Grandparents and my Dad Abie Garcia

Virginia Garcia-Lesperance

I am Virginia (Joanie) Garcia-Lesperance. I was born in the hospital in Mountainair, New Mexico in the early 1960s. I am the oldest daughter of Abie Garcia and Gloria Alderete-Garcia-Serrano. I am the oldest grandchild of Fidel Garcia and Antonia (Tonie) Chavez-Garcia and the second oldest grandchild of Pedro Alderete and Candelaria Montoya-Alderete.

I lived in Torreón with my family in a house right across the street from my grandma and grandpa Garcia when I was a child. When I was five years old, my family moved to Albuquerque so that I could attend school. My parents wanted me to have a good education in English. Spanish was still the main language in Torreón at that time. When my parents were young, they went to school in Torreón, and then they went to high school in Estancia. However, the schools were taught only in English, and the kids were not allowed to speak Spanish. Speaking Spanish in those days was definitely not encouraged. It was looked down upon, and the kids were not always treated well. Many of the kids had a hard time learning English and got behind in their studies. My parents did not want that to happen to me. Nowadays, so many people do not understand why so many New Mexicans do not speak Spanish.

After we moved from Torreón, we would go back and visit every weekend. We would spend the whole weekend there plus holidays. My sisters and I loved spending time at my grandma Tonie's house, and we loved eating at her house. She made delicious roasts and mashed potatoes. For Christmas, she made us goodie bags filled with hard candies, peanuts, fruit and big, round, colorful popcorn balls that she made herself. During the summer, Grandma Tonie would take me on a ride through Manzano to show me a house where her mom used to live. Then we would go to the drugstore in Mountainair to buy groceries, and she would buy me an ice cream cone. That drugstore is still there today.

Before heading back to Albuquerque, my sisters and I always looked forward to visiting my grandpa's bar. Towards the back of the bar and behind the long bar counter, there was a big glass cabinet that sat against the wall. The cabinet was full of chocolate candies, hard candies, gum, chips and beef jerky. My sisters and I were allowed to fill a small brown paper lunch bag full of whatever we wanted. I always chose chile chips, gum, chocolate candy bars and a coke. My sisters and I knew, we would always get what we wanted from my grandma Tonie and grandpa Fidel. We always thought of my dad's parents as the rich grandparents and my mom's parents...well... they just didn't have as much.

Spending Time with Grandparents and my Dad Abie Garcia

However, I did spend a lot of time at my grandma Candy's house too. At her house we ate beans, fried potatoes and sliced fried ring bologna on tin plates, and my grandma Candy made the best red chile. In the fall, we always had a *matanza* at both of my grandparent's houses, and all of my uncles, aunts and cousins would come to help.

We spent so much time in Torreón and the ranch, it was as if we had two homes. In the ranch, we had cattle to feed and brand and there were always fences to fix. My dad had a horse named Sunshine who was very tame. He was the horse all my cousins wanted to ride, but I do remember an incident with Sunshine. One time I was riding Sunshine at my uncle Fidel's (my dad's brother) house in Albuquerque when, all of a sudden, something spooked the horse. He just took off running with me on top of him. He ran me underneath the clothesline and then threw me off. Luckily, I didn't get hurt. My dad loved his horse, but he was very upset because I could have gotten hurt.

My grandma Tonie loved to ride horses. I remember one time my family and I were at the ranch when my grandma jumped on one of the horses and took off really fast on the horse. She must have been in her 70s at the time. Everyone was amazed and worried about her because she was riding so fast. Eventually, she came back and was fine.

I often went with my grandpa Fidel to the ranch, and he let me ride on the tailgate of the truck. The road to the ranch was a very bumpy, dirt road and when grandpa hit a bump on the road, I would fall to the ground. He would keep on driving, and I would have to run after the truck. He thought it was very funny to see me running after the truck, and so did I. Eventually, he would stop for me. I would get back on the truck, and I waited for him to hit another bump.

My dad always had a new truck with a camper when I was a kid, and he loved to go hunting, fishing and camping in the Manzano Mountains. He enjoyed taking my mom and my three sisters and me camping. It was always fun. My dad was a very social man who had many friends and enjoyed having a good time. He was handsome, was always well-dressed and was very creative and good with his hands.

My dad passed away when I was 11 years old. It was very hard on my mom and my sisters and me. After my dad died, life changed for us. We didn't go to Torreón that often anymore, and we no longer saw grandpa and grandma Garcia or the other Garcia relatives that often.

When I grew up and got married, I moved my family to Torreón. I live on my dad's property right next to the house I lived in as a child. My husband and I are currently, working hard, restoring the house. I am very proud of this land. I raised my children here, but after they finished high school, they decided to move to Albuquerque for school and work.

I married Pat Lesperance in 2011. He is from Tajique, the town just down the road from Torreón. When Pat was 15 years old, he drove with Pete Alderete, my mom's brother, to go work in Yosemite for the summer. Pat has many memories of my grandpa and his bar. Pat would often ride his horse from Tajique to Torreón to buy a six pack of Schlitz beer at my grandpa's bar. He remembers my grandpa always had a big baseball bat hidden behind the bar counter. Whenever there was a fight in the bar or the dance hall, my grandpa would bring out the bat and try to break up the fight with the bat. Pat also remembers one wedding dance in the hall, where the guys at the dance spent the whole night fighting. It was one continuous night of fighting. One fight would end and another would start. The guys from the small towns in the area didn't always get along, and they would fight with each other. According to Pat, the fights seemed to stop in the 1960s when people started smoking marijuana and calmed down. Pat also remembers another bar in town where the men hung out and played pool.

    Torreón is a town full of culture and tradition, but Pat and I have made our own traditions together. On Good Friday we make a pilgrimage to the nearby towns in the Manzano Mountains. We start in Torreón, and then we drive to Manzano, Punta de Agua, Mountainair, Willard, Estancia and Tajique, and we pray a Mystery of the Rosary at each church. This is a tradition we hope to continue. I feel very blessed and fortunate to live in this town that has been such a big part of my family for so many generations.

Abie and Eloy Garcia family picnic. Eloy Jr., Elaine, Judy Jeanette, Evette, Abie Garcia and Abie's red truck

Abie, Gloria, Joanie and Patsy Garcia

Gloria and Abie Garcia

Fidel Garcia's truck with cows in the back

My Fondest Memories Growing Up in Torreón, New Mexico

Rachel Garcia-Martinez

My name is Rachel Garcia-Martinez. I grew up in Torreón, New Mexico, and these are my fondest memories growing up there. My maternal grandparents, Melquiades and Leonor Trujillo, lived on a ranch about three miles from Torreón called El Cuervo, and this is where I was born in 1934.

I am the eldest of seven siblings. I have two brothers, Mel and Eddie, and four sisters, Rosalva, Lucy, Carmen and Lorina. There was a lot of love, fun and of course arguing when we were growing up, but we grew up as a very close knit family.

When I think of my childhood in Torreón, I automatically think of my dad, Ross Garcia, and my mom, Maria Rita Trujillo-Garcia. They were wonderful parents who instilled in me the moral values and character that made me the person I am today. My mom was a beautiful and gentle woman with deep spirituality. My dad was fun, strict and gentle, and he loved to sing and dance. I remember when we traveled away from home, we would sing in the car the whole way. I always danced a polka with my dad at the dances in my uncle Fidel's hall, and he would leave me breathless. He had more energy than I did. My dad was fun to be around, but he was very strict, especially with his daughters.

My dad was a farmer and cultivated pinto beans. I remember all the activity and hard work that went along with the harvesting of the crops. If the rains came and the crops were good, it was a good and profitable year. When my sister Rosalva and I were very young girls, we had to help hoe the fields. We would have to get up at the crack of dawn. I can tell you, we hated it. However, we learned how to work hard and to be responsible. Now our kids can't even rake the leaves.

When I was young, I spent a lot of time at my grandparent's ranch. I remember my grandfather Melquiades would hire young men from Manzano or Torreón to hoe the fields on his land. These men would stay at the ranch all week, and they were given room and board and $2.00 a day.

When I was growing up in Torreón, everybody living there was of Spanish descent, Catholic and pretty much of the same socio-economic standard and probably Democrat! Everyone was my *tío* or *tía* even if they weren't. There was never any fear of anyone ever hurting or harming us because we all knew, loved and respected each other. There was great respect within the family, and we were taught to respect our elders, school teachers, catechism teachers, priests and anyone in authority.

At the age of seven or eight, I made my First Holy Communion in the Catholic Church in Torreón. Father Jose Gauthier was the priest at the

My Fondest Memories Growing Up in Torreón, New Mexico

time. Making my First Holy Communion was a big, exciting day for me. It was the custom that after receiving the host for the first time, one would walk over to their relatives in the church and receive a blessing from each one. After mass, we had a big dinner at my house to celebrate. I'm sure the dessert was strawberry jello with bananas!

The social events in Torreón all revolved around religious activities. The annual *fiesta* to honor the town's Patron Saint of San Antonio was the big social event of the year. The *fiestas* at one time were celebrated in September because it was right after the harvesting of the crops, which was mostly pinto beans. Now the *fiestas* take place in June.

Our family and I am sure just like all the other families prepared for the *fiestas* the same way. First came the house cleaning, not only scrubbing floors but painting and sometimes even plastering the outside walls. This was done with mud and by hand. After the cleaning and painting came the baking of breads and cakes and, of course, *pastelitos* and *biscochitos*. Then came what was the most fun of all, the shopping for new clothes. We went shopping in Mountainair, or we shopped from the Montgomery Ward's catalog. Everyone had new clothes for *fiestas*.

The *fiestas* started on a Friday night with *Visperas*, which was a ceremony in the church. Everyone went to *Visperas* with a new outfit. Then came a large procession around the neighborhood adjoining the church. By the time the procession started, it was dark outside, so there were *luminarias* made of stacked wood that were lit up to light the way. There was a lot of singing and music, and it was beautiful and exciting. The music and procession GOT all the people in a very joyful mood, not only socially but spiritually. After *Visperas*, all the people went to the first dance. The dance was held in La Cibola dance hall. There was only one dance hall when I was a child. Years later, my uncle Fidel built a new dance hall and people then walked from one dance hall to the other. In other words, there were two dances going on at the same time.

The Cibola dance hall, as I remember, was a big building (I thought it was at the time) with long benches on both sides of the hall. Strangely enough, I don't know if it was only Torreón or a Spanish custom in small communities, but only the women and children sat on the benches. The men, both young and old, stayed in the entrance to the hall. From this vantage point, the men would seek out the available, single girls. When the band started playing, all the young men and husbands would come forth to ask for a dance. However, if they wanted to continue dancing together, the couple would stay standing until the next piece of music was played. Many a romance was started during the *fiesta* dances or other dances, as well.

The music for the dances and all the dances in Torreón was mostly provided by the local band called "The Happy Owls." Ross Salas, my dad's nephew, played the saxophone. His saxophone made all the difference in the sound and tone of the music. The music was happy and gay! (Gay at that time meant happy and joyful!) I remember right before a dance, "The Happy Owls" would go out late in the afternoon in a truck that had a long bed, and

Memories of Torreón, New Mexico

the whole band would play – starting from one end of town to the other. This was called *"El Gallo."* They would play loud, so it got everybody in a "happy and good mood" and ready for the dance. Everyone went to the dance, and all parents took their children to the dance. There was no such thing as babysitters then! Grandparents were there as well. The dances were usually over around midnight or thereabouts.

On Saturday there was the big *fiesta* mass and another procession followed that mass. Everyone went to the *fiesta* mass in their Sunday best or probably in a new outfit. After mass and the procession came the naming of the new incoming *Mayordomos* for the following year - an exciting moment. The *Mayordomos* are responsible for the smooth running of the church for the next year. If any repairs or any new projects are added to the church, the *Mayordomos* play a big part. As I recall, the outgoing *Mayordomos* always add something that enhances the existing beauty of the church. It is a gift, they personally and proudly give.

The outgoing *Mayordomos* select the incoming *Mayordomos*. I remember when my mom and dad received this honor. I think it was in the early 1940s. I remember how excited and happy my family felt.

After the *fiesta* mass on Saturday, everyone went to their own home for a big meal. In the afternoon there was another dance, and everyone attended and danced all afternoon. After that dance everyone went home for supper and to freshen up. Then they returned for the final dance of the *fiesta*. It was a weekend of religious and social celebrating. Everyone enjoyed themselves, danced, drank a little but no one lost sight of the real meaning of the celebration. The meaning was to give thanks to God and San Antonio for the blessings received during the past year. I am sure some people in the community suffered losses and disappointments during the year, but their faith never wavered and remained strong.

In February came Lent. Lent was a solemn occasion, but it was a celebration just the same. I remember being dragged to the Stations of the Cross every Friday afternoon. We could not pretend we were sick, tired or even state that we did not feel like going. We had to go, no matter what. The thing I remember and liked most about Lent was Holy Week, and it involved the sharing of food with our neighbors and relatives. We all had the same menu: *frijoles, chile rojo con torta, quelites, sopa, natillas* and *sopapillas*. On Palm Sunday we attended mass in Manzano so that we could get palms. Easter Sunday we went to church with our new clothes, but I do not remember any Easter egg hunts.

Corpus Christi Sunday in Torreón was another big event. People living near the church would set up an altar outside their home. The priest would then lead a procession walking to every altar. At each altar the priest would stop, and the people would receive a blessing. I remember this because many of us girls would dress as angles. We would wear long white dresses and wings, and we carried a basket full of confetti which we scattered throughout the entire procession route.

The other religious event I remember most clearly and which is

My Fondest Memories Growing Up in Torreón, New Mexico

most dear to my heart is the *Velorio* that my grandfather Melquiades and my grandmother Leonor Trujillo had every year on the 12th of December at El Cuervo. They started this devotion in 1918, and it was to honor the Feast Day of Our Lady of Guadalupe. This tradition came about as a result of my grandfather Melquiades becoming sick during the influenza epidemic of 1918. He recalls that when he closed his eyes, he would see the image of Our Lady of Guadalupe. He promised her that if he recovered from the influenza, he would honor her feast day with a *Velorio* for the rest of his life. He fulfilled this promise.

This event was particularly exciting for my brothers and sisters and me when we were growing up because it was like a big party. First came the *matanza*, the butchering of a pig, approximately a month prior to the *Velorio*. All the uncles, aunts, and the Trujillo cousins came to the *matanza*. Also, I remember my grandmother, my mom and my aunt Pablita would get together to make all the goodies for the *Velorio*. They would make *biscochitos*, *pastelitos*, cakes and *chile rellenos*. (Not like the *chile rellenos* we eat today. These were small and delicious and only made for special occasions.) Then came the thorough cleaning of the house!

Two days before the *Velorio*, brothers and sisters of my grandfather arrived from Punta de Agua, La Ciénega and the surrounding areas. Then came the big day, the 12th of December! This date is etched permanently in my mind! On the day of the *Velorio*, a special supper would be prepared because guests would start arriving around three o'clock in the afternoon. Most of the people came in horse-drawn wagons because very few people had automobiles in those days. Some years it was snowing or there was snow on the ground, but they still came.

At around eight o'clock in the evening, we all prayed the rosary together, and it included many beautiful prayers and songs. The rooms of the small ranch house were full. All of the men who had previously been outside around a big bonfire came in to participate in the praying of the rosary. After the rosary, the men went back to their bonfire, where I am sure a bottle of something was passed around. (I am sure it wasn't Kool-Aid!) Then came the coffee and goodies. Guess who was called in for coffee first? The men, of course. The last ones to come for coffee and goodies were us, kids. We did not complain, though. I guess we understood and had respect for our elders. Many people from Torreón came to the *Velorio*, and it was not uncommon for some people to stay the whole night, singing and praying, and then leaving after breakfast the next morning. I still remember Lita Benavidez (now Sedillo), Angelica, Adela Chavez and I staying up until early morning singing hymns throughout the night. The *Velorio* was always a beautiful event.

After my grandfather died, my grandmother continued this tradition. After my grandmother died, my mother, Maria Rita, continued the tradition. After my mom passed away in March of 2007, I inherited the beautiful statute of Our Lady of Guadalupe which has been in the family since 1918. I pray the Novena and Rosary every year, but I did not continue the *Velorio*.

Christmas in Torreón was a beautiful and quiet season anticipating the birth of the Baby Jesus and, of course, Santa Clause. We did not have the hustle and bustle that we experience today! I think my mother started preparing for Christmas a week before, not three months before like we do today. My dad would chop down a Christmas tree for us. The tree would fill the room with the smell of pine, and we would decorate it with small pieces of cotton and tinsel, and we would make decorations from red and green construction paper. We always thought it was the most beautiful tree. We prayed the *Novena* to *El Santo Niño* every night for nine days in the extra room called *el cuarto recivo*. There was no heat in this room, so it was freezing, but we were not allowed to complain.

Now comes the most beautiful memories I have of Christmas Eve. Not very many people will remember going out early in the evening and asking for *Aguinaldos, Regalo de Navidad*. It was like trick or treat but without the trick. We did not dress up like shepherds or angels or anything like that, but we kids walked to each house in Torreón asking for *Aguinaldos*. We would get goodies like *biscochitos, empanaditas* and maybe some hard candy. Then we would go to Midnight Mass and come home and eat *posole*. Before going to bed, we hung our stockings on the corners of a chair. These were not fancy stockings either, just our everyday socks. Probably some of them had holes! I remember Christmas morning, our "holey" socks had an orange, an apple, some nuts and hard candy that looked like little accordions. We did not get many gifts like our children get today. We got one gift and maybe...just maybe...a second gift. However, what a wonderful and beautiful Christmas we had. I still remember the beautiful *Nacimiento* that is still in the church in Torreón today.

One of the other happy events I remember during the Christmas season in Torreón was the *Pastorela*. It was a Spanish Christmas pageant celebrating the birth of Jesus, and it was held in La Cibola hall. I remember playing a role in one of these pageants, but I don't remember what part I played. I was a woman, but I don't remember who. I remember having to attend rehearsals. Maybe there is someone in Torreón around my age that remembers this event.

I have always preferred the winter months much more than the summer months because I love the snow. That brings me to the memory of riding in my grandpa's horse-drawn *trineo* from Torreón to El Cuervo in the snow. My grandparents would bundle me up in a coat and thick blankets, and I just loved riding in this sled.

In the month of May, I remember going to Manzano to bring the Blessed Virgin Mary to Torreón. We would walk the seven miles from Manzano back to Torreón carrying the Virgin. The week that the Virgin was in Torreón, there were several *Velorios*, and I remember attending some of them. It was a religious gathering, but also a social gathering. This tradition is still going on today.

One memory I have is of me winning a queen contest. Queen for

My Fondest Memories Growing Up in Torreón, New Mexico

what? I cannot remember. Was it for a *fiesta* or a political rally? I don't remember. What I do remember is that we all had a small can with a slit cut into the top so that people could put money into the can. Each penny counted as one vote. My aunt Gricelda put a one dollar bill in my can, and it may be the reason I won. I was never queen of anything ever again. There are things that one never forgets.

I will tell you about a memory that I have never forgotten. I have not lost sleep over it, but I can still remember it well. Lily Garcia-Chavez, my cousin, and my friend Lila Benavidez will probably remember this event. I was maybe eleven or twelve years old. There was going to be a party in my uncle Fidel's dance hall, but I do not remember the occasion. All of the young boys and girls from Torreón were invited, and I was very excited and looking forward to going. I guess, I took it for granted I would be able to go, and I guess it was ok with my mom because she bought some blue taffeta material to have a dress made for me. Rafelita Vigil made my dress, and it was absolutely beautiful. Then a terrible thing happened. My dad said I was not going. I remember begging and crying and everyone pulling for me to go, but when dad said, "No," it was NO! My grandma Lenore, my grandma Nemecia and my aunt Gricelda all told my dad, "*Dejala ir, toda la pleve va a ir.*" Later, I thought he didn't want me to go because there were going to be boys there. The Virgin Mary could have come down from heaven to intercede for me, and dad would have told her, "No." But you know that after one has children of their own, you understand. When we wanted to go somewhere and we asked dad for permission and he said, "Ask your mother" --- we knew we were going! My dad was strict with us girls, but we loved him dearly.

I want to share a rather rare and emotional occasion. Other people shared this same event as well. When my grandma Nemecia passed away in June of 1951, she was to be buried in the same grave as my grandpa Ross Garcia. He died February of 1914 (this was approximately 37 years later). I was there with my dad, and I am sure my uncle Ignacio and my uncle Fidel were also there. The grave was dug, and then someone opened grandpa Ross's coffin. I remember my grandpa's body was intact. I remember his mustache, some hair, his tie and he had a rosary around his fingers. Years later I heard a story that when they opened the coffin, he immediately decomposed. This is not true at all. He was and remained completely intact. There was a glass cover over his body, and it was broken exposing the upper part of his body. I don't know if the glass broke when they opened the coffin or whether it was already broken. There may be men living in Torreón today who were helping that day that still remember this.

My school memories...

I started school in Torreón at the age of six. My first teacher was Raquel Herrera. She liked me, but she did not let me get away with anything. I must have been a pretty naughty and rambunctious student because I felt the sting of her ruler on my hand many times. I would also be punished by kneeling in the corner of the room on a wooden log. I never complained to my parents about being punished at school because most likely, I would have been punished at home for misbehaving at school. I remained friends with Mrs. Herrera, and now I am friends with her daughters Dahlia and Bessie.

The other teachers I remember were Jose Sanchez, Lorenzo Sanchez and my first cousin Mary. My last teacher before starting high school was Demecio Perea. He was my eighth-grade teacher. Mr. Perea was the one that started calling me "Rachel" instead of "Raquel."

The first thing we did every morning at school was pray and say the "Pledge of Allegiance." Then we would sing, and strangely enough, I still remember one of the songs we sang. "Dixie Land" was a song we sang all the time. It was allowed and proper to sing it. I always enjoyed singing, and I must not have been too terribly shy because I always sang at Christmas school programs and other school activities.

My first language was Spanish, so learning English was strongly emphasized at school. When we had recess, we were not allowed to speak Spanish on the playground, and the teachers watched us and monitored this.

I vaguely remember what the school classroom in Torreón looked like. There was a wood burning stove in the corner of the room, and I remember a picture of George Washington hanging on the wall. I have often wondered what happened to that picture.

Now as I look back at my childhood days in Torreón, I think of all the wonderful friends I had and still have. I especially remember the sleepovers I had at Lita Benavidez's house. They lived in the center of town where all of the excitement took place. We would play "Kick the Can," and there were always lots of kids playing together. My mother and Lita's mother, Nicolasita, had been good friends since they were young girls. That made their daughters all close friends. Lita and I remain close friends to this day. I also liked to spend the night with Lily and Flora Garcia, my first cousins. I always enjoyed having breakfast at their house because they always had corn flakes.

1949 was the year my family moved to Los Alamos. This move was with mixed emotions and lots of tears. We were leaving the comfort and safety of our small Spanish community. We were leaving grandparents, uncles, aunts, cousins and friends. We were sad at first, but we soon adjusted because we did not have to haul water, chop wood, and we had an inside bathroom. Who would not like that! We moved in December of 1949, which was the middle of my freshman year at Estancia High School. I stayed with my grandma Nemecia until January, which is when the second semester started. The stay with grandma Nemecia was very pleasant. She was a kind, quiet, gentle, petite woman. I remember every night uncle Ignacio and aunt Mary would come to grandma Nemecia's house, and we would pray the rosary.

I started the second semester at Los Alamos High School. The high school in Los Alamos was very different than Estancia High School. I soon found out how behind I was. I will always remember Mr. Spence, one of my teachers. He spent his own time helping me get through my freshman year. However, I really had to burn the midnight oil with my studies to pass my

My Fondest Memories Growing Up in Torreón, New Mexico

freshman year. We adjusted to living in Los Alamos, and it was a good move for our family, but my roots remained in Torreón. Dad would take us to Torreón for wedding dances, *fiesta* dances and many other occasions.

As of today, I still remain close to my roots and the community of Torreón. My mom and dad are buried there, so part of my heart will always be in Torreón, New Mexico.

Just something brief about my life after Torreón...

In 1955 I met a wonderful guy from Raton, New Mexico, John Martinez. We got married in 1956. We were blessed with three children, J.D. (John David) Sandy and Lori.

Later, we were blessed with two grandchildren, Matthew and Allison, children of our son John David. Matthew and his wife, Maureen, live in Phoenix, Arizona and are the parents of three beautiful children, Madeline, Augustin and John, which makes me a great-grandma. Allison and her husband, Tad, live in Austin, Texas. No children yet.

Many years later Lori blessed us with twin girls, Elle and Jordyn, so now we have four grandchildren. Elle and Jordyn are now seven years old.

In 2014 my children and I experienced the most devastating and sad day of our lives. John passed away in July of 2014. We were happily married for 58 wonderful years, two years short of celebrating our 60th wedding anniversary, but God had something different on his calendar.

I love all of my grandchildren dearly, but Elle and Jordyn, my seven-year-old twin granddaughters, have brought a special joy and blessing to my life. These two little girls have helped me cope and adjust to living without John. Elle and Jordyn love to have "sleepovers" at Nana's house (they call me Nana) almost every weekend. They are so active and full of energy that when they leave, I am exhausted, but I look forward to more exhausting weekends. I hope they never stop.

J.D. and his wife, Julie, and Lori live in Albuquerque, not far from where I live, and Sandy lives in Bernalillo. I am very fortunate to have my children living close. We see each other almost every week.

Memories of Torreón, New Mexico

Rachel and Rosalva Garcia

My Fondest Memories Growing Up in Torreón, New Mexico

Statue of Our Lady of Guadalupe that Melquiades and Leonor Trujillo had for many years at El Cuervo.

Ross & Maria Rita

Ross Garcia Jr. and Fidel Garcia

Melquiadez & Leonor

Ross and Nemecia Garcia

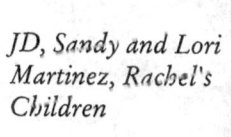

JD, Sandy and Lori Martinez, Rachel's Children

Elle and Jordyn, Rachel's twin granddaughters

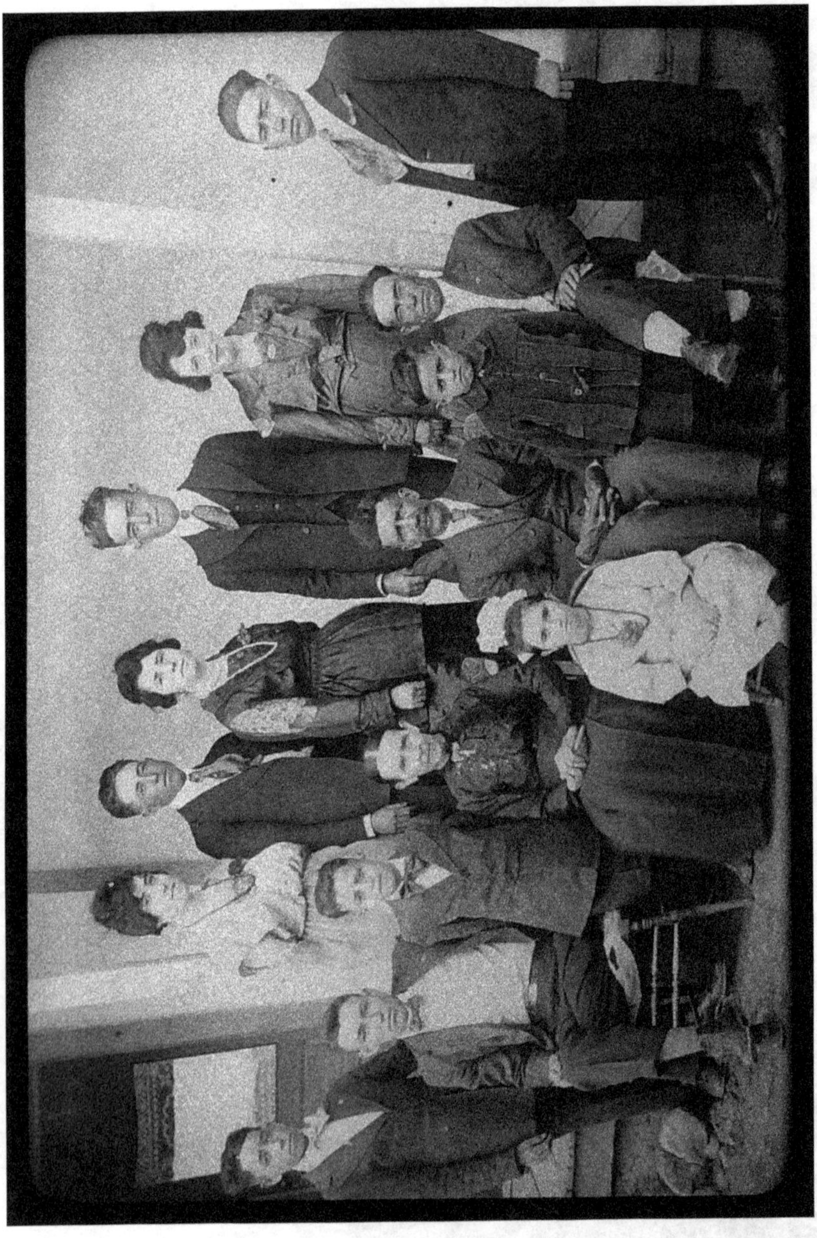

Family Picture back row L-R Gricelda Garcia-Zamora, Fidel Garcia, Juanita Garcia, Ross Garcia Jr., Delfinia Garcia (Eutemio's wife)

standing on the left Antonio Garcia

L-R sitting Pedro Zamora (Gricelda Zamora's husband), Ignacio Garcia, Nemecia Garcia-Lujan and her husband Valentin Lujan, Ross Salas (son of Juanita Garcia), Eutemio Garcia

standing on the right Jose Leon Lujan (Valentin's son)

sitting in front Nancy Salas (daughter of Juanita Garcia)

Gricelda, Fidel, Juanita, Ross Jr, Eutemio, Antonio and Jose Ignacio are the children of Ross and Nemecia Garcia. After Ross Sr. died, Nemecia married Valentin Lujan.

Capulin Jam

Cecelia Herrera-Sanchez

Growing up in Manzano, New Mexico in the 1950s and 1960s, my mom would make *capulin* jam for my brothers and sisters and me. It was a ritual event that she did before the end of our summer school vacation. My mom and my siblings and I would head for the hilly slopes to do our berry picking in mid-August after the monsoon season was over and the cherries were ripe and ready to be picked. Thanks to the rains which were a bountiful blessing, we were able to pick a lot of berries

The chokecherry or *capolin* is a suckering shrub or a small tree that grows up to about 16 feet tall. It grows wild alongside hilly slopes and in high elevations like Manzano. It grows best in moist climates but also tolerates a drier climate. The chokecherry is native to South America, North America and Canada. Native Americans used the leaves and bark for medicinal purposes and for food. They would also boil the berries and extract the juices to dye fabric. The cherry is about a quarter of an inch in diameter and ranges in color from bright red to black. It has a very astringent taste, somewhat sour and slightly bitter. The very ripe berries are dark in color. They are less astringent and sweeter than the red berries.

There was a *capulin* orchard in Manzano that was owned by the Turrietta family where my family would go berry picking. The Turrietta family was very kind to let us pick the berries from their trees.

The Turrietta's capulin orchard was located down the road shown in the picture below.

Capulin Jam

Every summer many of the families who lived in Manzano in those days went berry picking either at the Turrietta's orchard or further up in the Manzano Mountains. The Turrietta orchards were right behind the Turrietta house next to the creek that ran through the village. The roots of the *capulin* tree seek water, so this location alongside the hilly slopes was the ideal spot for them.

The day before our *capulin* adventure, we would start preparing. We would go out to the shed and look for different size buckets or anything we could find to put the berries in. The next day we took tarps, small ladders and we packed a lunch to take with us. We wore long sleeve-shirts, long pants and hats to protect ourselves from the mosquitos.

Our house was west of the orchards; it was approximately three-quarters of a mile one way. We would walk from our house to the orchards, but when you're a little kid walking about three-quarters of a mile seemed very far, especially on the walk back home carrying buckets filled with berries.

Sometimes if it rained the night before, the dirt roads would turn *caliche*. It was a sticky, muddy mess! The mud would stick to our shoes, and we would slip and slide all over the place. Walking back home carrying a few pounds of berries was not that easy for little kids to do in the mud.

When we finally arrived at the orchards, Tony and Eddy, my two older brothers, would unfold the large canvas tarps and spread them on the ground below the trees to catch the berries. Tony was the daring one; he would climb the taller trees like a raccoon without using a ladder. Eddy was the younger one, so he used the ladder to climb onto the smaller trees. My brothers would shake the branches and here came the cherries down on the tarps. The younger kids would then gather the berries in their pails. We also used long wooden sticks to knock off the berries from the taller trees, and we picked the berries right off the branches that we could reach. Sometimes we had to compete with the birds.

Alright, so not every day out there was totally hard work. When my brothers and sisters and I began to get tired, we would start to nitpick and compete with each other. We would brag about who had the most berries in their buckets. Sometimes our bickering would turn into a fight. We would throw *capulin* at each other and make a big mess until my mom, Manuelita, intervened and sent someone home. At times we were kind of like the Little Rascals, but most of the time we put in an honest, hard day's work. We made good team players! It is funny to think back now, how young we were at the ages of 8, 9 and 10 years old, but how much energy and determination we had for hard work and yet it was actually fun.

A few days of berry picking filled our tin tubs with this delightful berry which was enough to make plenty of jelly and syrup. My poor mom would stay up late at night getting the canning equipment ready that was needed for this long process. The next day she was up early and eager to start the day, and I never heard her once complain about how much work it was. My brothers and sisters and I all had a job to do. My job was to scrub and wash the mason jars, and then they would be boiled in a granite bathtub which was part of the sanitization process. My sister Diana would rinse and sort out the cherries and keep the equipment clean. My younger brother Arturo would dispose of the cooked down cherries that were not used. These were usually fed to the pigs.

When the cherries were ready to be cooked, mom would put them in a large cast iron kettle with water and boil them until they popped open and were soft. We could usually tell when the cherries were ready because an amazing aroma lingered throughout the house. The next step was to extract the juice from the cherries with a large strainer. Then the juice would be used to make the jelly, and the cooked down cherries were discarded. Then as I recall, my mom would add lots of sugar and pectin to help solidify the juice. This all cooked for a while until it began to thicken.

Once this process was done the next step was to pour the cooked juice into the sterilized jars and put the lids on them. The last step was to put the jars in a large pressure cooker filled with water and cook them for about 15 minutes so that the lids would seal tightly on the jars. This was the process of making *capulin* jam.

My family had peach, apricot, and apple trees, so my mother also canned peaches, apricots and apples. My dad, Antonio, planted all the fruit trees when he and my mom first moved into the house as newlyweds. I

Capulin Jam

suppose he was thinking then that they would need lots of fruit to feed lots of kids! Back in those days, women did a lot of canning, so they would have plenty of food to feed their big families throughout the winter months. Many of my mother's comadres in the community would trade canned foods with each other which gave them a variety of canned foods to feed their families.

    I have many wonderful memories growing up in a large family that I will cherish forever and that I now share with my two daughters. I will never forget the fun times we had growing up in a beautiful little village nestled in the foothills of the Manzano Mountains.

The Joy of My Youth

Andrea Lujan

I am Andrea Lujan. I was born in Torreón, New Mexico, and I lived there in the 1930s. My mother was Lola Chavez-Lujan, who was born in Willard, New Mexico. Her parents were Cristino and Carmelita Chavez of Willard. My father was Jose Leon Lujan. His parents were Valentin Lujan and Andrea Garcia-Lujan. Andrea's parents were Ignacio Garcia and Dolores Padilla-Garcia.

The church has always been a very important part of life for the people of Torreón. When my father was a boy, he served as an altar boy. When I was a child, my mom played the organ and sang the Mass in Latin prior to Vatican ll.

I lived in this small loving community of Torreón until I was 11 years old, and these surely were the happiest years of my life. It was a very carefree, wonderful time. All activities in my young life were centered around the church. We had wonderful celebrations that I will never forget. One of my favorite feast days was Corpus Christi. The priest would lead a procession around town with many people following behind. Many young girls dressed in white would walk along throwing confetti before the Blessed Sacrament which was placed in three different well-decorated altars.

The annual *Fiesta de San Antonio* was another one of my favorite feast days. On the night of *Visperas*, there was a procession around the church and *luminarias* were lit and placed along the way. It was a procession with a lot of beautiful singing and praying, and everyone had such a great time.

Because of the drought my father was forced to look for work elsewhere. My dad got a job working with the railroad, and we moved to the Barelas area in Albuquerque. After we moved, we didn't visit Torreón that often, but I never forgot where I came from.

I conclude by thanking all the people from Torreón who have been so supportive, kind and loving as I have lost my loved ones. From time to time, I always remember that peaceful, loving place, Torreón, New Mexico.

Riding Goats, Matanzas and Drinking Wine

Magdalena (Maggie) Lujan

I am Magdalena Lujan, better known as Maggie. I am a resident of Torreón, New Mexico, and I was born in the mid-1940s. My mother was Leonela Alderete, who was born in 1910 in Valencia, New Mexico, and my father was Melcor Lujan, who was born in 1905 in Tomé, New Mexico. At one time we lived about five miles east of Torreón on a ranch. My brothers and sisters and I were all born on the ranch, and I am the last born of ten children. My mama had two sets of twins, and I am one of them.

First born was my big, handsome brother Melcor Lujan Jr. Melcor married Fedelena Benavidez, a beautiful lady, who was a resident of Torreón. Fedelena was the daughter of Estaneslado and Nicolasita Benavidez, who were also residents of Torreón and who were wonderful people. Melcor and Fedelena had three daughters. *Las coloradas* is what we call my nieces Rita, Diana and Cathy. They are all very pretty girls. Unfortunately, Rita passed away several years ago. She left behind a lovely daughter by the name of Angelica.

After Melcor and Fedelena got married, they moved to Albuquerque and opened up Mel's Bakery in the south valley. They had the bakery for several years, and the tortillas they made were my mom's recipe. Melcor later sold the recipe to a well-known tortilla company in New Mexico. I worked in the bakery two years out of my life. I wrapped long john pastries, boxed them and delivered them to the snack bars at Rio Grande and West Mesa High Schools. I didn't mind helping them out at the bakery. It was fun. One day, I went to deliver long johns at West Mesa High School. After I had delivered them, I went to the bathroom. A lady came into the bathroom and asked me, "Why are you wearing pants?" "Well, ma'am," I said, with all respect, "Because I want to wear pants." She looked at me and said, "Follow me," and she took me to the principal's office. A mean looking male principal was in the office, and he said to me, "How many times have I told you, I don't want you girls wearing pants? Go back to class and tomorrow you wear a dress." I looked at him and asked him, "Can I say something?" He said, "Yes, and hurry up." I said, "Tomorrow I'm not going to wear a dress. First, because it's going to be Saturday and I delivery long johns and second because I'm not a student here." The teacher and the principal both apologized to me, and I said, "No problem, if you would have asked me who I was, we wouldn't have had to go through this." The principal said, "You're right." Anyway, that's what happened in those days. Good thing I wasn't wearing my mini-skirt or who knows what may have happened, *ha, ha, ha*.

Ida Lujan was born next. Unfortunately, I never met her because she passed away when she was just a baby. Next born was my sister Anna Lujan-Chavez. I was 10 or 11 years old when Anna got married. I didn't want her to get married. It was October when Manuel, Anna's fiancé, and his parents came over to my parent's house to ask for my sister's hand in marriage. At this time, the *calabasas* had already been harvested from the garden. When Manuel and his parents were sitting in my parent's *sala* talking with my parents, I took one of the pumpkins from outside, and I laid it on the floor next to Manuel and his parent's feet. I had heard that when you give a *calabasa*, the girl's family did not approve of the marriage, and they did not get married. My parents were embarrassed about what I did, and they wanted to kill me. Anyway, Anna and Manuel got married, and what a beautiful couple they were. Manual passed away July 5th, 2014. He was a wonderful husband, a very good father and a good brother-in-law. I called him my young daddy. When my daddy died, Manuel became my dad. He always helped me. He always made sure I had wood to keep my house warm in the winter. He called me "Black Stuff." (I loved it.)

Next born was Nellie Lujan-Gutierrez. I didn't want her to get married either, but I didn't do the *calabasa* thing to her fiancé, *ha, ha, ha*. What I did instead is when Nellie's fiancé came to our house to ask for her hand in marriage, I got into his car, and I hid in there and cried. When he was leaving and everyone was walking out of the house, my mama called for me. I hid on the car floor, and I found a 50 cent piece. I took the money and quickly ran out of the car. I was happy with the money I found. Soon after, I was also happy because Nellie married a good man. His name is Manuel Gutierrez. He is a good provider and a hard-working man. He is a good husband and a good dad to his six children. He is also good to me. He used to work in a bakery, and he always brought me a pecan pie. Recently, my sister Nellie has been sick, and he takes good care of her in all her needs. May God bless him for being him, a one-of-a-kind man. *Thank you, brother-in-law.* Nellie at one time owned a beauty salon, and I worked for her. I gave her a hard time, but she understood I was always kidding with her. She was a great boss. *Thank you Nellie for how good you were with me. Thank you for all your patience, your love, your kindness and your prayers.*

Next born was my brother Billy Lujan. He was a quiet man, but in his own way he reached out to others and to me. One time when I was a little girl, he bought me two small baby doll beds, two dolls to go with it and two baby bottles. At that time, I had two little kittens. I trained the kittens to lie down in the little doll beds, and I fed them milk from the little bottles. One day my brother Billy saw what I was doing and asked me, "Where are the little dolls I gave you?" I said, "These kittens are my dolls." He walked away nodding his head, saying, "You are too much." My brother Billy married Nancy Garcia-Lujan, a beautiful lady. They lived in Albuquerque but later on moved back to Torreón. Nancy's parents, Fidel and Antonia Garcia, were good to all the children in Torreón. As we passed their house on our way to school, they would call out to us. They owned a bar and always gave us candy from the bar. They had a peach tree, and Mrs. Garcia used to pay us to help her pick peaches from the tree. During the summer, Mrs. Garcia would open an ice cream shop in a little house right next to her home. Almost every day my mom would give me 25 cents, and I would walk to the shop to buy an ice cream cone. It was homemade ice cream, and she had several flavors.

My brother Frank was born next. He had a heart of gold. When we were young, we played together a lot. One time, my parents went to get groceries in Mountainair, one of the nearby towns. Mama told Frank to take good care of me while they were gone. Well, it had rained, and Frank and I decided to walk barefoot in the water puddles. We were both laughing, having a good time when, all of a sudden, I stepped on a piece of glass, and I cut my foot. My brother Frank ran inside and brought me a pan with some kerosene in it. He told me to put my bloody foot in the pan. He said, "Get well soon because when mama and daddy get home, we're going to be in deep trouble." I told him, "It doesn't matter anyway because we're going to get killed," *ha, ha, ha*! To this day, I still have a scar from that incident.

Next born were the twins Albert Lujan and Corrine Lujan-Peralta. Albert was raised with my grandma Reina and my grandfather Francisco Alderete in Valencia, New Mexico. They would visit us in Torreón, and my brothers and sisters and I would all play together. Albert was and still is a lot of fun. One time, we were shooting a BB gun, of course, I got in trouble when it was my turn to shoot because I shot Albert in the leg. Good thing he wasn't hurt that bad. When we were very young, Albert and I liked to ride our tricycles together. We would visit everyone in town. We would go from house to house on our bikes. My parent's house was catty-corner from the church on the south, and my auntie Carlota's house and my auntie Candelaria's house were right next to the church on the west. We would visit both of our aunties, who were both beautiful, kind ladies.

However, I do have a story about my auntie Candelaria. One day many years ago I was visiting with my auntie Candelaria and her granddaughter Joanie (Virginia) Garcia. Joanie was just a little baby at the time. That night Joanie got very sick. The next morning my auntie Candelaria came to see me and told me that I had given Joanie *el ojo*. The people used to believe, and I'm not sure if they still do today, but they believed at that time, if someone would admire a baby a little too much, you could give the baby *el ojo*. This caused the baby to become ill. Well, since Joanie got sick that night after visiting with me, my auntie Candelaria believed that I had caused her illness. She came to my house and told me to take a drink of salt water, gargle with it and then spit it on Joanie, so that's what I did. Joanie got better, but I'm not sure if it was because I spit on her.

Anyway, Albert and I would visit other homes in town. We were all friends or relatives in Torreón, and in every home the ladies were very nice and would feed us *biscochitos, pastalitos* or whatever they had. By the time Albert and I got back home for dinner, our stomachs were so full, we couldn't eat. These were all good times when I was a little girl. As I grew up, there were more good times, but I'll hit that card later. *(Smile)*

Memories of Torreón, New Mexico

My sister Corrine, Albert's twin, and I were terrible together. As kids, we would plan our day just before going to sleep the night before. In the morning mama would wake us up early. Hot chocolate and *sopapillas* would be waiting for us on the kitchen table. As soon as we woke up, we would ask my mama, "Let us do our chores and then please let us go play." We played with our cousins Christella and Hilda Alderete and Christina Perea, and our friends Antonia, Estella, Barbara and Viola. We played all kinds of games. We made cakes out of mud in mama's cake plates. Of course, I got in trouble for that. We would use ashes from the woodstove for the frosting on top of the cakes. We liked to play the game, *Red Rover*. "Red Rover, Red Rover, let Christina come over." When it was my cousin Christina's turn, we would let go of our hands, and she would fall. It is still funny to this day. *Sorry Christina! You know I love you!*

Auntie Carlota and uncle Jose Maria Perea were Christina's parents. Pablo was their son, and sometimes we all played together. We used to play in this old abandoned house that had belonged to my uncle Robert Lujan, who moved to Albuquerque. When he moved, the family left a lot of stuff in the house. I would take down the curtains and put them on my head and pretend I was marrying Pablo, and we would have a wedding procession. We made more cakes out of mud, and we pretended to eat them. We also liked to dress up an old coke bottle as the Virgin Mary, Nana Virgin, and we would go on a procession just like we did in church. As we walked along the way, we would pray and sing the hymns we learned in church. Corrine and I had the best time growing up.

My friends Dalia and Chavela and my sister Corrine and I liked to walk from one side of town to another. We walked a lot to the *arroyo*, and we played in the water. We would climb a big rock and slide down into the water. It was our slide, and we called it *la piedra rebalosa*. One day Adelina Montoya, a beautiful, wonderful lady who lived near the *arroyo*, saved our lives. She saw that a big *venida* was coming. She came running and yelled, "*Hijitas*, get out of the *arroyo*! There's a big *venida* coming!" The water was coming with great strength. It was loud, bringing down several tree branches with it. When we saw it coming, we got out of there as fast as we could. Our parents were very thankful that Adelina got us out of the water. She actually, with God's help, saved our lives because we could have drowned. After that incident, we didn't play in the *arroyo* as much.

One day my parents were having a *matanza*, and my mama wanted me and Corrine to take some *carne adovada*, *chicharrones* and *cueritos* to *nana* Concha and uncle Melcor Chavez. To get to their house, we had to cross the *arroyo*. At this time there was very little water in the *arroyo*, so we were jumping from one rock to another. We also stopped to do the rock slide because we hadn't been going to the *arroyo* that often since the *venida* incident. Anyway, guess who was carrying the food and what happened next? I was jumping from one rock to another when the food fell in some mud. I almost started to cry. Corrine said, "Don't cry." I said, "I'm going to be in trouble again." (I was in trouble a lot as you have probably noticed.) Corrine said, "Don't worry! They have killed you so many times, but you're still here." Corrine was a riot. She said, "Watch! We can solve the problem," and she washed the *carne adovada* in the *arroyo*, but the chile also washed off the meat. We finally got to my aunties house, and she welcomed us with open arms. When it was time to go, she said, "*Mis hijitas* you look so tired, your uncle will give you a ride home." When we got home, my dad and the other men were still outside making the last of the *chicharrones*. My uncle walked inside the house with us to thank my mom for the food she sent them, and he said, "I guess you didn't make *carne adovada* for the *matanza*?" My mom said, "Yes, that's what I sent you." Corrine and I looked at each other and thought, *Oh, No, here it comes. The cat is out of the bag*. Corrine and I started to walk slowly, outside. Then we heard mama say, "I had so many people helping me, I guess one of them gave you meat without chile." When Corrine and I got outside, she looked at me and said, "Seems like we handled this incident very well."

Other kids Corrine and I played with were our cousins Rita and Dorothy. They were the daughters of *nana* Concha, the aunt that I took the washed *carne adovada* to. One time we were all playing together and I decided to climb up the roof of an old barn. It was a roof made of wood, and I would walk across it, from one end to the other. Rita saw me on the roof, and she decided to climb up too. When *nana* Concha saw Rita on the roof, she panicked. She thought Rita would fall and get hurt, so she decided to climb up the barn herself to get Rita. When we saw *nana* Concha climbing up to the barn roof in a dress, we couldn't stop laughing. As she climbed up, her dress would fly up. When she got on the roof, she got on her knees and started to crawl, and her stockings ripped. When my mama found out what we were doing and saw *nana* Concha on the roof, my mama said to her, "Get down from there! You're the one that is going to get hurt!" Of course, I got in trouble again, *ha, ha, ha*!

When we were teenagers, there were dances at Fidel's hall in Torreón. Of course, Corrine and I wanted to go to the dances. We would ask our mama if we could go to the dance, and we promised to do all our chores. Mama would say, "Ask your daddy." Corrine would say to me, "Now, it's your turn. Do your crying act like you know how." I practiced so much, I was a genius, *ha, ha, ha*! I would get on my dad's lap, and look at him straight in the eye and tears would come rolling down from my eyes. My daddy would say, "You're already crying, and I don't even know what you want yet." I would say, "Ok, here it goes. Daddy, can Corrine and I go to the dance?" He would say, "Ask your mama?" We would say at the same time, "We already did!" So that's how we got to go to the dances. We danced and danced and danced. My cousin Hilda and I had a standing ovation. No one could do the twist like us, *ha, ha, ha*! *Remember Hilda, how Christella and Corrine were jealous of us? (Smile)*

I cried a lot when Corrine got married, but she was a happily married lady because our Lord gave her a good husband. I remember when Corrine got married. As the wedding ended, and she and her husband were leaving for their honeymoon, my mama was looking for me. I was sitting outside in the snow. I was sad because Corrine got married. My brother Billy came and found me, and he asked me, "What's wrong?" I told him, I was sad because Corrine got married. He gave me a hug and told me not to be sad. He then added, "She just got married, isn't she crazy?" Billy and Corrine are both gone now. Corrine was well-known for her quick craziness. She was so full of fun and laughter. She passed away in 2001.

My mother then had another set of twins which was my sister Theresa and me. Theresa was raised by my auntie Dolores and uncle Antonio Lujan. They lived in Torreón at one time, and then they moved to Albuquerque. They were great people. They used to bring Theresa to visit us, and we had a lot of fun dancing and doing other things together. I would also go stay with my aunt and uncle and Theresa at their home in Albuquerque, and we would all go to the movie theater together.

Then there is me the other twin. You have already learned a little bit about me. I have still to get to the real stuff. Up until the age of seven, I lived at the ranch. Living in the ranch was a lot of fun. We had cows, horses and chickens. Mama and daddy worked hard on the ranch. My daddy farmed and always had beautiful gardens. Once the crop was ready, mama started canning the crops. Once a year my daddy butchered a pig. A *matanza* is the best way to celebrate! It is awesome! Once a year my daddy also butchered a calf. It was a lot of work but entertaining and very delicious. When my family moved to the house in Torreón, daddy kept gardening and mama kept canning. We were always content. Sure, we had our ups and downs, but our faith was always there. Mama used to say, "Without God, we are nothing, so always remember everything comes from God. We have to thank God for all he does, and he gives us everything at a certain time." As a family we would all gather together, kneel down and recite the Holy Rosary. We were taught to pray to our Lord and ask him to help us in our lives if it is his holy will. At times I would get tired of kneeling down, and I would sneak out of the room to my bed. After the rosary, my father wasn't very happy with me, and I would get in trouble again.

There are a lot more memories, but I need to go back to the beginning before my parents got married. As a child, my daddy, Melcor Lujan, lived with his dad, Andres, and his mother, Juanita, here in Torreón. When my dad was six years old, his mom died. When he was 14 years old, he helped carry water to his daddy and to the other workers who were building our beautiful church here in Torreón. When my parents were courting, my daddy brought my mother to show her the house where they would live someday, and this is the same house where I live today. This house was built in the 1800s. It is catty-corner from the church and was once a big, one-room Spanish school house. My grandfather Andres and my grandmother Juanita were also residents of Torreón, and this is where they lived. My grandfather Andres was a teacher in the school. I remember my grandpa telling me as a child, "You're just a little girl, you have a lot to see in the world, and soon, cars will be flying." In my imagination, I thought that was fun. Before I knew it, a car became an airplane, sort of speaking. My grandpa Andres was a very religious Catholic. Our Lord blessed him with good health. He lived to be a century plus two more years. He composed a hymn to San Antonio, the Patron Saint of the church in Torreón. The song is called *La Entrega*. This song is still sung every year for the *fiestas* in Torreón when new *mayordomos* are chosen to be the caretakers of the church for the year. The ceremony is as follows: The current *mayordomos* stand at the entrance of the church along with the incoming *mayordomos* and *La Entrega* is sung as the new *mayordomos* are welcomed into the church. To be chosen as *mayordomos* of the church is a real privilege, and it is the prior *mayordomos* who choose the incoming *mayordomos*.

Anyway, as I mentioned earlier, dad took mom to the house where they were going to live someday after they got married. Dad asked mama, "How big do you want your kitchen?" "I would love a big kitchen," she answered. "Plus, I would like a kitchen woodstove," she said. From 1930 until 2016 the same woodstove is still in the same place and is still in good condition. This stove has cooked for armies of people, and it is still going strong. My mama did all her canning on this stove, as I still do. Mama loved her stove. She always told me to keep it clean.

Eventually, my parents moved into the house, and as time went by, my parents added rooms to the house because they had a lot of kids. Then we kids started growing up and spreading our wings. Mama used to say to us, "When you get married, always be good to your husband or wife because when you have children, you will love them a lot, but they are like little birds. When they grow up, they will leave their nest and fly away, but if you are good to your spouse, he or she will stay with you for as long as our Lord permits it."

Now for a little more about me. I went to grade school here in Torreón. The school is now the Torreón Community Center. When I was a young girl, I would play and do things by myself or spend time with my animals, as I still do today. I call my animals "My kidzzz." I recall very well, and I'll never forget my pet goat. I was probably between 10 and 13 years old at the time. My goat was a pretty, beige goat and his name was Chester. I got his name from one of the characters that was on the show *Gun Smoke*. The other goats I had were named Kitty and Matt Dillon also named after characters from *Gun Smoke*. I trained Chester. My dad made reigns for him, and I rode him like a horse. Mama would comb my hair in very long braids, and with these long braids, I would gently whip my goat to go faster. I rode him from my house, and then I would ride on the side of the highway and ride him to the other side of town, near the community center. I would stop at my sister Anna's house and get water for my goat. When my sister Anna saw me coming, she would say, "Oh, No, here comes Maggie with her goat." One day when I was riding my goat on the side of the highway, my brother Billy stopped me and asked me, "What in the world are you doing?" I answered him, "Nothing wrong. I'm riding my goat." I smiled at him and left on my goat. Tourists passing by on the highway would stop and tell me that my goat and I were cute, and they would take pictures of us. One day my mama was getting worried about me, and she hollered, "Maggie, Magdalena!" By the time I got home, my goat didn't run so fast. Billy had told my mother what I was doing, and I got in trouble. Mama said, "You're not going to ride that goat anymore." I asked, "Why?" I knew she didn't mean it. She said, "Ok, once in a while you can ride your goat." I said, "Ok," and I hugged her and told her I loved her. So I started thinking, and I planned the goat thing for the weekends that way I had more attention on the highway. *(Smile)*

One time my dad was outside our house having a *matanza*, and there were a lot of men helping him. My dad asked me to go inside the house and bring him back a gallon of wine. I went in the house to get the bottle of wine, and I came back outside with the wine and a *jumate*. The *jumate* was sort of like a long ladle. It had a long stick handle and a big cup at the end to drink out of, and it was always hung near the water tank next to the windmill. Everyone would come and scoop up water from the tank and drink water from the *jumate*. In those days there were no worries about germs. Anyway, I poured wine into the *jumate,* and I passed it around to each man to take a drink. After each man took a drink, so did I. I thought it tasted good, and before I took the bottle back into the house, I took another drink. I remember I felt tired and sleepy, and I didn't know what was wrong with me. I didn't know I was drinking wine. I thought I was drinking Kool-Aid. After a while, I heard my mama calling me, but she sounded very far away. My mama found me under the kitchen table, passed out. She asked me what I was doing there, and she told me to go to bed and lie down. I got up, and I fell. My mama said, "Oh, my *hijita*, you're sick. You have a fever, let me take you to bed." She took me to bed, and my daddy came in and asked where I was. He told mama to send me back outside with the bottle of wine. Mama told him, "Tell her yourself! She's sick in bed!" My daddy said, "Oh, No! She must have sipped the wine." Corrine laughed and said, "She's drunk!" That was crazy and funny, and to this day, I hate wine. Only then, I didn't know what it was, *ha, ha, ha*! *(Smile)*

Pedro and Gricelda Zamora owned a small grocery store in Torreón in the 1950s. For a nickel, I could buy ten little candies. Sodas were a quarter, and I could buy an ice cream bar for a dime. My mom would send me to the store to buy something, and when I got there, I would forget what she wanted me to buy. Of course, the ice cream, candy and soda I never forgot. I would tell Mrs. Zamora, "I forgot what my mama ordered." She would ask me, "Where do you have your mind, in your heels?" "No, in the ice cream," I would answer. She would laugh and give me *cariño*. Ice cream became a joke with me, but that's another story.

I wasn't the only kid in Torreón to get in trouble. The kids in Torreón were pretty good kids, but they did do things they weren't supposed to do. I remember one day when we were in grade school, some of us kids attended a *velorio*. Well, the man in the coffin still had his glasses on his face. I remember one of the kids went and stood at the coffin. She looked at the man and said, "He no longer needs these where he's going," and she took the

Riding Goats, Matanzas and Drinking Wine

glasses off the man's face and took off running. I think I remember who it was, but I will never tell.

Here is another event about my father I would like to share. Sometimes I would go with him to the ranch to take alfalfa to feed the cows. One day when we got to the ranch, I went straight to shoot the 22 gun, and my dad went to open the windmill. All of a sudden, I heard my daddy call for me really loud, "Magdalena!" It was strange because he wasn't a loud person, but then he repeated my name even louder. He yelled, "Magdalena! Run to the truck right now and stay in there!" As I was heading to the truck, I heard a loud noise. I quickly got into the truck, and I couldn't believe it. It was a stampede. The cows were running towards me and around the truck. It was an experience I will never forget. I have always liked watching stampedes on TV, but in person, it was the scariest thing. My poor daddy, he survived by running up the windmill. When it was over, he came running to me. He hugged me, and said, "Thank you for getting in the truck. We've completed the day. Let's go home, and thank God we're alright." Bless my daddy's heart. He then added, "Let's not tell mama about this yet, ok." I said, "Ok" and smiled. Days passed, and I couldn't wait to tell my friends what had happened. Finally, daddy told mama, and then I told all of Torreón, *ha, ha, ha!* (*Smile*)

Mama worried about us kids when we were growing up, and I understand that now, but we were safe in every way. We were never afraid of anything. Those were different times from what they are now. We never locked our doors when we went to sleep at night. We never took the keys out of our vehicles. Torreón was a safe place to live, and we knew our Lord helped us. I certainly know that only too well, for he does not send us more than we can handle.

I stopped making the mud cakes as I got older, and my daddy bought me a car. My friends and cousins would ride the whole Torrance County with me. Sometimes we would drive to Sherwood Forest, which was not far from Torreón. We would make sandwiches of potato chips to take with us and have a picnic.

I left home when I grew up, but not to get married. I left to go to beauty school. I got in trouble there too, but that is another story. (*Smile*) I lived away for 15 years, and I had my own business in Albuquerque. I worked all week, and during the weekend I would come home. After some time, I started seeing mama become ill and daddy up in age. On February 2, 1986, I decided I needed to come back to my nest. Torreón is a beautiful place, especially if you keep yourself busy. That I have done, with God's help of course. I like to work in the wonderful dirt gardening which I learned from my daddy. Then I do my canning which I learned from my mama.

One day in 1986 soon after I had moved back to Torreón, I was fixing dinner and making salsa. I sliced an avocado to eat with the salsa, and my mom and dad liked it. My mama said to me, "Put sliced avocados in a jar and leave it in there for at least five years to see what a mess you have made," and she smiled. She was a teaser. In 1989 my mama remembered better than

I did and asked me to go and get the jar of salsa with the avocado. We looked in the jar, and it looked fresh like I had just put the avocado inside the jar. The salsa that I make today comes from my beautiful mama whom I will never forget. Not just for the salsa but for a million more reasons. I have won Grand Champion and People Choice Awards at the Torrance County Fair for my salsa, thanks to my mama. In 2016 I entered the New Mexico State Fair for the first time, and I won First Prize for my layered pickle mix, my green chile, my pickles, my asparagus and my peaches. I also won Grand Champion at the Torrance County Fair for my layered pickle mix the same year.

    I couldn't have asked for better parents. Altogether, my parents lived a good life here in Torreón. They were hard-working, spiritual, humble and deeply kind to everybody, especially to their children. My mother with her personality gathered up friends like flies. All my brother's friends and my sister's friends and my friends simply adored my mother. She kept us going and always laughing. Dad was a more serious man, but sometimes he couldn't help it, he would burst out laughing about something. My mother and father may not have been very well-educated, but they were wise people. My mother always had something wise to say. She used to say, "Be nice and kind to people who are good and nice to you and when they help you in times of need, for they are not obligated." My father was also a very wise man, and I remember many times the teachers from Torreón would come to ask my father for information about a certain topic they were teaching. My parent's knowledge, sense of humor and wisdom also came alive in the way they treated their kids and others.

    I could go on and on. Growing up in Torreón was the best time of my life. My mama and daddy gave us a good life, and I am grateful to them forever. Living in the ranch and growing up in Torreón was wonderful, and still now, I can't complain.

    All of my brothers and sisters got married and had their families. I have the most awesome nieces and nephews. Now most of them have their own children, and they are great with me. They do lots of favors for me. I have three great-great nieces and nephews in Torreón. I have nicknames for them. Backwards is one of them, next is Alley May and then there is Jose Cuervo. I can't pass a week without seeing them. I simply adore them. They are my great-niece Sylvia's children. They are my kids. By the way, I just found out today that I am on facebook with my kids. They are not the only ones, I call my kids, but that is another story. All my brothers and sisters have wonderful children. As they were growing up, I babysat them. I would visit them, and they would visit me. With Nellie's kids, we played talent show and cowboys together. With Anna's kids, we played we were TV news announcers, and we played talent show. I was the head of ceremonies, and I would have to interview each of the celebrities. We had so much fun together. We also had pool tournaments. With Melcor's kids and his grandkids, I cooked with them, we watched movies, told stories, had good talks, and we ate the food we made. All are good memories. Corrine had two daughters, and I also had a lot of fun with them and love them. Now their children are so

Riding Goats, Matanzas and Drinking Wine

darling to me. Albert's children are also wonderful. I just adore them, and we have shared our good times together too. I have had good times with Theresa's boys and with their kids, my great-niece and nephew. Also, Frank's daughter and two sons are great. I love them all. Frank's daughter Beverly Ann is my *ahijada*. I confirmed her, and I did it with all my heart. I remember that day very well.

I will leave you with one last story. One year the *piñón* was in so I gathered up my sister Anna's kids, and we went to pick *piñón*. We packed a lunch and planned on having a picnic. We got to the place where we wanted to pick *piñón*, and we played, and we ate our lunch. All of a sudden, we all started to get sleepy, all eight of us, and we fell asleep. Well, we all woke up, and Gloria said, "Oh, No! Mom is going to kill us!" We were supposed to be home already. I had to think fast, so I told the kids to fill the five-pound can with dirt and then we covered the top with *piñón*. When we got home, Anna was already starting to worry about us, but when my mom and Anna saw the can full of *piñón*, they were so proud of us for picking so much. The following day, Anna came to visit my mom and she asked where I was. My mom said, "She's asleep. Poor thing she picked so much *piñón* yesterday, she must be tired. Anna said, "I understand she picked a lot of dirt," and she showed my mom the can of dirt. She said I was a bad influence on her kids, Manuel, Gloria, Theresa, Carlos, Theodore, Antonette and Leo. Now, they are all adults and awesome. *Thank you, my kids, for all the fun we had, not only then but other times as well, ha, ha, ha! God Bless you. (Smile)*

It has been hard losing mama, daddy, Corrine, Melcor, Billy and Frank and also some of my cousins, nephews and my niece, but we know that life goes on for us. With our Lord's help, we keep going and make the best of what we still have or even don't have. People come and go, things come and go, events happen, but our faith is what keeps us going. Faith helps us survive. Remember, it is important to take care of what you have because in a click of a finger, it is gone. We cannot change what our Lord does. It's our Lord's will and we have to accept it and just keep living as much as our health permits us. Perhaps, if I had grown up in another town, I would have gone through the same experiences, but all this happened here in Torreón, New Mexico in Torrance County. Today we keep our traditions alive through family gatherings, the church, and through our faith. As I mentioned before, keeping busy at all times is important, for our Lord does not send us more than we can handle.

Keep smiling and don't ever forget to pray and to ask God for his blessings and to grant you his most high reward someday, en la Santa Gloria. I don't know what will become of this story, but one thing I do ask is for our Lord to bless each and every one of you, living and dead en el mundo entero, Dios los Bendiga a todos. A special salute, gratitude y cariño to a lovely young lady, Judy Garcia, who made this book possible for everyone to enjoy. May our Lord always bless you and be with you, guiding you at your side. Thank you, Judy G.

Maggie Lujan and her award winning salsa!

Leonela Lujan

Maggie's stove

Maggie Lujan

Melcor and Leonela Lujan

Maggie's garden

Parish Priest of the Mission Churches Of Mountainair, New Mexico

Father Richard Olona

I am Father Richard Olona, and I was born and raised in Albuquerque, New Mexico. I was ordained as a priest on March 29, 1970, at the age of 25. In 1972 Archbishop James Peter Davis assigned me to the parish in Mountainair, New Mexico. The Mission Churches of Mountainair at that time were Torreón, Abo, Punta de Agua and Manzano which meant I would also be the priest in these towns. When I became a priest, I knew I wouldn't have any say in which parish I was sent to, and I was open to going anywhere. When I heard Torreón was one of the mission churches, I had to look it up on a map. I had never heard of this town. It is about a one hour drive from Albuquerque to Torreón, but once you get there, you are in a different world. I didn't know that just on the other side of the mountain was this town. It was a discovery for me. I knew of Manzano because my great-grandfather was born in Manzano. When the first Olona came to New Mexico from Spain, he settled in Tomé. From there the Olonas went to Manzano then to Puerto de Luna. My roots are in the southern part of New Mexico rather than in northern New Mexico, but I had never heard of Torreón.

I lived in Mountainair because that was where the main parish was, and from there, I traveled to the other mission churches to celebrate Mass. Once a month, I went to Punta de Agua and Abo, but every Sunday, I would have Mass in Mountainair at 8 am, Manzano at 10 am and then last was Torreón at 12 noon. After Mass at noon, I was always invited to have lunch at someone's home in Torreón. I remember I ate many times at Candelaria Alderete's house, but I ate with many other families as well. I was asked to lunch every Sunday, and I kept my little appointment book to remember where I was eating each week. I had wonderful conversations with the families, and I had some of the best meals ever. The women made wonderful beans, red and green chile, *enchiladas, sopapillas, tortillas* and all kinds of wonderful New Mexican food. I ate so often with the families in Torreón, I even knew all the names of their cats and dogs.

Mountainair and its Mission Churches was my first assignment as a priest, and the first assignment is always exciting. I had a lot of theological background, but the people had tremendous belief and faith. My job was to try and lead the communities, but it was a partnership. They learned from me, and I learned from them. One thing about the people of Torreón is that they taught me so much about life and community because in my book, church is community. You can have a building and not have community, or you can have community without the building. I was invited into the community, and it was marvelous.

Memories of Torreón, New Mexico

The people of Torreón lived like brothers and sisters; they were a family. Of course, they had their differences because all families do. This is part of life. If I had to describe this town, I would say, "It is a microcosm of New Mexico." If one wants to experience and know New Mexico, I would say, "Go to Torreón." In this small community is everything that we know of New Mexico, in terms of how you would describe New Mexico. You will find faith in God, culture, history, music, food, language, etc. Everything is right there in this little town. Torreón has never been touristic. It was founded at the base of a mountain where the village is centered, and the rich valley has always been used for farming and ranching. There aren't restaurants or cafes in Torreón, but the people gather together for a lot of the feasts and celebrations that are centered on the church. The church has always been the center of the social life in Torreón.

Every town is different and like a child to a priest. My parents had six children. They loved us all, but we were all different. Torreón had its own personality and so did Mountainair and Manzano and the other towns. Being a parish priest is like being a father. It is a very paternal relationship. As a father, you have to respect and take each parish for who they are. In the mission churches, the priest doesn't live in the community, so the people from the mission churches take a lot of responsibility for their community and their faith. The faith of the people is not only enriched by what the priest does by saying Mass, hearing confessions, baptizing babies and doing other spiritual duties but also by what the people do. The people of Torreón organized and prayed Rosaries in the church. They were really good about the religious formation of their children. They organized their teachers, their classes and they prepared their kids for Confession and First Holy Communion. They always made sure the little chapel was taken care of and cleaned. When a particular project needed to be done, the community took responsibility. In the four years that I spent in Torreón, the floors were buckling, and the parishioners took out the floors and redid them. They also put in a new heating system.

On Sundays everyone knew what their responsibilities were, and they made sure things got done. I would walk into the church and the *mayordomos* had the church open, heated and swept. The acolytes were always there ready and available with clean and pressed cassocks and surpluses. The lectors were there ready to read the scriptures. The choir, which consisted of the Benavidez sisters, was always there early before Mass, singing as the people came into the church. The music was a very beautiful, spiritual part of the celebration of the Mass. *Don* Perea would ring the bell a half-hour before Mass started, three times. Then he would ring the bell two times at 15 minutes till. He would ring the last bell at five minutes till, and the whole community would be called to Mass. The doors of the church were open to everybody. I remember there were grand older people and tons of little babies. People who had moved away from Torreón would return for Mass on Sundays, and the amount of people in town would double in size.

A nice memory I have is the summer I took a trip with the

Parish Priest of the Mission Churches Of Mountainair, New Mexico

parishioners of Torreón and the other mission churches. We hired a bus and a tour guide, and we went to Mexico City to visit the Shrine of Our Lady of Guadalupe. We also went to Puebla and to other sites near Mexico City. We were gone for about a week. It was a 24-hour straight drive and along the way we had a great time. We sang church songs and prayed and had great conversations. Some of the people who went from Torreón were Jose Maria and Carlota Perea, Candelaria Alderete and Ernesto and Carlota Vigil. There were about eight people who went from Torreón. It really was a great time for myself and for everyone who went.

Although the people were great to me and I had a great relationship with the families, things weren't always perfect. The teenagers liked to have their fun. One Saturday I was meeting a couple in Torreón because we were going to the movies in Albuquerque. I left my car in Torreón, and I went with this couple to Albuquerque in their car. When we got back it was late, and I went to pick up my car, and I went home to Mountainair. The next day, I went to say Mass in Torreón, and some of the ladies got after me for driving my car fast, up and down the highway the day before. I found out later that some of the teenagers had taken advantage of the fact that I had left my keys in the car. To leave my keys in the car was not a strange thing to do. This was a community where everyone trusted and respected everyone's property, so doors were often left unlocked.

As I spent time in these small towns in the Manzano Mountains, I was interested in doing what the people were doing. I wanted to be part of the culture and learn from their traditions. There was so much tradition and culture in these towns that I wanted to experience how things were done to know how things really were. I learned how to drive a tractor. I planted corn and beans, and I learned about animals. I was from the city, so I didn't know anything about these things. The *matanzas* were wonderful. I had never been to a *matanza*. They were a big, delightful event full of family and friends.

One of the outstanding qualities of the people of Torreón is that they have held on to their roots. They have not abandoned their traditions, their culture, their religion, their language and their history. I am very grateful to them because they have an awareness and love for their culture. Language is a big part of the culture, and I believe once you lose the language, you lose a lot of the culture. At that time, the teenagers were still speaking Spanish with their parents. They were perfectly bilingual because the language was still being passed down to their children.

My father was from Puerto de Luna, New Mexico, which is just south of Santa Rosa, and my mom was from Bernalillo, New Mexico. When my parents got married, they came to live in Albuquerque, where my brothers and sisters and I were born. As a child, my father always spoke English, and my mother spoke Spanish. My two grandmothers lived with us and only spoke Spanish, but my siblings and I answered in English. We would go back and forth in the two languages. As a child, I didn't know I was bilingual, it was just the way we spoke. When I went away to college and graduate school, I didn't have the opportunity to speak Spanish anymore. It wasn't until I got assigned to the churches in the Manzano Mountains and I had to say Mass in Spanish, hear confessions, preach and do other duties that I started using my Spanish. I never took a class in Spanish. I learned by speaking with the people in the small towns, and several people only spoke Spanish. I didn't have the local jargon, but I quickly picked it up. I am fluent in Spanish now because I had to use it.

Just like language, faith was something that was passed down from their parents. The kids learned their faith from their parents, and it was instilled into them as kids. The beauty of Torreón was that it was not only the faith of their parents, but it was also the faith of their extended family, friends and the people they went to school with. It just became part of them and part of their community. Torreón had a good quality of life that was held together by faith, and it still does.

Torreón is a bedroom community where people get up early and drive to Albuquerque to work and drive back home in the evening, and they think nothing of it. It is a very normal thing to do. The isolation of Torreón has created its uniqueness, but because of its proximity to Albuquerque, the people have also been able to be exposed to the things a bigger city has to offer. They are exposed to jobs, and the children are exposed to higher education. People go into the military, they travel and they work in government. They work for the forest service and hold many other jobs. They have the best of both worlds. They are able to experience the big city, and then they can come back and be themselves in their village. In the past, the people may not have been educated with college degrees, but they were educated in life. I enjoyed sitting down and listening to the wisdom of some of the older people. Politics were a big topic of conversation. They all knew their politics, and not everyone always agreed on the same issues. The land was very important to the people, and it still is. They are tied to the land grant and the forest. Without the land grant, they wouldn't have grown up in such a rich culture. The culture is the environment that one lives in and is raised in. The people of Torreón live in a richness of faith, culture and tradition.

New Mexico is a culture that you have to experience more than you can explain. You should go to a *fiesta* or to a *matanza* in one of these small towns to see how things are really done. To this day, I have close friends in Torreón who I met 45 years ago, and it seems like I run into people from Torreón wherever I go. It was a wonderful experience to be assigned to this place. Like I said before, one always wants a good experience for their first assignment. The people of Torreón were so good to me, but again it was about community. I opened up my hearts to them, and they opened up their hearts to me, and we had a wonderful time sharing our faith, culture, language and so much more.

Parish Priest of the Mission Churches Of Mountainair, New Mexico

Old Church in Torreón, New Mexico
University of New Mexico Center for Southwest Research, Juan Lucero files

Fond Memories of Jose Maria Perea and Carlota Alderete-Perea

Imelda Perea-Chavez

My name is Imelda Perea-Chavez. I was born in Torreón, New Mexico in the 1940s, and I am the daughter of Jose Maria Perea Sr. and Carlota Alderete-Perea.

My father, Jose Maria, was born in Torreón, New Mexico, August 25, 1894, and he passed away July 4, 1985. He was the son of Jose Perea and Escolastica Sanchez.

My dad was baptized by Antonio Perea and Maria Juliana Vallejos. He had two sisters and twenty brothers. My dad's parents and most of his siblings died of severe influenza outbreaks when he was a young child. In those days many people died from the flu. My dad used to tell me stories about the flu epidemic of 1918 and how the families of Torreón would collect old boards, and every night they would make coffins to bury the bodies that would die each day. After someone died, they would wrap the body in a blanket or sheet and bury them as soon as possible in the plainly constructed coffins. The Torreón cemetery, northeast of the Catholic Church, is where they were laid to rest.

I can remember dad telling me about only three of his brothers. One was uncle Francisco Perea, who lived in the northside of Torreón. The other brother was uncle Felipe, who had moved to Albuquerque, so we rarely heard much from him. The other was uncle Maclovio, who lived west of our house in Torreón. We kept in touch with him the most because he lived close to our family.

My dad and his brother Maclovio were left orphans at the age of seven and eight. They were left to live with an older brother Pablo Perea and his wife, Antoninita or *Mamasita*, the name my dad would call her. These were hard times for my dad and my uncle Maclovio and for everyone else who lost family due to the influenza outbreaks.

My dad and uncle Maclovio grew up very close to each other, and they took care of each other. At the age of eight, my dad was sent to earn his living and also to help support Maclovio. He was sent to work herding sheep at the Mestenio Draw Ranch near Willard.

At about the age of 18, my dad and uncle Maclovio moved to Arizona and worked as sheepherders. They worked for the Grand Canyon Sheep and Cattle Company and for the Hudspeth Sheep Company. My dad, being the responsible and organized person that he was, kept detailed records of events. I found a telegram my dad had sent to the Hudspeth Sheep Company in Seligman, Arizona. The telegram stated that he would have five men ready to start herding sheep in Arizona. Then in a letter I found addressed to my

Fond Memories of Jose Maria Perea and Carlota Alderete-Perea

dad from Hudspeth Sheep Company dated October 18, 1919, they were informing my dad that they would deliver five tickets to him, to give to the men. They were also instructing my dad to arrive at the job site before the five men crew. They were providing a place for him as *Caporal*, and he would get paid $75.00 a month.

My dad returned to Torreón in about 1926 and bought 50 acres of land for farming. He married Gregorita Torrez and became widowed one year later. He continued to farm and then got married for the second time to Flora Lucero. Flora passed away, and my father became widowed again.

Flora had a son named Jose L. Torrez. Jose (Joe) was born June 8, 1915, and was diagnosed with polio at the age of 9 months. He was orphaned at about the age of 12. At the same time that his mother died, his uncle Juan Agustin Lucero's parents also died. Agustin was 10 years older than Jose, and he became responsible for taking care of Jose as an older brother.

Agustin and Joe both lived in the little house known as the "Joe Torrez house" in Torreón. During the summer months, Joe's relatives would take him to El Paso, Texas for treatments on his legs. My father also took him to Denver for treatments. Joe was the most meticulous, orderly man that we had ever met. He knew where every item in his house was, and he could locate items as soon as they were requested. His mind was as clear as crystal when it came to remembering dates, times, names and other important information. He was just like his step-father, Jose Maria Perea. My father kept all kinds of records of all his children and God children, and he could tell you all the names and birthdates of each one. My dad was also an officer and a very active member of the San Jose Society of the church in Torreón. This is a league of the church that helped with the needs of the people. My dad kept records of the memberships, the traditions and the by-laws that had been established by the San Jose Society.

My mother, Maria Carlota Alderete, was born June 27, 1907, in Arroyo Colorado near Willard, New Mexico. She was the daughter of Francisco (Pa Kiko) Alderete and Reina Marquez. Her *padrinos* were Procopio Armijo and Amada Alderete.

As a young woman, my mom lived in the town of Valencia with her parents. Her dad, Francisco, used to herd sheep along with my dad. My grandpa Francisco wanted my dad to marry his older daughter Isabel, but my dad met my mom at a church gathering, and it was her that he wanted to marry.

When we were kids, my brother Pablo liked to follow my dad around as he went about his day, and he memorized all my dad's verses, prayers and jokes that he recited. Pablo, being so much like my father, learned the following verse and shared it with me as my dad had told him. My dad wrote the following verse along with a letter asking my mom to marry him:

Memories of Torreón, New Mexico

J-JUBILOSA EN LA PELUMBRA
O-O CIELO ESTRELLADO EN FLORES
S- SIEMPRE MIRA Y TE ALLUMBRA
E- EL ECHO DE MIS AMORES

Joyful Within the Shadows
O Heaven Flowered with Stars
Seeing Always and Finding Light
Echo of My Love

My parents were married February 15, 1932, in a small church in Tomé, New Mexico. They made their home on the outskirts of Tomé in a two-room ranch house. They planted corn, cane, peas and beans from which they made their living. Two years later, they moved to their ranch on the southeast side of the town of Torreón. Here they raised three daughters, Reina, Clara and Bernice and one son, Jose Maria Perea Jr. Four years later, they moved to a two-room house in the town of Torreón where they raised three more children: me, Pablo and Christina.

As a child, I remember mom canning all the vegetable that grew in our backyard garden. We bought our fruit from uncle Max Chavez and aunt Victoriana. They would sell fruit from their old army truck that their son Filomeno drove through town for them. My mom canned peaches, apples, pears, and apricots and she made the best jellies you could imagine. Sometimes dad had us fill up five-pound cans full of pinto beans, and he would take the cans to Davalos in Torreón and sell them for a quarter each. Davolos was the store that aunt Gricelda and uncle Pedro owned. Uncle Pedro was hilarious. My mom would send me to buy soap and the brand of soap they sold was called "G and P." Uncle Pedro would say, "Oh, you want to buy Pedro and Gricelda soap?" My dad would also go by horse and wagon to the Salinas area near Willard and trade corn or beans and other vegetables for salt.

When my brothers and sisters and I were young, my dad took us to the ranch by horse and wagon. My dad would ask me to sit next to him as he held the reins from the two horses that pulled the wagon. He knew I was always afraid, so he would ask me, *"¿Qué, tienes miedo hijita?"* I always answered, *"¡No, pero hay que tremblores!"* Dad would laugh and hold me close to him. The horse and buggy or wagon was pretty much the only means of transportation in those days.

My mother was a very great seamstress, and growing up she made us beautiful dresses and even our cheerleader outfits. She made the prettiest patchwork quilts, and she was always hand embroidering cup towels or other things for the house. My mom was very charitable, and she always gave away her quilts that she made. If you told her you liked something she made, she would say, *"Lleva te lo."*

In the fall after the chile crop was ripe, my mom went to spend two or three weeks in Valencia helping my grandma Reina and grandpa Francisco tie up chile *ristras*. Dad kept up the crew here at home, and while mom was away, we practiced rolling *tortillas* and cleaning house. This is how we learned to keep house and cook.

We had no running water in our home. Therefore, we had to haul water from a well south of our house that belonged to Andres Lujan, who by the way lived to be 102 years old. This well supplied water to most families in Torreón. Our baths consisted of warming up water on top of the woodstove and then pouring the water into a round tub. We only had one day of the week to take a bath. Usually, it was on Saturday. The oldest child would take their bath first. We would add a little bit of hot water to the same bath water, and you can imagine how the water looked after the sixth child took their weekly bath. As for our toilets, we had to use the outhouse. It was the "*escusado de viento*" as my dad would call it. At night or during emergencies, we had to use the WHITE *VASIJA*. To have to empty the pot the next morning was a joy no one wanted to be in charge of. It was NOT fun, but we survived. These days we have way too many luxuries. We never seem to have enough.

Growing up in Torreón was fun! We lived right next door to uncle Pedro and auntie Candelaria and about a half a block north of auntie Leonela and uncle Melcor. On the westside of our house was uncle Maclovio and aunt Rosalia, so we always had plenty of relatives to visit and cousins to play with.

All of our cousins and friends would get together to make *zancos*. They were big walking stilts made out of wood, or sometimes we made the *zancos* out of vegetable or fruit cans. We liked to pretend that the *zancos* were our high heels. Another thing we liked to play was church. We would dress up a coke bottle with rags or paper or whatever we had to look like our Blessed Mother. We climbed on top of the chicken coop, and this was our choir. We would sing hymns like "*Bendito, Bendito, Bendito sea Dios,*" everyone knew that hymn.

My family didn't have a telephone or a television set in our home. We were poor but rich in love of family. However, I do remember a radio that my parents had. Dad would listen to Spanish music and would take off dancing. We all loved to be twirled around. It was so much fun! Mom listened to a Spanish story everyday at about 1:00 p.m. The name was "*El Derecho de Nacer.*" Once in a while, we were treated to watch the *I love Lucy Show* on a black and white TV at our aunt Gricelda Zamora's home next door. We were taught to call every older person "aunt and uncle". We really thought they were our aunts and uncles.

We grew up next door to the Catholic Church, and my mom and dad were very spiritual people. My dad told me how he would follow his older brother Pablo throughout the day, and this is how he learned all his prayers. Some of my best memories of my childhood were when my family would visit the Blessed Sacrament at church each morning and when my parents would gather up all of us kids to pray the Holy Rosary after supper. Dad would get upset if any of us kids did not attend Mass or other church activities such as Novenas or Rosaries. If the church bell rang, we had better be there or else.

Dad never spanked us, but when he spoke, we listened. We knew he meant business when he spoke.

As one of Dad's church ministries, he was in charge of ringing the church bell. He would ring the bell to inform the community that church services would be starting soon. The different bell tolls held different meanings. The *doble* was to inform everyone in town of a community member passing. One of the other bell tolls was to acknowledge our May Pilgrimage.

During the month of May, *El Mes de Maria*, our community would get together for prayer and devotion, and we had our annual May Pilgrimage. Families from Torreón and the other nearby towns like Tajique, La Canada de la Perra, La Canada de la Zorra, Chilili, and Escabosa would walk to Manzano to pick up the statue of Our Lady of Sorrows and take her out to make her yearly visit to the church in Torreón. This antique, miraculous statue spent most of her time in the Mission Church of Manzano.

Once the people picked up Our Lady from Manzano, they would turn around and walk back to Torreón carrying her. On the walk back, people would join the pilgrimage to fulfill their promises to our Blessed Mother. The elders would sing the *alabados*, and the little children would take turns ringing a little bell to let the community of Torreón know that they would be arriving soon. They walked a total of 14 miles to and from Manzano.

My dad and my mother-in-law Lourdes used to tell me stories about how this miraculous statue had tears in her eyes all year round. Then at the beginning of the month of May, as the people from Torreón and the surrounding areas got ready for their annual pilgrimage, the Blessed Mother would show her beautiful little smile.

Some people prayed to Our Lady of Sorrows in thanksgiving for a certain miracle, and some would make promises to our Blessed Mother with so much faith and devotion. Some people called her "The Little Doll" who sent them rain. Dad would say, "What a blessing to see such love and happiness between a mother and her children." This little statue was the pride of the people from the little villages in the area. Some people do not understand what devotion and faith the people from the past had. Our Blessed Mothers visit to our community is a tradition that has been observed for more than 150 years.

For years my dad led the praying of the Rosary as the people walked along carrying our Blessed Mother. At the age of 84, my dad was still carrying on this tradition. Sadly, during that year's pilgrimage, I noticed that my dad's health was declining, and he was working hard to catch his breath. Following this pilgrimage, I promised my dad that I would continue this tradition.

What followed during the 1970s is that the tradition had threatened to end when my mother-in-law's health started to decline, and she could no longer complete the walk. Lourdes was always very devoted to our Blessed Mother as she continued to follow in the footsteps of our ancestors. Lourdes asked Flora Alderete and me to continue the tradition and thus far, we have been able to. We have also tried to keep the traditions of reciting May and October Rosaries, Novenas and other church activities.

The *San Antonio Fiestas* are another beautiful memory. My dad taught us beautiful novenas and *alabados* that are still being sung and prayed today during *fiestas*. In the past, the traditional *fiesta* meal was held at the home of the *mayordomos* and only family members were able to participate. These days we have a nice lunch in the community center for the *mayordomos*, and everyone is invited. Many families make the trip to Torreón from Albuquerque, California, Colorado, Arizona and from the other parish communities in the area to celebrate with us.

For Christmas my parents gathered up all us children, and we recited the Holy Rosary, a tradition never to be forgotten. After praying the Rosary, we would sing hymns and Christmas carols, all in the Spanish language. My dad had a green hymn book called *"El Pueblo Canta."* From this book, he taught us the Spanish songs, and this is how I learned to read in Spanish. My dad always had something to teach us. He was a very smart man even though he only completed the fifth grade in a one-room school house in Torreón. Both my parents spoke only Spanish, and that is the language we spoke at home. When my brothers and sisters and I started school, we had to learn English.

In 1984 my parents took their first and only vacation in their lives. The trip was to see the Metropolitan Cathedral in Mexico City. They were accompanied by their good friends Ernesto and Carlota Vigil, my aunt Candelaria Alderete, their nephew Leroy Alderete and his wife, Lorella, their niece Gloria Garcia and Concha and Cecil Chavez, among many others. Most outstanding of all is that three of their favorite priests went along as well: Father Richard Olona, Father Mike O'Brien and Father Salazar. The first Hispanic Archbishop of the State of New Mexico, Archbishop Robert Sanchez, also went. This trip was their most interesting and rewarding experience of their entire lives.

My Dad always autographed all of his favorite books and his belongings. The following was written in his own handwriting in his hymn book:

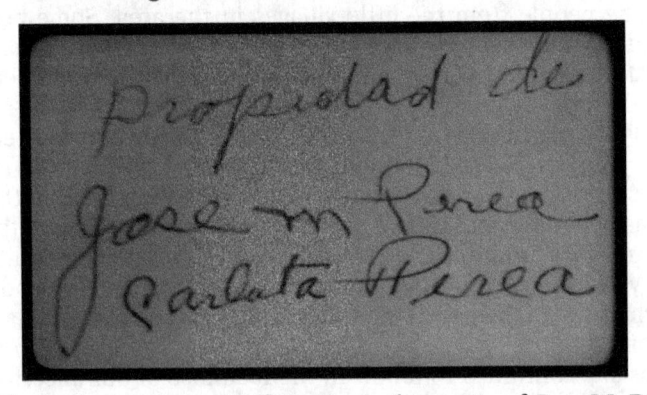

Propiadad de Jose M. Perea y Carlota Perea (property of Jose M. Perea and Carlota Perea).

The inscription written in his song book is as follows:

Si este libro se perdiera
Como sucede, suceder,
Le suplico al que lo allare
Que me lo sepa bolver.

y si fuera de unas largas
o de poco entendimiento
le suplico que se acurde del
Septimo Mandamiento.

If this book should get lost
as it may successfully happen
I beg you, if you find it
that you will know to return it

Fond Memories of Jose Maria Perea and Carlota Alderete-Perea

If you practice stealing habits
or of little understanding
I beg you that you remember
the Seventh Commandment
thou shall not steal

My dad also kept records as follows:

EN EL AÑO DEL SEÑOR DE 1894 NACIÓ JOSE MARIA PEREA EL DÍA 25 DE AUGUSTO. (In the year of our Lord 1894 was born Jose Maria Perea the 25th of August.)

Dad's verse at his grave is as follows:

No Dejen Pasar El Tiempo
Que El Tiempo No Da lugar
Es Ligero El Pensamiento Pero
Nada Puede Ascer Si Dios
Dice Que No Hay Vida No Hay
Plaser

Don't let time get away
Time doesn't wait for you
The mind is light, but
nothing can be done, if God
says there is no life, there is no pleasure

    Jose Maria Perea and Maria Carlota Alderete-Perea lost their first child, Antonette. She was stillborn. My mom and dad talked about the loss of another daughter, Clara. She passed away at the age of seven. What follows are the families of my parents, Carlota and Jose Maria's children: Reina, Jose Maria, Bernice, Imelda, Jose Abilio (Pablo) and Christina.

    Reina married Elfego Chavez, and they live in Torreón. Elfego worked for the railroad and the United States Forest Service and is currently retired. Reina retired from the ring fabricator in Mountainair. They had two sons, Norbert and Thomas, and five daughters, Carmen, Lupe, Linda, Cathleen and Jessica.

    Their first daughter Carmen has two daughters, Stephanie and Cynthia, and a son, Christopher. Christopher and his wife Jennifer have a son, Thomas Christopher, and they live in Belen. Stephanie lives in Albuquerque with her son, Joshua, and she is currently employed as a teacher with Youth Development Incorporated. Cynthia is married to Nicolas Medina. They have one daughter, Isabeya, and they live in Los Lunas.

Cynthia is a physical therapist.

Lupe married Irvin Vigil. They live in Albuquerque, and they have two daughters, Tanya and Tiffany. Tanya teaches pre-school for Rio Rancho Public Schools, and Tiffany currently attends Central New Mexico Community College.

Linda married Paul David Herrera. They have a son, Isaac, and a daughter, Sofia, and they both attend college in Boulder, Colorado.

Norbert retired from the United States Air Force and is now employed by the United States Government in San Antonio, Texas. He is married to Elva, who is also employed by the United States Government. They have a daughter, Erica, who is a second-grade teacher and a son, Norbert Jr., who has a daughter, Aundrea.

Cathleen Chavez married Donald Gurule, and they have a son, Elias. Cathleen is employed by Bernalillo Public Schools and has been teaching for the past 20 years. They reside in Corrales.

Reina and Elfego also had another son, Thomas. Thomas drowned in an accident in Ramah Lake. Thomas was born Tuesday, February 2, 1965, and passed away Wednesday, November 11, 1998. Thomas left behind a daughter, Desiree, who lives in Los Lunas. Thomas was employed as a firefighter with the Albuquerque Fire Department.

Jessica, the youngest, is a cosmetologist in Albuquerque. She married Mark Barboa, and they have two sons and a daughter, Michael, Steven and Joslyn.

Jose Maria Jr. (Joe) married Susie Chavez, and they live in Torreón. Joe retired from the United States Forest Service, and Susie retired from the United States Postal Service in Torreón. They have six children: John, Evelyn, Johnny, Arlene, Mary and Jerome. Their first child John passed away when he was five days old.

Evelyn is married to Kevin Kelsey, and she has two stepchildren who live in Albuquerque. Evelyn is employed by Presbyterian Medical Hospital as a Registered Nurse.

Johnny is married to Shana Brazil, and they have six kids: Kara, Andi, Tasa, Jade, Beca and Traye. Everyone except Jade has graduated from high school, and they are all attending college. Johnny is the County Executive Director for the Farm Service Agency in Estancia. Johnny and his family live in El Cuervo, which is just south of Torreón.

Arlene is employed by the Mountainair District Forest Service, and she lives southwest of Torreón.

Mary married Tim Carlson, and they live in Albuquerque with their two children, Chloe and Lucas. Mary is employed by the Bureau of Acclamation Association in Albuquerque.

Jerome, the youngest, lives in Denver, Colorado and is employed by Urban Outfitters.

Joe and Susie have a nice second home in the foothills of the Manzano Mountains, and they still own the former land that my parents used to live on.

Bernice married Cecilio Gabaldon, and they have one son, Cecil James. Bernice was employed as a health assistant with Albuquerque Public Schools (APS) and retired after 25 years of service. She is currently employed with the Child Find Program. Cecilio Gabaldon was born June 11, 1939, and passed away November 19, 2006. Cecil James is married to Liza Estrada, and they have a son, Marcario Jose, and a daughter, Ariana Salome. Cecil is currently employed by ARCA in Albuquerque.

Imelda (me) married Leon (Leo) Chavez. We have three children, Ramona Natividad, Lee Anthony and Charlene Barbara. I worked for the Estancia school system for 14 years and for the Farm Service Agency in Estancia for 24 years. I retired August 29, 2008. I currently volunteer my time working in the Torreón Community Library. I also serve as secretary, treasurer and bookkeeper for the Torreón Mutual Domestic Water Association.

My husband, Leo, began working the summer of 1954 at the age of 14. His first job was as a laborer for a crusher company. This company was located between Tajique and Chilili, and they crushed rocks for gravel. At the age of 17, Leo dropped out of Estancia High School in order to join the labor union. He told the labor union he was 18, and he got a job at Hydro Conduit in Albuquerque. Almost all the men from Torreón have worked at Hydro Conduit at one time or another.

Leo then moved in with his grandmother Concepcíon Chavez in Albuquerque and attended the Technical Vocational Institute (TVI). He

Memories of Torreón, New Mexico

trained as a cement finisher and was then employed by Pickens and Bond. He has also worked with other contractors doing cement finishing jobs. Some of the job sites he has worked on were the Winrock Shopping Center, the Dukes Stadium, Presbyterian Hospital, Intel and many others. Although Leo retired at the age of 65, he continues to work on our ranch. He still does cement finishing projects, and at the age of 74, he is very active.

Our eldest daughter, Ramona Natividad, graduated from Estancia High School. She attended New Mexico Highlands University and earned a Bachelor's Degree in Business Administration. She was employed with the State Employment Commission and ended her career with the Mid-Region Council of Governments. She is retired and lives in Albuquerque.

Our son, Lee Anthony, graduated from Estancia High School and enlisted in the Air Force at the age of 17. He has been stationed at Lackland Air Force Base in San Antonio, Korea, the Netherlands, Nebraska, Germany, Kansas and Colorado Springs, Colorado. He retired from the Air Force in 2007, and he is now employed with the Missile Defense Center in Colorado Springs. Lee married Donna Flauding, and they have two children, Matthew Ryan and Amanda Lynn. Matthew lives in Alaska, and Amanda will be attending graduate school at Case Western Reserve University in Cleveland, Ohio.

Our youngest daughter, Charlene Barbara, graduated from Estancia High School and attended New Mexico Highlands University, where she earned a Bachelor's Degree in Education. She taught physical education and was a coach for two years in Questa, New Mexico. She returned to Albuquerque and was employed by All Faiths Receiving Home for 14 years, where she helped neglected and abused children. She earned a Master's Degree in Social Work and is currently employed by the Division of Vocational Rehabilitation (DVR) in Albuquerque.

Jose Abilio (Pablo) married Kathleen Garcia, and they have two children, Jose Maria Perea III and Antoinette. Jose is a graduate of the University of New Mexico and lives in Albuquerque. Antoinette married Mark Valenzuela, and they have three children, Madalen Clara, Marcos and Mercedes Estrella. Antoinette is a principal with Albuquerque Public Schools.

Christina married Richard Eddie Vigil, and they have two children, Angela Renee and Richard Conrad. Angela lives in Denver, Colorado and Richard lives in Albuquerque.

Fond Memories of Jose Maria Perea and Carlota Alderete-Perea

Jose Maria Perea and Carlota Alderete-Perea

Memories of Torreón, New Mexico

Jose Maria Perea and Carlota Alderete-Perea

Carlota Perea, Leonore Otero, Candelaria Alderete, Carlota Vigil in Mexico City

Trip to Mexico City with Father Olona

Nicolasita Benavidez, Lourdes Chavez, Carlota Perea

Antonita (mamasita) Perea, she raised Jose Maria and uncle Maclovio

Uncle Maclovio Perea

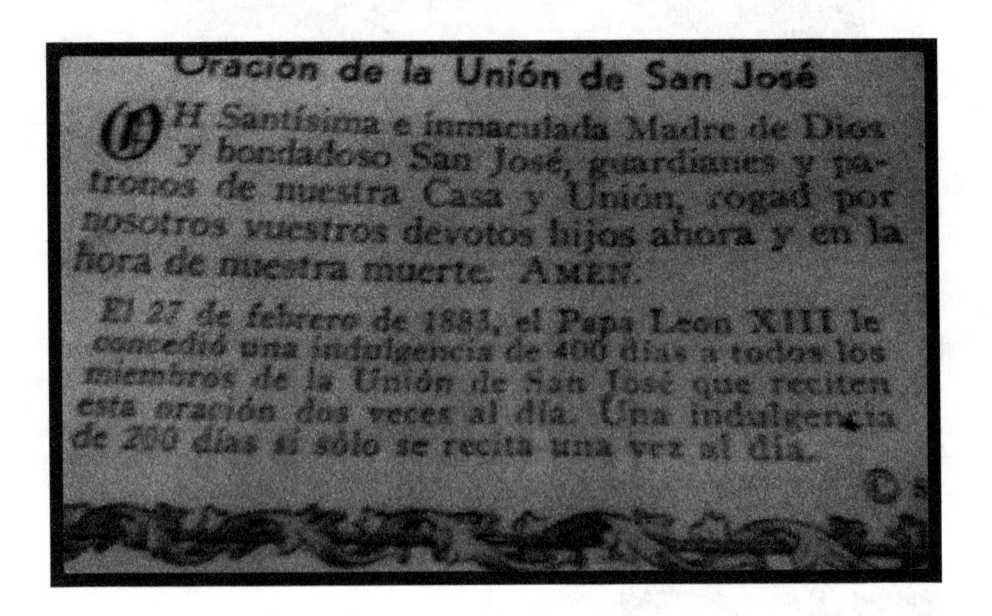

Oración de la Unión de San José

OH Santísima e inmaculada Madre de Dios y bondadoso San José, guardianes y patronos de nuestra Casa y Unión, rogad por nosotros vuestros devotos hijos ahora y en la hora de nuestra muerte. AMEN.

El 27 de febrero de 1883, el Papa Leon XIII le concedió una indulgencia de 400 días a todos los miembros de la Unión de San José que reciten esta oración dos veces al día. Una indulgencia de 200 días si sólo se recita una vez al día.

Society of San Jose prayer

Back row L-R Melba Vigil, Gloria Vigil, Floria Alderete, Imelda Chavez, Front L-R Glenda Lujan, Theresa Lujan, Susie Perea, Reina Chavez

Our Lady of Sorrows at the Ten Pines cesteo

San Jose Society Members 1937

Top Row

1. Unknown
2. Antonio Garley
3. Arestio Lopez
4. Jose Maria Perea Sr.
5. Flavio Torrez
6. Francisco Chavez
7. Antonio Chavez
8. Ross Salas
9. Tedocio Herrera
10. Trinidad Chavez
11. Unknown
12. Unknown
13. Florencio Chavez
14. Sarafin Perea
15. Melquerez Chavez

Second Row

1. Eliseo Garcia
2. Eutimio Garcia
3. Melcor Chavez
4. Otavianio Garcia
5. Jose Zamora
6. Jose Jesus Chavez
7. Leonires Garcia
8. Max Montoya
9. Ambrocio Perea
10. Feliciano Chavez
11. Ignacio Garcia

Third Row

1. Jose T. Lujan
2. Francisco Lujan
3. Melcor Lujan
4. Emeterio Montoya
5. Delfin Chavez
6. Pablo Zamora
7. Demecio Perea
8. Estaneslado Benavidez
9. Juan Chavez Apodaca

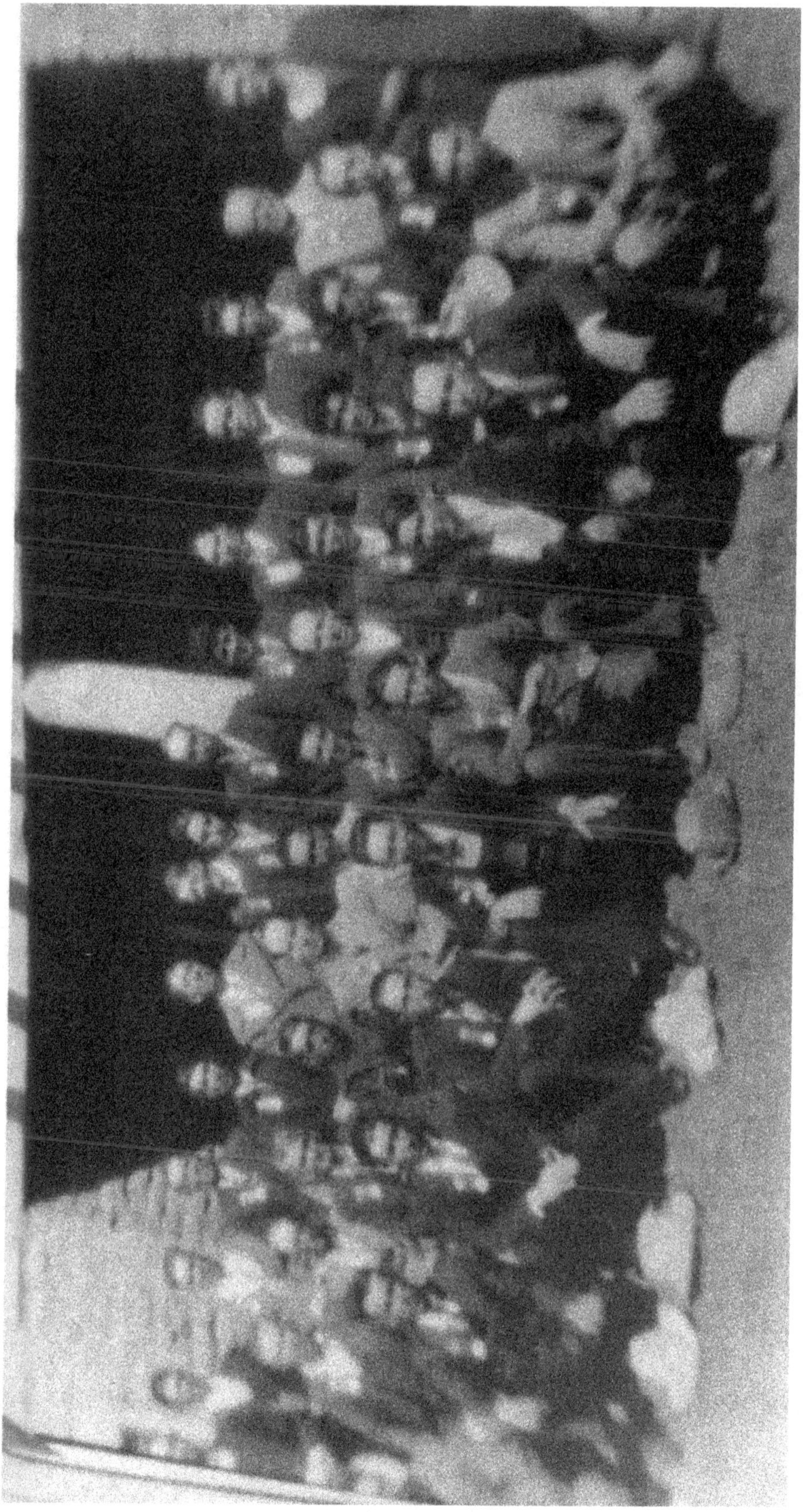

Current San Jose Society Members present for photo Phil Lucero, Ernest Gallegos, Willie Chavez, Paul Garcia, Herman Salas, Luis Benavidez, Eddie Padilla, Feliciano Chavez, Leon Chavez, Fidel Chavez Jr. Delfin Romero, Frank Lujan, Vicente Alderete, Ezequiel Chavez, black hat, Elfego Chavez, Willie Romero, Ray Garcia, Jushua Garcia

Serving as an Altar Boy

Eloy Sanchez

My name is Eloy Sanchez, and I lived in Torreón, New Mexico from 1958 through 1967. I attended Torreón Elementary School from 1958 through 1960 and Estancia Junior High School from 1961 through 1963. I graduated from Estancia High School in 1967. I consider myself very fortunate to have grown up in a small town like Torreón. I have very fond memories of my childhood growing up there.

Religion:

In our family, as in most families in Torreón, the Catholic religion played a central role in forming an excellent foundation of moral, spiritual and ethical upbringing. The Catholic religion was the main activity that brought families together in spiritual and communal gatherings. For most junior high school aged boys, serving as an altar boy was a special opportunity to serve the community and assist the priest in conducting Mass. I remember when it was finally my turn to start learning to be an altar boy; it was very exciting and all very new to me. During my training, my group would meet at the church, and our altar boy teacher was Manuel Chavez. Manuel was an excellent teacher; he made sure all the kids got along, and he conducted organized and orderly training sessions. He would bring the altar boys together for Latin education and Mass role play. We would work on the required Latin phrases that were part of specific functions during Mass, V*isperas*, a Rosary or other services. During the 1950s and 1960s, all Mass services were conducted in Latin; it was only in the mid-1970s that the Mass was changed to English or in the current local language of the community, which in this case was Spanish. The bulk of the altar boy training was always for the Mass service. During the Mass, the priest would recite the required readings and chants in Latin, and the altar boys would respond accordingly also in Latin. The altar boys were paired together in sets of two or four depending on the type of Mass. For regular Sunday Mass, two altar boys served. If it was a High Mass, four altar boys were used. I was usually paired up with my brother Frank, my brother Norbert or my good friends Jimmy Garcia, Pete Alderete, Pablo Perea, Joe Manuel Zamora, Gilbert Chavez, Leroy Chavez or Clem Perea.

The best and most important position of an altar boy was the keeper of the incense. The incense urn was very decorative, and it was made of stainless steel or silver. It opened at the top and inside the urn were red hot coals that were kept hot by constant motion. This was done by using the long chains attached to the urn and constantly swinging it side to side. The keeper of the incense was bestowed upon the top altar boy and the one with the most seniority. I remember Pablo was the top altar boy and was in charge of the incense. After a specific chant or prayer preceding the blessing of the altar, Pablo would come with the incense urn and present it to the priest. The priest would open the top, and he would place one or two spoons of incense on the hot coals. The urn was then handed over to the priest. With a swift movement, the priest would use the incense urn to bless all four corners of the altar and the center. He would then bless Pablo and then give Pablo the urn. Pablo would then take the urn, and with the same swift movement, he would bless the priest. Then he would turn away from the altar, walk over to face the entire congregation and with the same swings, he would bless everyone by starting with one movement to the left, one to the center and one to the right. The art of blessing with the incense urn had to be learned, and it needed to be performed with the utmost grace. Some of the duties we had as altar boys involved the following:

We would light the candles before the service.

We would ring the altar bell as the priest would unveil the chalice and place the veil on the altar.

We would act as thurifers, burning incense during a procession.

We would administer the water to the priest as he would wash his hands.

We would ring the bell at Sanctus and Canon of the Mass.

During Communion we would follow the priest with paten in hand and the other hand over our breast.

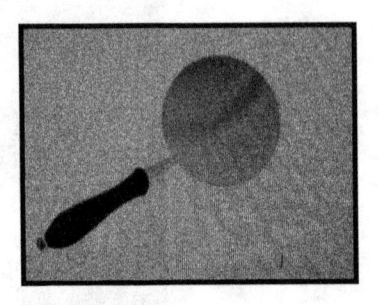

Serving as an altar boy wasn't always serious business. On a few occasions, Father Wilkinson, the parish priest assigned to the church, would take the altar boys from Manzano and Torreón on a trip to watch a movie at the Kimo Theater in downtown Albuquerque. That was a special treat because most of us had never seen a movie on a big screen in a theater. Father Wilkinson was a very special person that could relate to young people in a kind, caring and special way. Simply said, Father Wilkinson was a priest that all of us kids liked and looked up to. I give special thanks to Manuel Chavez, who was a great mentor that gave many hours of his valuable time to provide a very important service which was much needed at the time in Torreón. I had many great experiences and great times while serving as an altar boy. The things I learned back then have remained with me throughout my entire life, and for this experience, I am truly grateful.

Serving as an Altar Boy

L-R Jimmy Garcia, Eloy Sanchez, Nash Salas, Dennis Alderete, Milton Garcia

Changes from 1942-2016

Stella Sanchez

I am Stella Sanchez, and I was born October 25, 1942, at my maternal grandparents, Juan and Juanita Romero's, home in Estancia, New Mexico. I am the fourth oldest child of eleven children born to Jose and Carmen Sanchez.

Dr. Willoughby was the attending physician who did home deliveries at the time. He worked at the Mountainair Hospital and served the surrounding area. Dr. Willoughby also treated diseases. Today it is not common for doctors to make home visits and many specialize in a particular area of medicine. At that time there were also *curanderas* healing with herbs, eggs, fire, flowers, etc. When I was young, I believed *curanderas* were doing witchcraft. Today I have great respect for them. Many are very successful healers, both emotionally and physically.

As a newborn, I was taken to live with my family on a ranch two miles west of Torreón. The 250-acre ranch belonged to my paternal grandparents, Francisco and Manuelita Sanchez. The land was obtained under the Homestead Act. In those days, you could work the land and pay taxes, and then you would become owners of the property. The house my family lived in was a white, rock house that had been constructed by my *tío* Severio and my *tía* Sofia. It was about a third of a mile away from my grandparent's house.

My grandpa Francisco had one of the most prosperous ranches in Torrance County. The ranch was awesome! It had a pond, an iron workshop, an orchard, a garden and there was a big garage where my grandpa kept his wagons. The garage was made of adobe and had many *vigas* across the ceiling to support it. These *vigas* were carved by my grandpa and the lumber to make the vigas came from the ranch. In those days, everything was made to last a long time. Today it seems everything is made cheaply so that we can replace it as soon as possible. As an adult, I remember going back to the ranch and being utterly amazed at the talent and creativity that my grandparents had. I then realized why my brothers and sisters and nieces and nephews are all so artistic and creative.

My grandpa had fields of pinto beans, corn and alfalfa. In the summer, he would have to hire men to pull weeds from the corn and pinto bean fields. He prepared for the great depression of 1929 by storing huge amounts of food, and his family never suffered from hunger during that time. During the depression, my grandfather also gave generously to others.

As a child, I would slip away into my grandmother Manuelita's kitchen for breakfast. My grandmother was an excellent cook. She would get up early and start baking delicious biscuits and coffee rolls. She also made

Changes from 1942-2016

homemade butter and cottage cheese and canned fruits and vegetables which were kept in a large cellar. To me, it seemed like a grocery store. Today we have refrigeration, and we live close to stores, so we have no need to store in large amounts. Food in those days was organic, without preservatives, additives, hormones or pesticides, which made foods much healthier than what we have today. My grandmother also had herbs growing inside the house, so her home always smelled like fresh herbs.

My favorite place at the ranch was the orchard. There was a bed in the middle of the orchard where I would take naps. I found peace being in nature. I would climb the fence and pick cherries until my grandmother would tell me to get off the fence. The windmill was special to me. I remember once, I took my clothes off and covered myself with mud. My grandmother dunked me into a can of water, washed me and then spanked me. In those days, a spanking was not considered child abuse but rather a form of discipline. It was common for parents to give grandparents, teachers and relatives the authority to discipline their children. Rafael, the son of my aunt Sofia and uncle Severo, lived most of the time with my grandparents. All of us kids loved him dearly. He was our playmate, but when he got annoyed with us, he would lock us all up in the outhouse. Sometimes we were locked in there for hours.

My grandparents had three different wagons, and I loved to ride in them. They went to Mass in Torreón and to get the mail in Torreón by horse and wagon, and I went to elementary school in Torreón by horse and wagon. At that time winters were severe with large snow storms. Due to the severe winters, I missed a lot of school in the first grade. Consequently, because I missed so much school, I failed the first grade. Lucky for me, so did all my classmates. My father, who was a teacher in Torreón, went from the ranch to the school house on horseback that year.

I lived on the ranch for seven years then my parents purchased the home of my *tío* Jose Leon and *tía* Lola Lujan in the town of Torreón. When I was a child, my parents did not worry about me as I played in the area around town. Children could be gone from early morning to sunset playing in the *arroyo,* the fields and homes of friends and relatives with no worries. The people in Torreón were honest and trustworthy, and nobody ever locked their doors because we all trusted each other. As a child, I felt much love and concern from the people of Torreón.

I had a lot of fun playing with my friends. I would play with my friend Irene at her mother, Nicolasita Benavidez's, home. We would spend hours putting on long dresses and hats pretending to be rich and elegant. During the summer evenings, we enjoyed playing baseball while our parents shared stories about witches and ghosts. People were very creative about making up stories for entertainment. Today, TV does not allow much time for visiting neighbors. However, I do remember getting our first TV set and how at one time it did bring us together.

When television was invented in 1927, it was only in black and white with a small screen. My family was the first family in Torreón to buy a television in 1950. Families would come to watch TV in our home. We shared our excitement about everything we saw because it was so new to us. Shortly after, most families purchased a TV, and I missed watching TV with my friends.

Daily, I remember skipping and picking field flowers on my way to church to visit the Blessed Sacrament. Religion was the first priority in my family and faith was given to me by my parents and grandparents. On Saturdays there were two things that I had to do. One was to take a bath and the other thing I had to do was go to confession. Most of the homes at that time did not have indoor bathrooms, so my mother would set up a tub in the kitchen. She would warm up the water on the stove and pour it in the tub. My brothers and sisters and I would all take a bath in the same water. When I was the last person to take a bath, I'm sure I was left with scum. Today I feel I live in luxury.

After I took my bath, I went to confession. I remember the first time I went to confession. I went with one sin. I believe I confessed that I had said a lie. I confessed to the priest my one sin, and he told me, "Next time bring more sins." I remember my father would often read from the book called *Examination of Conscience,* and I memorized as many sins from this book as possible. Next time I went to confession, I had a list of sins to confess. I even confessed that I had committed adultery.

At that time confession used to be something that I felt obligated to do. Now it is one of the most important things in my life. For me it is very healing to go to confession. I now go to confession face-to-face with the priest, and I am able to confess and look at my behavior, my motives, my fears and my actions towards my sins.

Angie Sedillo-Salas, Irene Benavidez-Zamora and I were cheerleaders in the eighth grade. I still remember the uniform we wore. It was a green skirt and white blouse. The basketball tournament that year was in Mountainair and I decided to smoke. My aunt Elizia Romero caught me smoking and took me by the ear into the bathroom. She told me she would tell my father if she ever saw me smoking again. In those days, pulling the ear was a common way of disciplining children. There was fear and respect for parents and other elders, and by the way, I never smoked again.

During the 1950s there were no telephones in Torreón. To communicate with their girlfriends, young boys would peep into the girl's window to announce their presence and get their attention. I remember I would slip out for a kiss while my father was watching television. My brother Tony tried making an alarm system with cans by placing them on top of the house. Had it worked, Tony would have made good money selling them because every home had window peepers.

I remember the summer Tividad Chavez died at the age of 16. He died from an accident while cutting wood in the mountains. A tree fell on him, and he was taken to the hospital where he soon passed away. Tividad and I were good friends. I would meet him at the *arroyo,* and we would dance. He was a great dancer, and because of him at age 73, I still enjoy

Changes from 1942-2016

dancing. In those days, the deceased person would be brought in a coffin to their home, and their body was left overnight for a *velorio*. I remember all the teenagers gathered at Tividad's grandmother Concepción's home to sing *alabados*. I remember the sadness I felt because of his death, but I also felt the love and unity of all the teenagers singing and praying together. When someone passed away, all the people in Torreón would come to support the family by bringing firewood, food and drinks. The men would make a bonfire outside and pass the time talking, while the women would be inside the home praying, singing and conversing. Funerals were very different from what they are today. Relatives and friends of the deceased would cry out loud and talk to the dead person. Grief was expressed loud and natural. Today I see little emotion expressed. I feel tears are a precious gift from God. Life has great happiness and great sorrow. I allow my tears to flow, and I grieve my losses in order to experience joy in life.

I attended high school in Estancia, and I had to ride the school bus to get to and from school. Looking back, I see how at times I would act immature. I would drop my books out of the bus window, two or three times, before arriving back home to Torreón. I tortured our bus driver, Mr. Bozo Sturges. He must have been a saint, as he would stop the bus and I would run out to get my books. I thought he was prejudiced against Hispanics, but in reality, he was patient and kind.

My school lunch often consisted of *tortilla* sandwiches, now known as *burritos*. I was ashamed to be seen eating a *tortilla*. I wanted white bread. As a result, I kept my *tortilla* sandwich inside a paper bag and ate with the bag close to my mouth so that the other children would not see the *tortilla*. I know I was not the only one who did this. Today children love *burritos*, and homemade *tortillas* are a treat.

Throughout my school years, I was not confident in my learning abilities and did not do well in my studies. At home Spanish, our native language, was spoken. I did not speak English when I started school. I believe the language barrier hindered my education. I was fearful to ask questions and give book reports, and at times I could not express my thoughts in English. I decided to stay in school to have fun and to enjoy myself. As a result, I have many wonderful memories of times spent with my friends. Although, I believe I graduated from high school with a fourth-grade level education.

Things changed in 1964 when I entered the Benedictine Convent in Clyde, Missouri. While at the convent, it was customary to have table readings during the meals. When it was my turn to read, I stumbled with every other word and cried during the entire meal instead of reading. After that painful experience, Mother Superior Pascaline said, "I have been observing you, and I know you have the potential to learn. You will learn." I attended classes with my peers, and my reading and confidence improved. I feel deep gratitude for the five years of convent life, but I left the convent with the desire to get married.

My mother became a widow at the age of 40 years old. She was a strong woman. She did not drive at the time, but she was determined to learn. I took her to the baseball field behind the Torreón Elementary School to teach her. She was apprehensive and fearful. She would put the gear in reverse and drive at a high speed without looking in the rear-view mirror. She was speeding all over that baseball field, and then she would slam on the breaks. The first time she got on the highway, we went to the grocery store in Mountainair. When she was trying to park, she hit the wall of the store and made a dent on her car. Eventually, she became a good driver.

  I want to pay tribute to my mother, Carmen Romero-Sanchez, who raised eleven children as a widow. My mother raised her children on her low-income as a part-time postal worker. She did not receive social security from my father's employment as a teacher because in those days, they did not have social security. As my brothers and sisters grew up, they and their spouses Carlos and Isabel, Fermin and Ramona, Tony and Severina all helped financially. My mom told all her children that when we graduated from high school, we would be responsible for getting a job and supporting ourselves. A few days after graduating from high school, we all went to Albuquerque or to Santa Fe to work. My mom didn't give me any money after I graduated or enable me in any way. I took the first job offered, and I started supporting myself.

  I have a story of struggle, tears, survival and success. I believe that my suffering produced endurance and character and from character, came hope. I am proud of my siblings. Some attended college and paid for their education while working full-time and supporting their families.

My sibling's successes:

Carlos is a college graduate and was President for Duke City Lumber Company.

Tony worked for the State of New Mexico as a computer programmer and was often called to different state offices as an advisor. Tony is now deceased.

Ramona worked for Sandia Base and Peanut Butter and Jelly School as a bookkeeper. She has made beautiful wedding gowns for her family members and friends. She made me a very beautiful wedding gown and veil when I got married.

Stella (me) worked for St. Joseph Hospital and the University of New Mexico Physician's Association. I billed Medicare, Medicaid and insurance companies. Billing Medicare was difficult because the Federal Government constantly changed laws and regulations.

Virginia is a certified massage therapist.

Frank is self-employed. He is the owner of a construction company and

Changes from 1942-2016

professional buildings.

Eloy (Art) is a college professor in the state of Oregon.

Norbert is a college graduate and was a registered nurse.

Agnes was a director of a state agency.

Bernadette is a college graduate and was a school counselor and a New Mexico State Senator.

Joseph is an artist who works with wood. He carved the Stations of the Cross and Jesus Resurrected Sculptures for the St. Joseph Catholic Church in Albuquerque.

When mother died all of her cookbooks were given to me because I enjoy cooking. To my surprise, all the cookbooks were filled with prayers. I realized mother had prayed for all of us constantly and that is the ONLY reason we persevered. Mother was a private person regarding religion and her prayer life. She trusted God.

I am proud and happy I grew up in Torreón. I am grateful for the memories and traditions that were passed down to me. I have much gratitude for my family and friends and the fun, love and laughter I received from the people of Torreón. Torreón was a wonderful place to grow up. I praise God for blessing me abundantly. Thank you for asking me to share.

First Communions, Funerals and Feast Days

Ramona Sanchez-Lujan

My name is Ramona Sanchez-Lujan. I was born in Torreón, New Mexico in 1941. I am the daughter of Jose Sanchez and Carmen Romero-Sanchez. I am the third child of eleven children, and I am the oldest daughter. My brothers and sisters are Carlos, Tony, Stella, Virginia, Frank, Eloy, Norbert, Agnes, Bernadette and Joseph.

What I remember most about Torreón is how all the activities of the community were centered around our church, *La Iglesia de San Antonio*, which was a Mission Church of the church in Manzano, *Nuestra Señora de Dolores*. I really don't remember going to Mass before making my First Holy Communion, but after I went every Sunday. Making my First Holy Communion was a very special event. All the girls wore white dresses and veils, and the boys wore suits, white shirts and ties. My mother bought me a new white dress, a veil, shoes, and I think I even had long white stockings. I remember, I was concerned about not eating or drinking anything after midnight the night before I was to make my First Holy Communion, and I worried I would forget. At that time we were required to fast from food and water after midnight. If we didn't fast, we wouldn't be able to receive Holy Communion for the first time. During the Mass, we all held candles that were lit, and we were warned about burning someone. I spent a good part of the Mass worrying and being careful while I held my candle.

My First Communion day was also my Confirmation day. The Archbishop was there, and during Mass we were called up to the communion rail. The Archbishop asked some questions from the catechism book, and he asked some children to recite certain prayers. I remember one little girl did not know the Act of Contrition, so the bishop asked her *madrina* to say it. Her *madrina* got so nervous that she stumbled and couldn't finish the prayer. The bishop asked someone else to say it. It happened to be my *madrina*, Aunt Adelaida Perea, and she said it perfectly. I was so proud of her. Of course, I was very relieved that he didn't ask me because I didn't know it that well either.

A few weeks later when I went to confession and was asked to say the Act of Contrition, I couldn't remember the prayer. The priest told me to go home and tell my mother I didn't know it. I didn't want to admit that to my mother, so I found a prayer book that had the Act of Contrition in it. The next time I went to confession, I took the book with me and read the prayer from the book. I did that a few times until I learned it.

Sunday was the most special day of the week, and on Saturday we prepared for Sunday. In the morning, we cleaned the house, baked a cake

First Communions, Funerals and Feast Days

(maybe), and sometimes my mother baked bread. In the afternoon, we took our baths and washed our hair. Taking a bath was no simple matter. The water had to be warmed on top of the stove. We had a round tin tub which served as a bathtub. When we were very young, my sister's Stella and Virginia and I took our baths together. After our baths, our mother would put our hair in curlers. Most of the time at around four o'clock in the afternoon, we went to confession. Most of the girls went to confession with curlers in their hair, but some had torn pieces of cloth around their hair which served as rollers. They were the ones that had the nice long *rizos* and looked so pretty. I always wanted those nice long curls, but my hair never got long enough for that. My hair was so thick and tangled so easily that I would cry when my mom combed my hair. As a result, my mom would cut my hair short. Consequently, no *rizos*.

On Sunday we rushed around getting ready for Mass. El *primero*, the first church bell, would ring about an hour before Mass, a reminder that there is Mass today and we need to start getting ready. *El sequndo*, the second bell, meant the priest was there, and we better start hurrying up. *El tercero*, the third bell, meant ¡Apurecen! Ya dieron el tercero. We had better be out the door, there goes the third bell. After Mass we went home and had a nice Sunday dinner. Sometimes the priest would come over and eat with us after Mass. My brothers and sisters and I were to be on our best behavior, and we waited until the adults ate before we could eat. We would peek and see if they were almost finished. Sometimes, we would send one of the younger siblings to go see how the adult dinner was progressing, and sometimes they would report, *"Todavía huy pan."* We devoured that bread when we had it. We didn't get store bought bread very often. After Sunday dinner, we usually went to visit our friends and relatives. We did not work on Sundays as it was a day of rest. Sometimes relatives from Albuquerque came to visit. Sometimes I went to my friend's houses to play. Most of the time, I would go to Bernie Perea's or Gloria Alderete's house. On Sundays, we got a nickel to spend at *prima* Gricelda's store. How to spend that nickel was a major decision. Most of the time, I opted for a *Big Hunk* or a *Sugar Daddy* because they lasted a long time. Sometimes I bought two for one cent candy because I could get a lot of candy for a nickel.

On weekdays one of the things we often did was stop by the church for a visit. We had to make sure we had a scarf or bandana to put on our head because women had to cover their heads inside the church at that time. Sometimes we didn't have a scarf, so we improvised by putting on a Kleenex or leaves from a tree.

Funerals were a big part of life in Torreón. When someone in town died the church bell would toll. One of us children would be sent to the church to find out who had died. Soon after, our parents would go over to the deceased person's home to offer condolences and to see to the needs of the family. The men from town would dig the hole for the burial, and the women would cook and take food to the family. The next night there would be a *velorio* at the home of the deceased person. Everyone from town would attend and prayed, drank coffee and spent time with the family. On the third day, they had the funeral Mass. We all attended the funeral even if it was a school day. The children would then return to school after the funeral and burial. One day when my dad was the principal of the school in Torreón, the superintendent stopped by the school unannounced. There were no students present because there had been a funeral. Uninformed of our traditions, the superintendent asked my father where the students were. My father explained that they, along with their teachers, were at a funeral. Not to my surprise, the superintendent suggested that as a principal, he should encourage the students to attend school instead of a funeral. I doubt my dad actually encouraged the students not to go to the funeral because this was part of our culture.

The important events in the church were Lent, Easter, Corpus Christi, the *Fiestas de San Antonio* and the months of May and October. During Lent we had to give up something, most of the time it was candy. We prayed the Stations of the Cross every Friday in church, and all the people in town attended. *Prima* Meres, who had a very beautiful sing-song voice, led the stations. She was perfect for the station prayers. Of course, all the prayers and songs were in Spanish. My mom always said the most holy days, were Holy Thursday, Good Friday, Holy Saturday and Easter Sunday. On Thursday, Friday and Saturday, we didn't have church services in Torreón, so we went to church in Manzano during the three most holy days. Sometimes after Mass on Holy Thursday, my parents would take us to visit different churches. I loved it when we were able to go to Albuquerque and visit several churches there. We would go inside the church, stay about five minutes, then drive to the next church.

The Adoration of the Blessed Sacrament was followed by services on Holy Thursday, and this event lasted until Good Friday. On Thursday night after we all had gone to bed, my parents would get up sometime in the middle of night, drive to Manzano and spend time with the Blessed Sacrament. Sometimes they got up early on Good Friday, at about two or three o'clock in the morning, and spent time with the Blessed Sacrament at that time. My Dad liked going during the early morning hours because he said very few people could go at that time. Sometimes some of us children would go along, but it seemed that my parents stayed there an awfully long time. I would get restless, but I felt guilty because after all, Christ died for us, the least I could do was stay awake.

On Good Friday, we went to Church for the *Siete Palabras*. This service was quite long, about two hours with lots of words. On Holy Saturday our house was quiet. It was supposed to be a day of reflection. We stayed home, and we weren't allowed to play too much. I mostly reflected on my new clothes that I would be wearing the next day. Finally, it was Easter Sunday. Oh, how great that was! We put on our new Easter clothes. It was now time to put away our winter clothes, wear our summer dresses and we could go back to eating candy.

The month of May was dedicated to the Virgin Mary. During this

First Communions, Funerals and Feast Days

month we prayed a Rosary every evening at the church in Torreón. *Prima Meres* led the Rosary, and most of the people from town would attend. During the month of May, it was a nice walk to and from the church, and after the Rosary we would get to spend time with our friends. This I always looked forward to.

On the first Saturday of May, some of the people from Torreón would walk seven miles to the church in Manzano to pick up our *Nana Virgen*. Then many of us would walk back in procession to Torreón carrying this delicate Statue of Our Lady. There was a lot of praying and singing on the way. Midway, we would stop at Los Pinitos for a break and a snack. We would then continue on our way to the church in Torreón where some of the people would be waiting for us. We would bring the statue into the church and pray. People in the community would take turns taking the statue to their homes overnight for a *Velorio* and to pray the Rosary. The Statue of Our Lady would stay in Torreón for a week and then she was returned to the church in Manzano. I love this tradition. It is a tradition that is still being held today, and I try to attend every year.

The Feast of Corpus Christi was very special. It was held every year in the month of June. We prepared for this Holy Feast by cutting up pieces of paper into confetti. Some of the people in town prepared altars in the front of their homes. These altars were beautifully decorated with white or colorful tablecloths and flowers. The day of Corpus Christi, we had Mass and then a procession around the neighborhood. A *paleo* was used during the procession. It was made of white cloth and was decorated with lace and gold-colored fringe. Under the *paleo*, the priest carried the monstrance with the Holy Eucharist and the altar boys carried incense. At each altar, we stopped and prayed the Divine Praises, then the priest blessed all of us with the Holy Eucharist. As we walked along the procession, little girls dressed in white and carrying baskets filled with confetti sprinkled the confetti along the way. Some of the girls were dressed as angels wearing long, white gowns. On their heads, they wore gold tinsel formed into the shape of a crown. They also wore wings which were made out of cardboard and covered with crepe paper. They looked very special. I remember wearing my white dress and having a basket filled with confetti. I dreamt of the day I would be an angel, but for some reason that day never came. I don't know how the angels were picked, but I never was. This celebration is still held every year.

The *Fiestas de San Antonio* in September was probably the most anticipated holiday in our town. We prepared for the *fiestas* by getting new clothes. We looked forward to the carnival, though small, it was exciting. We had a few rides and a *ruleta*. The *fiestas* started on Friday night with Visperas, a church service and a procession. Don Apolonio played the violin during the *Visperas*, and this is the only time that I remember him playing. The way of the procession was lit up with *luminarias* made of *ocote*. The *luminarias* would burn as we walked from the church, down the main street, around Rocky Street and then back to the church. As we walked some of the men would fire shots up into the air, and although we knew they were coming, we were still startled by the shots. After the procession was the *Vispera* dance. Sometimes we had two dances. One at the San Jose Hall (the Cibola Hall) and another one at Fidel Garcia's dance hall. We girls stood at the back of the hall hoping the boys would ask us to dance. We didn't like to sit because the boys had to cross the hall to ask us to dance, and if they were shy, they wouldn't do it. Saturday we had another Mass and another procession. As we walked out the church to walk in procession, there was Fidel Garcia instructing us, "*Las mujeres adelante, los hombres atras.*" Some young men would carry the *paleo*. This was an important job. Under the *paleo*, the *mayordomos* carried the *Santo de San Antonio* and a framed picture of San Antonio during the procession. We went around the neighborhood the same way we had gone the night before. As we reached the doors of the church, the procession stopped, and the choir sang hymns to San Antonio. After the singing, the current *mayordomos* turned over the *Santo* to the incoming *mayordomos*. After Mass we went home to eat. We then went to the carnival and played the *ruleta* and then went to the afternoon dance. At this dance there were mainly teenagers, and we had so much fun. Then we went home again for dinner, and back out again for the *fiesta* dance. Those two days were wonderful!

Another special month was the month of October, which is the month of the Rosary. During this month the community would gather together at the church to pray the Rosary.

Other memories:

It was at a *fiesta* dance that Fermin Lujan, my husband, asked me to dance with him. I was so excited. After that dance, Fermin and I started dating. Fermin and I dated for five years before we got married. During our dating years, we never lacked for chaperones. If we were sitting outside our home in his car, we could count on Stella and Virginia to come and sit in the car with us. My brothers Frank, Eloy and Norbert would also come around and check on us. One time Fermin asked my mom if he could take the "girls" to a basketball game. My mother asked, "All of them?" She meant Virginia and Stella. Frank and Eloy also asked if they could go with us. I told them, "Only, if Fermin invites you." They put on their good clothes and stood by the door, hoping they would be asked to go. Fermin did not realize they were waiting for an invitation. We started to drive away, and then I said, "*Pobrecitos,* the boys wanted to go too." Fermin turned the car around and went back and picked my brothers up so they could go with us.

During my teenage years, my father had a brain tumor and was diagnosed with brain cancer. This was a very hard time for our family. At that time cancer was a death sentence. There was no chemotherapy or radiation or really no treatments available. My dad tried herbs and eating healthy foods to cure the cancer. Someone told him that drinking warm, fresh blood from a recently killed deer was known to cure cancer. Since he was willing to try anything, he agreed to drink some. Manuel Chavez and Orlando

First Communions, Funerals and Feast Days

Lujan heard about this, and they volunteered to bring him some blood. I remember they brought some warm blood in a thermos bottle, and he drank it, "Aaagh."

The community came together to help our family during the time of my dad's illness. My mother ran the post office in Torreón, and she had to take time off to go to Albuquerque during my dad's surgery and recovery. Rafelita Vigil was an angel to us. She moved in with us and stayed for weeks. She ran the post office and took care of the younger children while we went to school. My dad eventually came home, but he never recovered. About a year later, he got very ill and was dying. Friends and family from the community helped take care of the younger children while my dad was sick. Especially helpful were Prima Meres and Antonia and Fidel Garcia. For about a month, the *socios* from the *Sociedad de San Jose* would come and pray the Rosary with our family almost every night, and then they would stay the night so we could get some sleep. My aunt Elena, aunt Adelaida and aunt Corina all took turns coming to help my mother take care of my dad. Two weeks before my dad died both sets of grandparents came to stay. At that time, the community provided a place for some of us to sleep as there were a lot of people in our home. I was at *prima* Gricelda's house the night my dad died. I will forever be grateful to the many people who helped us during my dad's illness and afterward. Thank you is not enough.

Fermin and I got married in 1961 in our San Antonio Church in Torreón. We moved away and never lived there again, but Torreón never moved away from us. It is still very much a part of our lives. The church of San Antonio is still very special to me. When I am in Torreón, I always stop at the church for a visit. It feels so peaceful. For me, it is the most special church in the world.

Ramona Sanchez-Lujan 17 years old

Ramona 10 years old

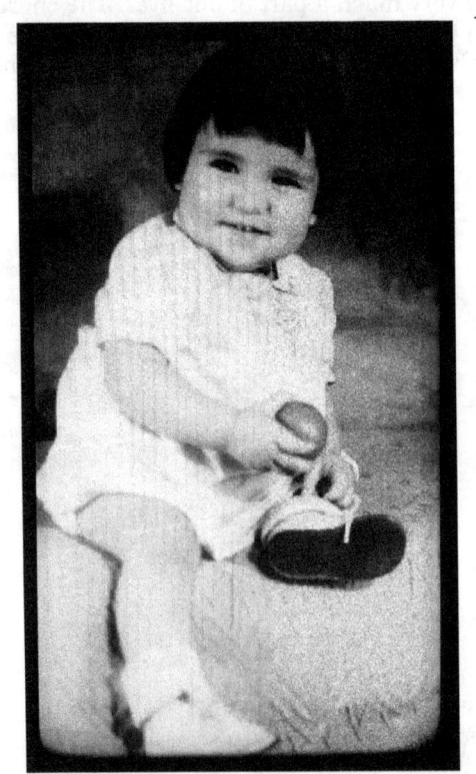

Ramona Sanchez

Running Against Horses and Threshing Beans

Jesus Trujillo

I am Jesus Trujillo, and I was born in Torreón, New Mexico in 1937. I am married to Elesia Barela, who was born in Tajique, New Mexico in 1940. I am the oldest son of Sosteno and Rosalia Trujillo. My father Sosteno Trujillo was born in 1910 at El Rancho del Tule which was located between Estancia and Willard, New Mexico. My mother Rosalia Chavez was born in Torreón, New Mexico in 1911.

My mother was the daughter of Jesus Chavez, who was born in Torreón in 1872 and Felicita Chavez, who was also born in New Mexico. My *tata* Jesus became a sheepherder at a very young age, and he became blind at the age of 33. They say that the glare from the snow made him lose his eyesight. I remember he talked a lot about *El Ojo de Barendo*, now McIntosh, which is where he herded sheep.

My *tata* Jesus was also a runner. According to him, he would run from *El Ojo de Barendo* to Torreón when his *remuda* came to relieve him from his duties. According to my mother, Rosalia, one time the people of Torreón matched my *tata* up to run a race against a horse. They gave my grandfather a lead, and he won. The story goes that he took off his pants and ran in his underwear. My grandma Felicita made his underwear *del saco de harina*. The brand name of the *harina* was "M." According to my mama, my *nana* Felicita was so embarrassed that the letter "M" was on his underwear. She thought the people would say that she didn't wash the *saco de harina* before making the underwear.

My father was the son of Melquiades Trujillo and Leonor Perea. My grandpa Melquiades was born in the town of Punta de Agua, New Mexico in 1884. My grandma Leonor was born in Torreón, New Mexico in 1884. My grandparents met in El Pino, and they homesteaded 160 acres under the Homestead Act. They called their ranch "El Rancho del Tule" because of the wild tulips that grew in the area. The water on the land was four to six inches from the surface, so at this time the land was good for grazing but not for farming.

Grandma Leonor, being an heir of the Torreón land grant, inherited 40 acres of land in El Cuervo. For many years, my grandparents would come and farm the 40 acres. They finally sold El Rancho del Tule and permanently moved to El Rancho de Cuervo. They became bean farmers, and they built a house that still remains today. My dad was 18 years old when his family moved to El Rancho de Cuervo. I remember my dad telling me that once in the early 1930s, there were four bean threshing machines that someone was bringing up from the Estancia Valley, but they could not reach the foot of the mountain because of the tremendous amount of beans in the valley. It was early November, and the beans were piled high at the ranch. My dad and my grandpa had to open up the piles of beans to let them air out. Grandpa Melquiades then heard that there was a *trilladora* for sale at the place of Juan Cruz, called El Gato. My grandpa went and bought the *trilladora* and brought it back to the ranch. According to my dad, they threshed all the beans and also the neighbor's beans. They threshed about 7000 sacks of beans that year. Then the drought came in 1951, and that was the last year they farmed at El Cuervo.

    El Rancho de Cuervo became known for the *Velorio de La Señora de Guadalupe* which was celebrated each year on the 12th of December. People from Torreón and the surrounding ranches would come walking to pray the rosary at my grandparent's house. They even came when there was snow on the ground. They would all come wearing their *chopos de guangoche*.

Trujillo Family Velorio at El Cuervo

Carmen Trujillo-Luna

My name is Carmen Trujillo-Luna. I am 73 years old, and I have retained many memories of my life in Torreón. I am the daughter of Sosteno Trujillo. Sosteno is the son of Melquiadez and Leonor Trujillo, who owned and lived at the ranch El Cuervo, which was located on the eastside of Torreón. This is the land my father and grandpa farmed for many years.

My parents moved to Estancia in the early 1950s from El Cuervo because my dad could no longer make the land yield beans. My father then took a job with the New Mexico Highway Department, where he retired from 25 years later.

My mother Rosalia was a typical housewife. It is unthinkable how much work a woman did in those days. They worked sunup to sundown, from washing clothes by hand, before the wringer washing machine appeared, to *barriando lana* with those long sticks. I partook of that chore, and it wasn't long before your arms went to sleep. These women also raised many children. There were *chinches* and *piojos* to contend with, but we youngsters didn't bat an eyelash! It was all so normal!

I will recount one lovely tradition of our Trujillo family. During the years of 1918-1919, the mountain towns of Torreón, Manzano and other towns were hit pretty hard by the influenza epidemic. My mother would recall how people in Torreón would go to the cemetery to bury a family member, and when they returned home from the burial, they would find another family member dead.

My grandpa Melquiadez would go in his *carro de caballo* and take eggs and milk and other foods that were produced at the ranch and give them to the families of the sick. As the family history goes, he too became sick towards the end of the epidemic. In his fevered delirium, he made a promise! He asked, Our Lady of Guadalupe to heal him. In return, he would keep a *velorio* to Our Lady on her feast day, the 12th of December, for the rest of his life. (I am not sure if I am correct in saying the following. It seems to me Our Lady, under the title of Guadalupe, was not that well-known in our communities at that time.) Where did my grandpa hear of her? Again, I beg your indulgence in making such a statement. However, my grandparents held a *velorio* for our Lady of Guadalupe for 60 years. I cannot believe my grandfather had such commitment, especially since it was such a BIG family event. So much work went into it.

My family would prepare for weeks, making mountains of *pastelitos* and cakes, and an *altar* was built in honor of Our Lady. The *altar* was a beautiful, holy apparition. In later years, my *tía* Maria Rita Garcia would come from Los Alamos to help my grandmother construct the *altar*. On the eve of December 11th, my family would eat supper together and then waited for guests to arrive. Those who came would stay up all night eating, praying and singing in Spanish. During these times is when I learned to read and write in Spanish. We youngsters tried to stay up all night. Sometimes we succeeded, and sometimes we failed. At first light, my grandma would wake us up to sing the *alba*. We sang, *"¡Cantemos la alba ya viene el día, daremos gracias Ave Maria!"* Then we prayed the Hail Mary.

In 1967 when my second child was about three months old, my grandparents held their last *velorio* in Torreón. As they were becoming elderly, they moved to Los Alamos and celebrated our Lady of Guadalupe at my *tía* Maria Rita's home in Los Alamos. The *velorio* was a glorious event for 60 years at El Cuervo in Torreón and then later on in Los Alamos.

The Catholic faith has always been that holy, affirming, life-giving source that has allowed us to persevere in prayer for 2000 years. Glory to God and our Lord Jesus Christ.

Vigil, Garcia, Lujan Family

Selina Vigil-Lujan

I am Selina Vigil-Lujan, and I was born in Torreón, New Mexico in 1940. I am married to Rosendo Lujan, who was also born in Torreón.

I am the daughter of Ernesto Vigil, who was born August 30, 1915, in Torreón and Carlota Garcia-Vigil, who was born October 3, 1917, in Los Ojitos near Manzano, New Mexico. My parents had four sons and three daughters: Ernie, Dan, Abie Gabriel, me, Carol and Onila. We had a wonderful and healthy upbringing.

My dad was the son of Antonio Jose Vigil and Rosarito Lujan-Vigil. My grandfather Antonio was orphaned as a child, so he had to start working at a very young age. He was a sheepherder and a farmer. In the 1920s he would go to the mountains to cut *vigas* which were used to build the church in Torreón. In the 1950s or so, my grandpa Antonio opened a bar in Torreón that was called the Torreón Bar. My *nana* Rosarito did what most women did in those days, she took care of the home and kids.

When I was a child, my grandpa Antonio would put his hand on my nana's head and say, "When I met your *nana, había hallado un tesoro."* Whenever someone did something for my grandpa, he would say, *"Dios te lo pague y Dios te bendiga."* When my grandparents were newly married, they would go to Albuquerque by horse and wagon to sell wood and to buy groceries. Whenever we went in the wagon somewhere, my grandpa would say, *"Que Dios venga con nosotros, Dios adelante y nosotros atras."* For one of my grandparent's wedding anniversaries, they went to Mexico City and traveled throughout Mexico. My grandparents lived in Torreón for most of their lives.

My *nana* Rosarito was 84 years old when she passed away. After she passed, my grandfather and his daughter, my *tía* Alicia, went to live in Albuquerque with his other daughters, my *tía* Teresita, my *tía* Lupita and Lupita's husband, Flavio Martinez. My grandfather Antonio was 102 years old when he passed away.

My mother, Carlota Garcia-Vigil, was the daughter of Jose Angel Garcia and Soledad Vigil-Garcia. They had three daughters and three sons. After my mom was born, my grandparents Soledad and Jose Angel moved from Los ojitos to Belén and then to Albuquerque. I don't know what my grandfather did for a living, but I know he was bedridden at a very young age. My grandmother was a homemaker, and she did odd jobs for people. She washed and ironed clothes and cleaned houses.

At the age of six, my mom went to stay with her *tío* Volais and her *tía* Carolina Sanchez in La Arroyo Colorado which was near Manzano. My mom became very close to her *tío* Volais and *tía* Carolina, and she never wanted to return home. Growing up my brothers and sisters and I were also very close to *tío* Volais and *tía* Carolina. We called them p*apa* Sanchez and n*ana* Nina, and we loved them very much.

My dad worked as a farmer and a rancher. He would hire men to help with the planting, hoeing and the harvesting on his ranch. He also helped run his dad's bar in Torreón. My mom was a housewife, and part of her duties were to cook for the workers on the ranch. When she wasn't cooking for the hired help, she was sewing or cleaning or doing other chores. She used to make quilts, she embroidered and she made our clothes. She also liked to bake, read, and she always had a vegetable garden. When it was harvest time, she canned and dried fruits and vegetables, and she made *capolin* jam and jellies from chokecherries. My parents would kill chickens, and then we would pluck them and can them. We also canned beef, pork and chile. Where my mom found all the time to do everything she did, I don't know. When the drought came in the 1950s, everything changed. It got so hot and dry that my father could no longer make a living as a farmer and rancher. He went to work for the State Highway Department and was stationed in Moriarty. He worked on I-40 east and at the Galisteo Road to Santa Fe.

Rosendo and I have been married for 55 years. Before we got married, I made drapes for American Furniture in Albuquerque, and Rosendo worked construction. After we got married, we made our home in Albuquerque but had a ranch in Torreón, so we would go to Torreón every weekend to feed the cows and horses. Rosendo also went to the ranch during the week, very early in the morning before going to work. We lived in Albuquerque for ten years then we moved back home to Torreón in 1967 when our son Matthew was born. Rosendo then went to work for the County Road Department. Later, he went to work for the County Sheriff's Department, where he retired from after 25 years. While living in Torreón, Mr. Ralph Dial, who was the school bus driver at the time, was selling a school bus. We bought the school bus, and I started driving the kids from Torreón to school in Estancia. I drove the school bus for 20 years.

Rosendo and I had three children. In 1960 my first child was a full term stillbirth. My second child was Matthew, who was born in 1967. Matthew went to school in Estancia up until his sophomore year. His junior year he went to Albuquerque to work for the summer. He decided he wanted to continue working, so he stayed in Albuquerque, and he graduated from Albuquerque High School. After he graduated from high school, he went to the National Guard. He then went to the police academy and became a police officer for the Albuquerque Police Department (APD). He was with the department for 25 years. He retired from APD and then went to work for the Corrales Police Department. He recently spent two years in Afghanistan working with a private contractor. Matthew is now taking classes and working towards becoming a journeyman or electrician. He is married to Peggy R. Lujan, and they have two daughters. Shelby Lynn, their oldest daughter, went to the University of New Mexico for a year and is now in college in the San Francisco area. She works with a model agency in talent sales where she frequently travels to Canada, Australia, Hawaii and around the United States. Mckayla Renea, their younger daughter, is 10 years old and has already received many belts in Karate.

My daughter, Roxanne Kathleen Burchell, was born in 1969. She went to school in Alamosa Colorado on a scholarship, and then she went to dental hygienist school. She is married to Ray Burchell, who is also a dental hygienist. They have two daughters, Taylor Rae Abagail and Leah Marie. Taylor Rae Abagail is 16 years old and attends Albuquerque Institute for Mathematics and Science (AIMS) in Albuquerque. She also works as a lifeguard at West Mesa High School. Leah Marie is 13 years old. She also attends AIMS and is a cheerleader.

Ernie, my older brother, married Melba Chavez-Vigil. They have three sons and one daughter and five granddaughters. Ernie retired from Sandia Base, and Melba retired from Albuquerque Public Schools. Melba passed away May 26, 2016, from complications of Leukemia.

Carol Vigil-Chavez, my sister, is married to Carmel Chavez. They both retired from Sandia Base. They have four sons and four grandchildren.

Onila Vigil-Garcia, my sister, is married to Mariano Garcia, who retired from Sandia Base as a security guard. Onila worked at a jewelry store and for Albuquerque Public Schools. She now works as a real estate agent. They have two sons and two granddaughters.

My brother Dan is married to Donna. Dan attended the University of New Mexico then moved to California where he is a therapist. Dan and Donna have a daughter, Alexandra. Alexandra has one son.

My brother Abie is married to Antonette. Abie attended the University of New Mexico where he studied architecture. He currently works for the State of New Mexico as an inspector. Abie and Antonette have a daughter, Zarah, who is attending the University of New Mexico.

When I was born my *nana* Nina and *papá* Sanchez took my brother Gabriel, who was about two years old at the time, to live with them. They took him to makes things easier on my mom because she already had several kids to care for. Gabriel grew up with my grandparents, and he never wanted to come back home. When Gabriel was about 13 years old, my *nana* Nina passed away. My *papa* Sanchez then adopted Gabriel. In 1960 after Gabriel finished high school, he joined the marines. He later worked at Sandia Base, where he retired from after many years. He never married. He developed multiple sclerosis, and he lived alone for many years with this disease. He refused to give up. He would say he could do anything just like anybody else.

It just took him a little longer. He was a very talented woodworker, and he made beautiful furniture. Everyone in my family owns several pieces of furniture made by Gabriel. The baptismal font that the priest in Torreón uses to baptize babies was made by Gabriel. The Cross outside the front of the church was also made by him. Gabriel died in 2008 at the age of 70. He died four months after my dad died. My dad died at the age of 93. My mom died in 2007 at the age of 90. My parents were married for 74 years.

L-R Rosendo, Selina, Roxanne, (back) Matthew Vigil, Carlota and Ernesto Vigil

A Little Extra

Glossary
Legend to the map of Torreón
Map of Torreón
La Entrega de San Antonio

Glossary

abuelo- grandpa
acequia- irrigation ditch
aguinaldos- going out and asking for small gifts on Christmas Eve
ahijada- goddaughter
alabados- Spanish hymns
alba- morning song
¡Apurecen¡ Ya dieron el tercero. - Hurry up! There goes the third bell.
arroyo- stream
atole- a drink or cereal made from blue corn
barriando lana- beating the rugs
(el) basudero- dump
biscochitos- cookies
(una) borrega- a sheep
la botiquita- drugstore
bueno- ok
cajete- tub
calabacitas- a dish of squash and corn
caliche- clayish
calabasas- big pumpkins
campito- camp
camposanto- cemetary
¡cantemos la alba ya viene el día, Daremos gracias Ave Maria!-We sing the coming of a new day. We give thanks to Ave Maria!
cantina- bar
caporal- main boss, forman
capulin- chokecherry jam
caramelo- sugary
carnal-brother, bro
carne adovada- meat marinated in red chile
cariño- affection
carro de caballo- horse and wagon
casa vieja- old house
cesteo- a rest, a break
chica- girl
chicharrones- fried pieces of pork
chile rojo con torta- chile and egg dish
chile rellenos- stuffed chiles
chile ristras- a string of chile
chinches- bed bugs
chopos de guangoche- shoes made of gunnysack

coloradas- the red heads
comadre- godmother, friend
¿cómo estás, mi hijita? - How are you, my girl?
(el) Coronel- colonel
corridos- ballads
(la) Cuaresma- Lent
(el) cuarto recivo - living room, room where you receive guests
curandera - traditional folk healer
curanderismo - the practice of folk healing
cuentos- stories
cueritos- pork skin
Dejala ir, toda la plev(b)e va a ir. - Let her go, all the young kids are going.
del saco de harina- from flour sacks
deputados- deputies
Dios te lo pague y Dios te bendiga.- May God repay you and bless you.
dispensa- pantry
doble- double
¿Donde están?- where are you?
embrujado- bewitched
empacho- blockage of undigested food
empanaditas -sweet meat pies
en el mundo entero, Dios los Bendiga a todos.- In the whole world, May God bless everyone.
en la Santa Gloria- in Heaven
escapotes- scrapes of wood
escuela- school
escuelita- little school
escusado de viento- toilet in the wind, outside toilet
esque- so they say
Esta cantina es mia.- This bar is mine.
fiesta- party
frijoles- beans
(la) galera- a room
los garrapatas- the ticks
gauriniciones- harness
(la) grande seca- the big drought
güero- blond
había hallado un tesoro. I had found a treasure.
¡hay vamos¡- we're going
Hay viene Parras con su guitarita.- Here comes Parras with his guitar.
hermanos- brothers
hijole- gosh
hombres- men

horno- adobe outdoor oven
(la) Iglesia- church
jondable- water hole
jumate- big spoon, ladle
Lleva te lo.- Take it.
luminarias- lights
madrina- godmother
mal de ojo- evil eye
mantoncito- edge of the mountain
manzanilla- chamomile
(la) maquina de rajar- sawmill
maranito- little pig
marcarnoria well-wisher
maromero- circus guy
matanza- butchering of a pig
mayordomos- caretakers of the church
menudo- tripe
mis- my
mis hijitas- my girls
mis recuerdos de Torreón- my memories of Torreón
mochila- backpack
molacho- someone missing a tooth
molletes- sweet bread
montecito- edge of the mountain
montones grandotes- big mountains
mucho cuidado- be careful
(Las) mujeres adelante, los hombres atras.- Women to the front, men to the back.
nacimiento- nativity set
nana- grandma
natillas- custard
¡No, es mia! - No, it's mine!
¡No, pero hay que tremblores! - No, but I am shaking!
Nuestra Maria Santísima- Our Blessed Mother
Nuestra Señora de Los Dolores- Our Lady of Sorrows
ocote- dry, quick burning wood
(el) ojo - the evil eye
oye- hey
pachetas- overalls
padrino- godfather, best man,
pájaro- bird
paleo- canopy
papá- dad
papas con caldo- potatoe soup

Para lo! Para lo! - Stop it! Stop it!
pastelitos- small fruit pies
perrodos- black stink bugs
piedra lisa- slick, smooth rock
(la) piedra rebalosa- the slippery rock
piñón- pine nuts
piojos- lice
platón- deep dish
pobrecitos- poor things
(Las) Posadas- re-enactment of the birth of Christ
posole- hominy
prendorio- engagement party
primo- cousin
promesa- promise
(el) pueblito de- small town of
(la) pumpa de agua water pump
Que Dios venga con nosotros. Dios adelante y nosotros atras. -That God will come with us. God in the front and us in the back.
¿Qué tienes miedo hijita? - Are you afraid daughter?
¡Qué turn, ni qué turn! – What turn! There is no turn.
questasita (cuestasita) de pierda- hill made of rock
¡Quiero ir a mi casa! ¡No voy a beber más! - I want to go home! I'm not going to drink anymore!
rancheras- traditional Mexican music
regalo de Navidad- Christmas gift
remuda- replacement
resolana- a place where the sun hit
rizos- curls
rosas de castillas- roses
ruleta- roulette wheel
Sabado de Gloria- Holy Saturday
Sala- living room, hall
sala de Fidel- Fidel's dance hall
San Antonio de Padua- St. Anthony of Padua
santo- saint
(el) Santo Niño- Holy Child
Santo Rosarios- Holy Rosaries
sapos- toads
¡Se cayó! ¡Se cayó! - You fell! You fell!
Se quebro la cola.- You broke your butt.
(la) seca- the drought
serruche- hand saw
sierra-mountain range
Siete Palabras- the Seven Last Words of Jesus on the Cross

Sociedad de San Jose-Society of St. Joseph
socios- members
sopa- bread pudding
sopapillas- fried bread
susto- becoming ill from a terrible freight
tamales- meat wrapped in pastry dough
tapolio- tarp
Tarre (tan) bonita la Lupe, lavame los trastes.- You're so pretty Lupe, wash the dishes for me.
tata-grandpa
terrenos- land
tía- aunt
tienda- store
títeres- puppets
Todavía hay pan.- There's still bread.
torta con juevo- red chile with eggs
¡Tranca el refrijador, ya viene la Lupe! - Lock the refrigerator. Here comes Lupe.
Treame la farrola o una vela y enciendelo.- Bring me the flashlight, lantern or a candle and light it.
trilladora- thresher
trineo-sled
valise- suitcase
Vamos afuera para ver quien es.- let's go outside to see who's there.
vasija –pot
velorio-wake, a vigil
venida- flood
Vía Crucis- the Stations of the Cross
vigas- wood beams
(el) violin- the violin
visperas- vespers
yerba buena- mint
zancos- stilts

Legend to Map of Torreón, families in the 1940s
Eloy Garcia Sr.

1. Teodoso Herrera
2. Jesus Montoya
3. Melquidez Chavez y Corrales
4. unknown
5. Abdon Castillo
6. Don Paz Sedillo
7. Manuel Brown
8. Los McKaffee
9. Silverio Martinez
10. Doña Felicita
11. Demecio Perea
12. la sala Cibola de San Jose
13. la maquina de rajar
14. Alfredo Chavez
15. Patrocinio Lujan
16. Manuel Archuleta
17. Roberto Lujan
18. la pumpa de agua- a well was here that belonged to Andres Lujan, people would come for water here
19. cantina de Antonio Jose Vigil
20. Ramon Sanchez
21. la tienda de Pedro y Gricelda Zamora
22. Elizeo Lopez
23. Melcor Lujan
24. Pablo Zamora
25. Juan Lujan
26. Pedro Alderete
27. Jose Maria Perea
28. Eufelia Zamora
29. Maclovio Perea
30. Juanito Lujan
31. Doña Rebecca
32. Jose Sanchez
33. Daniel Otero
34. Vicente Chavez
35. Jose Amable Perea
36. Francisco Lujan
37. Elias Garley
38. Unknown
39. Unknown

40. Vantentin Tapia
41. Jose Zamora
42. Ruiz Salas
43. Melquidez Trujillo
44. Manuel Vigil
45. Roman Lujan
46. Juan Lujan
47. Juan Vigil
48. Ross Garcia
49. Brablio Otero
50. Melcor Chavez
51. Donociano Montoya
52. Onofre Montoya
53. Vicente Montoya
54. Florencio Chavez
55. Lorenzo Sanchez
56. Ross Salas
57. Carlos Salas
58. Sam Vigil
59. Sosteno Trujillo
60. Los Hulbinas
61. Jose Torrez
62. Don Sarafin Perea
63. Pablo Torrez
64. Juan Augustine Lucero
65. Melquidez Chavez y Benavidez
66. Chon Salas
67. Juan Jaramillo
68. Ignacio Garcia
69. Nemecia Garcia- an horno was located here, there were about three hornos in town
70. Antonio Maldonado
71. Juan Chavez
72. Estanislado Benavidez
73. el pool- there was a pool hall here at one time, we hung out here on the porch
74. Don Salvador Chavez
75. Manuel Chavez
76. tienda de Pedro Zamora
77. Don Andres Lujan
78. La Iglesia de San Antonio
79. Antonio Chavez
80. Juan Chavez y Apodaca
81. casa vieja de Juan Chavez

82. Jacoba Chavez
83. Juan Jose Montoya
84. Amadeo Sanchez
85. Los Vigils
86. Polonio Sanchez
87. Los Gallegos
88. Jesus Candelaria
89. la tienda de Don Jesus Candelaria
90. Antonio Zamora
91. Eutimio Garcia
92. coral de Fidel Garcia
93. Mucario Gabaldon
94. Fidel Chavez
95. Arcenio Chavez
96. el ranchito de Carlos Maldonado
97. Feliciano Chavez
98. Elizeo Garcia
99. Dona Trinidad
100. Antonio Chavez y Benavidez
101. la cantina de Fidel Garcia
102. Fidel Garcia
103. la botiquita- little house where my mom sold ice cream
104. Ignacio Salas
105. Vito Salas
106. Prudencio Hulbina
107. Leopoldo Chavez
108. Julian Trujillo
109. Celso Gomez
110. Feliberto Montoya
111. Manuel Antonio Perea
112. Raymundo Maldonado
113. Macario Hulbina
114. Abenicio Gallegos
115. Petrita Gallegos
116. Antonio Garcia
117. El Pino donde llevaba a San Antonio a un pilgrimage
118. El Camposanto de la placita de Torreón
119. Luis Salas
120. Carlito Maldonado
121. la escuelita 1st-3rd grade
122. la escuela 4th- 8th grade
123. Ernesto Vigil
124. Antonio Jose Vigil

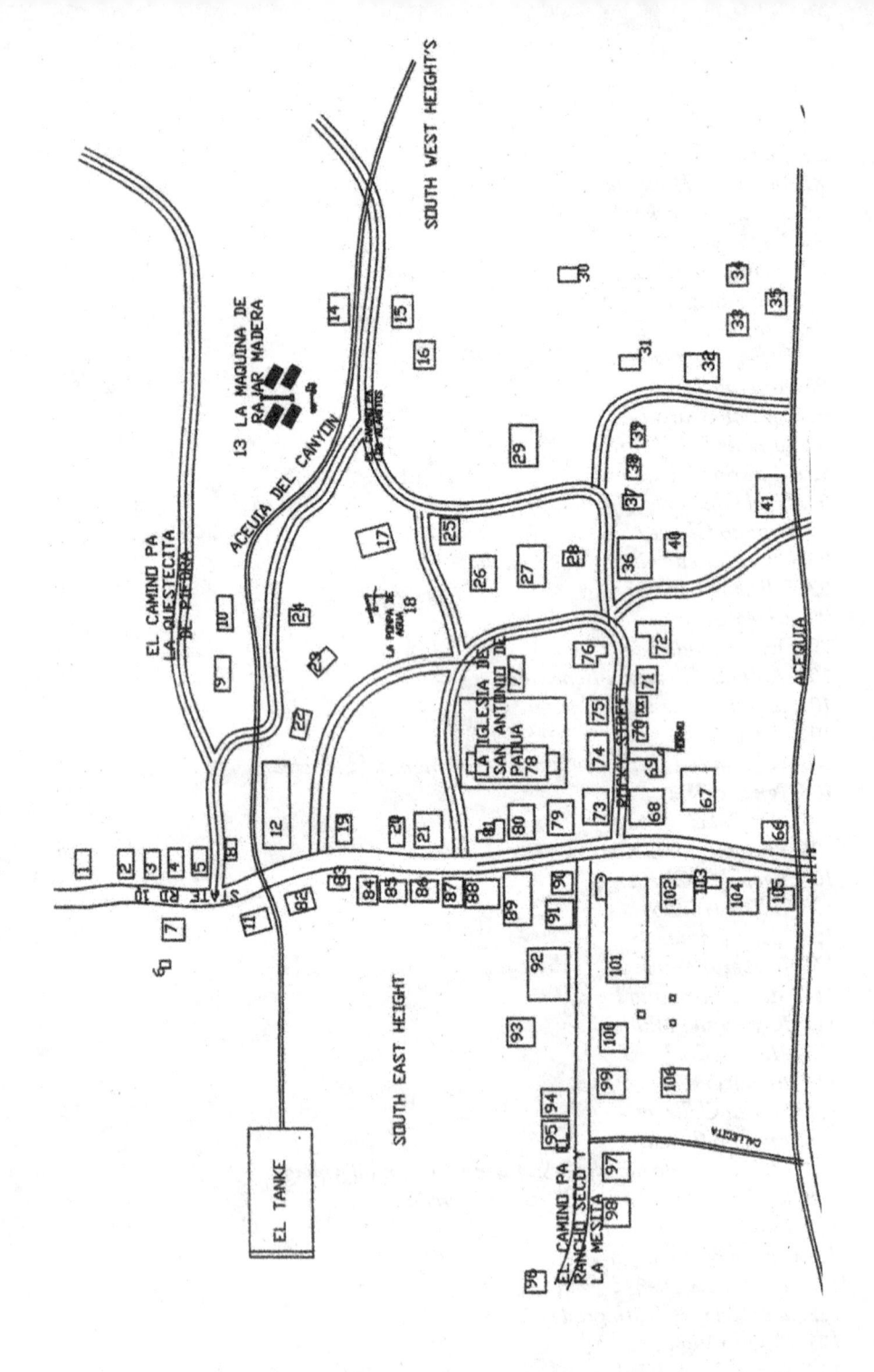

NORTH

EL CAMINO PA LA CUESTECITA DE PIEDRA

ACEQUIA DEL CANYON

13 LA MAQUINA DE RAJAR MADERA

LA BOMBA DE AGUA 18

LA IGLESIA DE SAN ANTONIO DE PADUA 78

BIRCH STREET

STATE RD 10

ACEQUIA

SOUTH WEST HEIGHT'S

SOUTH EAST HEIGHT

EL TANKE

EL CAMINO PA RANCHO SECO Y LA MESITA

CALLECITA

Map: Torreón area

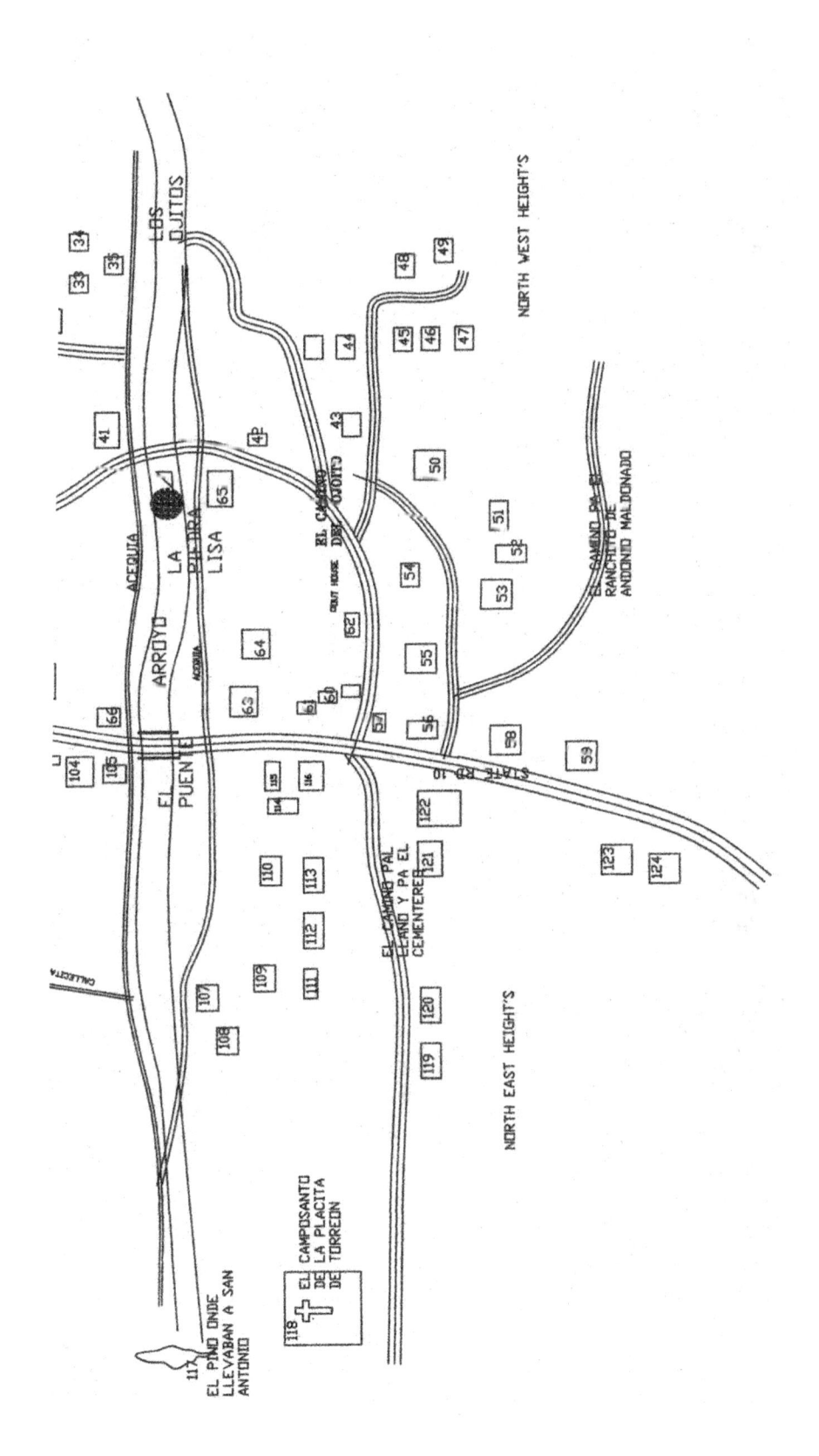

LOS OJITOS

- 33, 34, 35
- 41, 42, 43, 44, 45, 46, 47, 48, 49
- 50, 51, 52, 53, 54, 55, 56, 57, 58, 59
- 62 (COURT HOUSE)
- 63, 64, 65
- 60, 61
- 66

ACEQUIA
ARROYO LA PIEDRA LISA
ACEQUIA
EL CAMINO DE LOS OJITOS
EL PUENTE

NORTH WEST HEIGHT'S

EL CAMINO PA EL RANCHITO DE ANTONIO MALDONADO

STATE RD 10

- 104, 105, 106
- 107, 108, 109, 110, 111, 112, 113, 114, 115, 116
- 119, 120, 121, 122, 123, 124

CALLECITA

EL CAMINO PAL LLANO Y PA EL CEMENTERE

NORTH EAST HEIGHT'S

- 117 EL PINO DONDE LLEVABAN A SAN ANTONIO
- 118 EL CAMPOSANTO DE LA PLACITA DE TORREON

La Entrega de San Antonio

Año de 2016
Yo te entriego Santo Hermoso
Los Mayordomos que entraron
Te reciben con gran gozo

A la puerta de la Iglesia
Lugar donde van llegando
Que los Mayordomos nuevas
Alli los estan esperando

El día 13 de Junio
Como lo voy a esplicar
Vamos hacer una entrega
Al patron de este lugar

Yo te entriego Santo Hermoso
Como Santo verdadero
Tu no concedes la vida
Para el año venidero

Antonio Santo y Glorioso
Tú me estas acompanando
El día 13 de Junio
Cuando te este yo entregando

Salimos de la Iglesia
Todos en la procession
Toda la gente venilla
Con Nuestro Santo Patron

Los Mayordomos entrantes
De todito corazon
Como perla de diamante
Reciben a su Patron

Estas fiestas las Festejan
Aqui a Nuestro Patron
Yo creo que a El le agraden
Que vamos con devoción

De la mesa de altar
Todos de buen Corazon
Ahora vamos esperar
Una Santa bendicion

Adios Santo Milagroso
Adios Santo Verdadero
Espero verte otra vez
En el año venidero